# THE ILLUSTRATED
# WHO'S WHO IN
# MYTHOLOGY

## MICHAEL SENIOR

CONSULTANT EDITOR
## GEOFFREY PARRINDER

Macmillan Publishing Company
New York

Macmillan Publishing Company,
A division of Macmillan, Inc.
866 Third Avenue, New York NY 10022

First published in Great Britain by
Orbis Publishing Limited, London 1985

Library of Congress Catalog Card Number 85-18814

Printed in Yugoslavia by Mladinska Knjiga

printing number
  2  3  4  5  6  7  8  9  10

**Library of Congress Cataloging in Publication Data**

Senior, Michael 1940
    Illustrated Who's Who in Mythology
    I. Mythology-dictionaries.    I. Title
BL303.S46    1985    291.13    85-18814
ISBN 0-02 923770-X

*Page 1:* Sun-disc containing the sacred eye of Ra, the sun-god of
the ancient Egyptians. Detail from the Book of the Dead, Papyrus
of Hen-taui, 21st Dynasty.

*Frontispiece:* Sandstone sculpture of the Hindu god Ganesha,
7th century AD.

# CONTENTS

# INTRODUCTION

In a book of this kind the principal problem is that of selection, and that problem comes in two forms. First there is the general question of definition – what counts as mythology? Second, assuming that to have been satisfactorily settled, there is the internal question within each mythology, as to who is to be included, who to be left out. After all, not everybody gets into a Who's Who. I want to be clear about the principles I am using on both these points.

## MYTHOLOGY AND ITS NEIGHBOURS

There is a habit of mind which leads us to suppose that if an item belongs to one domain it cannot at the same time belong to another. This, if it were so, would lead to an enormous set of difficulties, since mythology (it must be said at once) has undetermined boundaries. As soon as one sees, however, that there is no real problem about holding dual nationality, these troubles fortunately disappear.

Mythology has borders with, most obviously, religion, history and folklore. In each of these cases it is a matter of an overlap rather than a defining line. In many cases (though not, as we shall see, in all) one is relieved of the responsibility of deciding whether an item is either/or by recognizing that it is both. A figure can at the same time bear mythological characteristics and belong to a clear religious system – indeed a great many do. And whereas some personages belong very clearly to history and to history only, and some are pure and uncomplicated folktale material, there are some which come out of history bearing mythical qualities and some which can play a purely folktale role in a certain context while serving a mythic purpose in others.

Given then that we do not have to worry about whether an individual belongs to some other sphere as well, what is it that decides us when we say that he, she or it belongs to mythology? First, to clear the ground, let me say what it is not. The word 'myth' has taken on inconvenient connotations of falsehood. To describe something as a myth has come to be a way of saying that it is fanciful, fantasy, delusion. This use is a secondary meaning, and forms no part of the way the word is used here. Indeed, rather the opposite is the case: to say of something that it is mythic is to ascribe to it, correctly, a very hard core of truth. To be part of mythology an idea or a character has to be true in the old sense of being accurate, of hitting its mark. It has to be a finely tuned, precision-made tool for serving an important and highly specialized purpose.

*History and folklore are the close neighbours of the myths recounting the exploits of heroes that are a feature of all cultures. Theseus, the hero of the city-state of Athens, represents a common type, semi-divine, favoured by the gods, precocious in bravery and the champion of his people, yet fated to a tragic end. Kylix found at Vulci, showing the deeds of Theseus, including the slaying of the Minotaur.*

7

Perhaps the best phrase to sum all this up is 'symbolic significance'. If an image or an episode, a character or a set of circumstances, bears symbolic significance, then it belongs potentially to mythology, quite apart from any other sphere it may belong to.

The word 'potentially' there signals a qualification. Like some forms of art this material must first stand the test of time. It may indeed be tempting to speak of recent events or figures of history as belonging to a mythology, but in doing so one is consciously extending the use of the term, using it, as it were, allusively or metaphorically, and to do this habitually would be to risk diluting its accuracy.

This discussion may seem mildly academic, but it is highly relevant to the question of what to include, what to exclude, from this book, an area in which we have had to make some real, and very practical, decisions.

Take the matter of religion: are there cases where something is so much essentially a part of a living religion that it would be wrong, or misleading, to label it as mythology?

Certainly many of the mythological elements in cultural systems which would be universally recognized as such are also part of a religion. That is no problem when the religion in question is no longer believed in. But that is an accident of time, and it means that belief by itself cannot be the criterion.

All the systems which make up the subject-matter of this book have been believed in at one time or another, and indeed some of them are believed in still. The gods have been worshipped at their temples, the heroes venerated as exemplars. Yet in these cases we feel confident in saying that the characters belong to a mythology.

Why then would we feel uncomfortable about saying that in other cases? This manner of working backwards from a decision to see how one made it is not as philosophically dubious as it might sound. One can best arrive at a generalization by considering examples. I would feel that there was something wrong in including in a work devoted to mythology the living religions of Christianity and Islam. Yet elements of Buddhism, Hinduism, Judaism and Zoroastrianism do not seem out of place, and these are clearly living religions. Many of the African religions treated here are still very much alive, and it would be patronizingly ethnocentric to hold them in a different category.

It would appear, then, to be a matter of proximity. Choosing to exclude something from mythology and confine it to religion, or, come to that, to history, is to make a statement about one's point of view, rather than one about the symbol-system concerned. It would be unrealistic, because illogical, to pretend that one can view things other than from a certain place and time. Viewing mythology is no different in this respect to any other activity. I am, by definition, here and now.

*Buddhism has been influenced by and left its mark on the mythologies of many eastern cultures. In Tibet, to which the religion was introduced from India, it developed its own distinctive character, with the absorption of pre-Buddhist mythological and religious elements and the elaboration of traditional Buddhist lore. A 14th-century Tibetan gilt and partly painted statue of Shakyamuni, the Buddha who, according to Tibetan belief, came to teach the present world-age.*

In the developed countries of the twentieth century both Christianity and Islam are contemporary with relatively new and still current civilizations, and it must be for this reason that they are too close in time and place to be viewed as mythologies. Certainly the same could be said of Buddhism, if one started from a different standpoint; and it must be said that in these terms that is a marginal case. Yet it is in the traces that it bears of a more ancient culture that Buddhism qualifies, and Christianity's base in Judaism (for instance) means that elements of Christianity, and come to that Islam, are in fact here included.

Some systems, such as Judaism, are so unequivocally ancient, that certain elements in them have had time to harden over the millennia into a form which we can perceive as something we would wish to call myth. This does not in any way obstruct their functioning as living beliefs. I repeat: there is no incompatibility there. A personage can perfectly well be at the same time the object of doctrinal and credal reverence, and the bearer of mythic significance.

Christianity and Islam are perhaps only special in this spectrum because of their relative youth. If I were invited to revise this 'Who's Who' in two thousand years time I should no doubt have to reconsider this decision, and would very probably be inclined to put them in.

## WHO IS WHO

To return, meanwhile, to the practical problems before us, there are significant differences between the world's mythologies which make it difficult in a work such as this to achieve a balance. Yet in a way the nature of the problem produces its own solution.

Some mythologies are more developed than others, either through being more fully recorded, or through belonging to a more complex or sophisticated culture. Some are more literary, some more centralized, and hence more highly structured. In these there are generally more named characters, and more given data either existed, or remains available, about the names. One finds, therefore, that the characters in such traditions appear to have more status, more importance, more fullness of form, than the characters in others. If, as a result of this, the heroes of Greece or the gods of Egypt get more space here than, for instance, the spirits of the African bush, it is perhaps on the one hand an unfair advantage mainly due to literacy. Yet on the other hand it is a fair reflection of the real identity of the raw material itself. It reflects in physical form what there is, how things are, in the distribution of images across the world's cultures.

Within each mythology, similarly, a character will end up here with as much space as seems justified by the attention paid to him, her, or it, the things said about them, the information known about them, within their own system. The space they demand, through the subject-matter available, is a true reflection of their relative internal importance in the mythology.

## THE PROBLEM OF TRANSLITERATION

It is hard enough sometimes to decide on the correct spelling of one's own language, let alone on that of one making use of quite different sounds. For a long time anthropologists and philologists attempted their own approximate equivalents. The advance of a scientific attitude in this as in all spheres of knowledge has led to a move towards standardization. I have tried as far as possible to identify the current recognized standard, which one hopes, for the sake of future consistency, will remain the orthodoxy in this matter. Since many works and sources still use variants from the past, I have occasionally mentioned alternative spellings, in cases where these are common in the literature.

## THE SOURCES

Where there is a clear main source which would be available to readers who wish to pursue a character further, I have mentioned it at the end of the entry. The criterion for deciding whether such are primary enough to be authentic statements of the tradition, rather than reports from outside it, is that they should belong to the national culture concerned, though of course in many cases their actual cultural context is one which has been changed by the advent of Christianity.

Sometimes the preservation of the record of a culture's mythology is largely, or even mainly, the work of one man. In Greece, of course, we owe our confidence in our knowledge of the basic tradition to Homer, who was dealing with a period some five hundred years before his time, and with the beliefs current then and still extant when he composed. We have other early Greek writers, such as Hesiod, for comparison; and the long classical tradition, in which the dramatists worked largely from the matter preserved by those two, confirms our understanding. The later development of Graeco-Roman material is effectively collected by Ovid, whose lifetime spanned the turn of the era. It is remarkable, but true, that

*The mythology of Greece has been immeasurably enhanced by the quality of the major literary sources, including Homer's* Iliad *and* Odyssey. *In Homer's account, the wandering Odysseus performs prodigious feats of heroism yet reveals engagingly human weaknesses. Black-figure skyphos, c. 350-40 BC, with a caricature of Odysseus and the enchantress Circe.*

*The literary sources of Hindu mythology include the* Ramayana, *an epic that tells the story of Rama, an incarnation of the god Vishnu. This 17th-century wooden sculpture depicts the hero with his dead wife, Sita.*

although this process took place over a period of more than seven hundred years the authenticity of the record is not diminished. Nor has the fact that each of these great writers embellished the matter with the delights of his own artistry distorted its underlying structure.

Elsewhere lesser men than Homer have played his role in establishing the mythology of their lesser cultures, providing the base for its development, the touchstone of its authenticity. Closer to home, we have the example of the work of Geoffrey of Monmouth, compiled from early sources and from current tradition, with the aid of his own vivid imagination, in the first half of the twelfth century. Fortunately we have enough other material to be able to identify the strands of original tradition in that large and rather wayward work, *The History of the Kings of Britain*. But to some extent Geoffrey made things into mythology which might otherwise have remained pseudo-history or lore. He heightened their significance and gave them national status. In his 'History' he put together a body of truly British material which thereafter had to be viewed as mythology.

The same identifying process was achieved even more strikingly by the Icelander Snorri Sturluson, who compiled a near-complete record of the pre-Christian tradition of Scandinavia in about the year 1220. Although this can be checked against, and to some extent supplemented by, the remains of the poetic tradition from which Snorri worked, and although omissions can be filled by the much duller work of the twelfth-century Danish scholar Saxo Grammaticus, it is to the production of Snorri's book, known to us as *The Prose Edda*, that we owe our considerable knowledge of the ancient tradition of northern Europe.

In other cases the material itself has remained intact from the start, and has not needed such compilers to excavate and conserve it. The *Rig Veda*, for instance, preserves the elements in the Hindu religion of India which originated among the Indo-European peoples of the second millennium BC in much their original form. Of course not all primary sources are so awesomely ancient. The sacred book of the Quiché Maya of Mexico and Guatemala, for instance, known as the *Popol Vuh*, was written down by them in the sixteenth century of this era, though from oral traditions which no doubt were as old as the race itself. To some extent, indeed, the process of collecting authentic traditional material and safeguarding it in written form still goes on. Whether myths are still being developed or founded is another matter, and all one can say is that if they were we should be too close to the process to be able confidently to say so. One thing that is certain is that the interest in them endures, as well it might, since their subject-matter is, almost by definition, permanently relevant.

*Note: All cross references are printed in capital letters.*

## AARON
Brother of MOSES, in the Hebrew stories recorded in the Old Testament, and assistant to him in the deliverance of the Israelites from their bondage in Egypt. He came to be a priest of the people, but led an idolatrous movement by representing YAHWEH in the form of a golden calf during Moses' absence. Nevertheless he later became reconciled with God and features as a patriarch in the Hebrew genealogy.
*Exodus, Leviticus*

## ABEDNEGO
In the Hebrew story of DANIEL he features with two companions, and shares with them the test of the fiery furnace. See MESHACH, SHADRACH.  *Daniel*

## ABEL
Younger son of ADAM and EVE, in the Hebrew story of the creation as recorded at the beginning of the Old Testament. Like his elder brother CAIN he was born after their parents' exile from the original state of grace. In the main episode of his story he and his brother bring offerings to YAHWEH. Cain however is a tiller of the soil, whereas Abel is a pastoralist who brings an animal from his flock, and Yahweh favours this and rejects Cain's produce. In anger and envy at this discrimination Cain kills his brother Abel. The myth represents, among other things, a deep-seated rivalry between the settled agriculturalists of Canaan and the invading Hebrew tribes with a pastoral way of life.
*Genesis*

## ABRAHAM
Formerly Abram. A major character of the Old Testament, an ancestral figure in the early history of the Hebrews. In the first sources in fact he was himself called 'the

ABOVE: *Aaron, who with Moses played a major part in the deliverance of the Israelites from their bondage in Egypt, performed a number of miracles with his rod.*

Hebrew'. The figure is said to have originated in Mesopotamia, his home country in the story, possibly being based on a historical character of the early second millennium BC. He represents an ideal for his people, subservient and responsive to his God, devout believer, upholder of moral worth. His link with Hebrew tribal genealogy passes through his son ISAAC to his grandson JACOB. See also HAGAR, SARAH.  *Genesis*

## ABSALOM
Son of DAVID, in the Hebrew stories recorded in the Old Testament. He conspired to usurp his father's throne, gaining popular support by his strong personality and good looks, but was in due course overcome and killed by the loyal forces. In a gesture of selfless forgiveness, his father lamented his death.
*2 Samuel*

## ABUK
The first woman, in the cosmogony of the Dinka tribe of the Sudan area of Africa. She was created of clay along with her partner GARANG. In a main part of her story she was said to have caused a version of the Fall by grinding more corn than the one grain a day stipulated by God, which up to then had been enough for the pair to live on comfortably.

## ACHACHILAS

Also known as Acacila. In the beliefs of the Aymara Indians of Bolivia, these are the spirits representing the high mountains, thought of as having the form of old people who dwell underground. The Indians believe that they have the power to govern the weather and cause rain and other conditions.

## ACHILLES

Son of the sea nymph THETIS and PELEUS in Greek mythology. Although his father was a mortal prince, he possessed almost complete immortality through being immersed by his mother as an infant in the river Styx. This however left a mortal portion, the heel by which she held him. Achilles played a leading role in the Trojan War, though he had at first been reluctant to go because of a premonition of his mother's that he would not come back. At Troy he led the force known as the Myrmidons, and himself stood as the Greek champion against the Trojan hero HECTOR. A quarrel with AGAMEMNON over a woman at one point threatened the Greek cause, when Achilles, in high temper, withdrew his troops. Inevitably he died by eventually being struck in his mortal heel. Achilles is the perfect Greek hero, down to the human touch of his bad temper; strong, brave, amorous, straightforward, doomed.

HOMER: *Iliad*

## ACTAEON

A hunter, in the mythology of the Greeks. He is best known for having had the misfortune accidentally to see ARTEMIS, the goddess of hunting, bathing naked. Outraged, she turned him into a stag, and he was torn to pieces by his own hounds.

## ADAD

A Babylonian storm god, in the pantheon of the early people of Mesopotamia. He was responsible for bad weather.

## ADAM

The first man, in the Hebrew story of origins as recorded in the Old Testament.

He was made by God out of dust and given a paradisal garden as his home, in which all things were for his provision except for the fruit of one tree, which was taboo. Along with his consort EVE he transgressed this stipulation, and when they ate it they at once lost their previous moral innocence, and also incurred the anger of God. Expelled from the garden they were condemned to work in order to survive and to suffer hardship and sorrow.

*Genesis*

## ADAPA

A Mesopotamian character, he was the creation of EA, and was given by him great wisdom; he then served Ea as a provider, largely in the role of fisherman.

BELOW: *The Greek hero Achilles, here slaying Penthesilea, Queen of the Amazons, whose female warriors had gone to the aid of Troy in the Trojan war. Black figure amphora, 540 BC.*

15

## ADITI

Mother of VISHNU, in the Hindu beliefs of India, and a mother-figure generally among the gods. In one of her manifestations she is also said to be the mother of KRISHNA, one of Vishnu's incarnations. In the Vedas, however, she is described as being Vishnu's wife.

*Rig Veda*

## ADONIS

A Greek adoption and adaptation of the Syrian-Babylonian deity TAMMUZ. The name means 'lord', and may therefore originally have been a title. His main significance is that he is doomed to spend half the year in the underworld, half on earth, thus clearly symbolizing seasonal cycles. (Compare PERSEPHONE.) Because of his unusual beauty he caught the attention of the love-goddess APHRODITE, and in doing so attracted the jealousy of her lover ARES, god of war. One day when Adonis was out hunting Ares took the form of a wild boar and attacked him, and he bled to death.

## ADU OGINAE

The leader of the first race of men, in the stories of the origins of the Ashanti people of West Africa.

## AEGEUS

In Greek mythology, the king of Attica, and father of the hero THESEUS. Burdened by the dreadful tribute exacted by MINOS (the despatch to Crete of young Athenians at regular periods as a sacrifice to the bull-god) he reluctantly allowed Theseus to go as a member of the tribute to try to bring it to an end, and he leapt to his death from the Acropolis when he wrongly thought that the mission had failed. He gave his name to the Aegean Sea. See also ARIADNE, ASTERION.

## AEGIR

In Scandinavian myth, a giant who is lord of the sea. A type of demigod, of a lower status than the AESIR, he lived in a magnificent palace luxurious with

gleaming gold. This theme of sea-gods living in halls full of riches may be a reference to the treasure lost in shipwrecks. (Compare ALCINOUS, MANANNAN.) Aegir has a wife, RAN, who entraps seafarers in her net, and nine daughters who are the Nordic equivalents of mermaids.

## AEGISTHUS

In Greek mythology, he was the lover of CLYTEMNESTRA, queen to AGAMEMNON, embarking on a liaison with her while her husband was away at Troy. Aegisthus conspired with the queen to murder the king on his return, after which crime he married her and thus became himself king of Argos. They were both killed by Agamemnon's son ORESTES, avenging his father's murder. See also ATREUS, THYESTES.

AESCHYLUS: *Agamemnon*

## AENEAS

The main hero of Rome, approximating in stature to the great adventurers of Greek tradition, in which in fact he occurs in the *Iliad* as one of the Trojans. In the Roman expansion of his story he came to Italy after the fall of Troy and unified the natives. The Romans regarded him as the ancestor of their people and a number of noble families claimed descent. VIRGIL: *Aeneid*

*An Eskimo shaman's mask probably used in ceremonies to influence good and evil spirits, such as the benevolent Agloolik.*

## AEOLUS

In Greek mythology, he was the guardian of the winds, which he kept confined on his floating island of Lipari (or Aeolia, in the *Odyssey*), releasing them one by one at his discretion or at the request of the gods. He occurs most prominently in the episode in which he befriends ODYSSEUS and his companions on their ill-fated voyage.    HOMER: *Odyssey*

## AESCULAPIUS

The Roman version of the Greek god of healing, ASCLEPIUS.

## AESIR

The family of the principal gods of Scandinavia, chiefly ODIN, THOR, BALDER and TYR, who lived in a fortress called Asgard. They may be compared to the inner circle of Olympian deities in Greek myth. The fortress of Asgard was said to lie in Asia, or Asaland.
SNORRI STURLUSON: *Prose Edda*

## AGAMEMNON

A major figure of Greek mythology, the king of Mycenae and Argos, and High-King of the Greeks. Commander-in-chief of the massed force which left for Troy, Agamemnon is the embodiment of political power, the human equivalent of Olympian ZEUS. At the same time he is (as is the way with many Greek heroes) tragically doomed, destined to play his part in working out the curse on the family of his father ATREUS. Putting military and national requirements ahead of personal ones, he sacrificed his daughter IPHIGENIA in order that the fleet might sail for Troy, and received requital for this when his disaffected wife CLYTEMNESTRA and her lover AEGISTHUS murdered him on his return from the war. At Troy he appears as dictatorial but respected, a slightly distant and intimidating figure.
AESCHYLUS: *Agamemnon*; HOMER: *Iliad*

## AGLOOLIK

In the mythology of the Eskimos of North America he is regarded as a spirit who lives below the ice, the guardian of the young seals, and viewed as being a benevolent influence.

## AGNI

An ancient god of fire, in the early mythology of India, a god both of the fire of the hearth and the fire of sacrifice, also bearing its associations of destructive power. In later Hindu mythology his sacrificial connections became dominant, and to some extent his functions merged with those of INDRA. He is represented as having three (or two) heads, and sometimes four arms, and is usually depicted accompanied by a ram.
*Rig Veda*

*A two-headed statue of Agni, the fire god of Hindu mythology and one of the most important deities in the religion of India.*

## AHAB

In Hebrew stories, as recorded in the Old Testament, he was the king of Israel at the time of the prophet ELIJAH, who rebuked him and his queen JEZEBEL for following false gods, and was persecuted for doing so. Ahab of the Old Testament is based on a historical character of ninth century BC.

*1 Kings*

## AH KINCHIL

God of the sun, in the beliefs of the Maya people of Mexico, thought of as similar in appearance to ITZAMNA. At night when the sun passes under the earth he becomes the terrible jaguar god.

## AH PUCH

Or Ah Puh. God of death in the beliefs of the Maya Indians of Mexico, ruler of an underworld kingdom.

## AHRIMAN

In the Pahlavi (Middle Persian) cosmogony of Iran, the externally existent spirit of evil, a being therefore coeval with the good god OHRMAZD, and by his freedom a check on Ohrmazd's total power. The world was created as a trap for Ahriman, who became ensnared in this material universe, and man was placed in it as an ally of Ohrmazd against him. The two great antagonists, principles of good and evil, are embattled in the medium of Ohrmazd's created world, and at the end (the era of which is prefigured by the birth of ZARATHUSHTRA) a final battle will lead to the ridding of the world of the forces of evil, and the restoration of creation to its original state of purity and bliss. See also ANGRA MAINYU.

## AHURA MAZDA

Commonly known as Mazda, also spelt Mazdah. The major god of the ancient kingdom of Iran. In the earliest texts he appears as Mazda Ahura. He is the Wise Lord, the good god of Zoroastrianism, and opposed to the evil spirit ANGRA MAINYU. The two occur in Pahlavi (Middle Persian) doctrine as OHRMAZD and AHRIMAN. Mazda

*A relief on a cliff face at Naqsh-i-Rustem showing the evil Ahriman being trampled by the horse of Ahura Mazda, the good god of Zoroastrianism. Second quarter of the 3rd century AD.*

*The Japanese god Aizen-Myoo, although terrifying in physical appearance, has a benevolent nature in which physical passion is refined by intellectual desire. Wooden statue of the Kamakura period, 14th century.*

is the ultimate creator of all things and of life, and the upholder of the world. He allows man in his creation the free choice between good and evil, but the progress of the world, in his plan, is towards good, and this he encourages with reward and punishment. Only the righteous will become immortal. He speaks to the world with this message through his prophet ZARATHUSHTRA. Historically the rise of Mazda to this supreme position was due to his adoption as their patron deity by the kings of Persia.

## AHURAS
Gods (one of whom is MITHRA) subservient to the good and supreme deity AHURA MAZDA, in the Zoroastrian religion of Iran. They are combatant with Ahura Mazda on the side of good against the forces of evil represented by the DAEVAS led by ANGRA MAINYU (Pahlavi AHRIMAN). Compare Hindu ASURAS.

## AIPALOOKVIK
A sea spirit, thought of as being hostile to men, occurring in the tradition of the Eskimos of the North American continent.

## AIWEL
In the tradition of the Dinka people of Sudan, in Africa, he is the son of a river spirit. He was noted for possessing magical powers and formed the centre of a saga of pastoral rivalry and migration. The hierarchical structure of Dinka clans derives from him.

## AIZEN-MYOO
In the tradition of Japan, this god spans the border of physical and intellectual desire: the transition from sexual indulgence to the wish for true knowledge. Although he is depicted as being terrible in appearance, he nevertheless is thought to have a benevolent nature, showing great compassion for mankind.

19

LEFT: *In the Homeric account of the Trojan war Ajax was a major figure among the Greeks. On this amphora painted by Exekias he is shown with Achilles playing a board game.*

BELOW: *Ala, the earth and mother goddess of the Ibo people of Nigeria.*

## AJAX

Aias to Homer; one of the leading Greek heroes of the Trojan War. When **ACHILLES** died Ajax was defeated in a contest for possession of his armour by **ODYSSEUS** and according to later poets his fury at this drove him to suicide.

HOMER: *Iliad, Odyssey;* SOPHOCLES: *Ajax*

## AKSHOBHYA

In Tibetan Buddhism, and in the whole of Mahayana, or northern, Buddhism, as practised in China, Japan, etc., he is one of the group of five Buddhas which formed together a major cult, the others being **SHAKYAMUNI**, **AMITABHA**, **RATNASAMHAVA** and **AMOGHASIDDHI**. The name Akshobhya means 'Imperturbable'.

## ALA

An earth and mother goddess of the Ibo people of Nigeria. The provider of fertility and plenty, she also rules the land of the dead. Compare Greek **DEMETER**, **PERSEPHONE**. Her cult is popular and widespread and her priesthood influential in Ibo lands.

## ALBERICH

In German mythology, he was a dwarf whose function was the guarding of King **NIBELUNG**'s treasure. The story which tells how this was stolen from him by **SIEGFRIED** is well-known through Wagner's Ring Cycle. See **ANDVARI**, the Scandinavian equivalent.

## ALCESTIS

A heroine occurring in Greek myth, seen as the epitome of selflessness. She devotedly volunteered to die in place of her husband, later being rescued from Hades by **HERACLES**. EURIPIDES: *Alcestis*

## ALCINOUS

King of the Phaeacians, a seafaring people who occur in the mythology of the Greeks as hosts to **ODYSSEUS** towards the end of his voyage. A descendant of **POSEIDON**, the sea-god, Alcinous lives in an upright and civilized style in a magnificent palace, full of gold. HOMER: *Odyssey*

## ALCMENA

A heroine of Greek mythology, Alcmene in Homer. She was the mother of **HERACLES**,

by ZEUS. In the main episode of her story Zeus swore an oath when she was due to give birth that the child born that day would rule over his neighbour. His jealous wife HERA arranged for the birth to be delayed and another advanced, with the result, typical of the irony in Greek myth, that Zeus' ordinance led to his son's domination by his cousin EURYSTHEUS.

HOMER: *Iliad*

## ALL-FATHER
A name for ODIN, in the mythology of the Scandinavians.

## ALOM
A mother goddess in the beliefs of the Maya Indians of Mexico. The name comes from *al*, 'son', and *alan*, 'to give birth', and means 'She who bore sons'. *Popol Vuh*

## ALULUEI
A hero of the mythological tales of Micronesia in which he is a sea-going adventurer, connected by the natives with their all-important sea-canoes.

## AMATERASU
The major deity of the Shinto religion of Japan. Goddess of the sun, she was herself said to have been born from the left eye of IZANAGI. She became the ancestress of the emperors (see NINIGI) and is still much worshipped in the Shinto religion, having a major shrine at Ise, a great religious centre visited by ten million pilgrims a year. During one episode of her long-standing conflict with her brother SUSANO, god of storms, she retreated in anger into a cave, causing the world to grow dark, only being tempted out by the efforts of the other gods, whereupon she saw herself in a mirror they had made. This is now kept at Ise, among the imperial regalia, and forms an important part of the imperial treasures.

## AMBROSIUS
Or Aurelius Ambrosius, the name given by Geoffrey of Monmouth to a composite figure drawn both from early British history and from Celtic legend: that is,

from post-Roman leader Ambrosius Aurelianus on the one hand, and on the other hand the early prototype of MERLIN named EMRYS. In the story Ambrosius was a forerunner of ARTHUR as king of Britain, and it was on his instructions that Merlin built Stonehenge.

GEOFFREY OF MONMOUTH: *History of the Kings of Britain*

## AMERETAT
One of the AMESHA SPENTAS, figures in the Zoroastrian religion of Iran. The name Ameretat is translated as Immortality, and the quality represented by the personage is therefore attributed to AHURA MAZDA.

## AMESHA SPENTAS
Also spelt Amesa Spentas, and alternatively known as Ahaspends or Amahraspands. These figures occur in the Zoroastrian religion of Iran. Translated as the Bounteous Immortals, they are the spirits which form the medium through which God (AHURA MAZDA) works in the world, to some extent elements of the godhead himself, in other lights seen as abstract qualities separated from him and become independent beings.

## AMITABHA
One of the five Buddhas of Tibetan Buddhism, and of northern or Mahayana Buddhism generally – as found in China, Japan, etc. The group of five together form a central focus of worship. The name Amitabha means 'Boundless Light', and he is represented as a meditating Buddha. See SHAKYAMUNI, AKSHOBHYA, RATNASAMHAVA, and AMOGHASIDDHI.

## AMMA
The creator God, in the beliefs of the Dogon people of West Africa. His action lies behind the more developed images of the NUMMO.

## AMOGHASIDDHI
One of the five Buddhas which together form a central focus of worship in Tibetan Buddhism and in Mahayana, or northern,

Buddhism generally. Along with
RATNASAMHAVA, Amoghasiddhi is an
addition to an earlier group of three,
SAKYAMUNI, AMITABHA and AKSHOBHYA. The
name means 'Perfect Accomplishment'.

## AMON

Sometimes Amun. An Egyptian deity,
originally a local god of Thebes; he rose to
major prominence in the hierarchy of
Egyptian gods through being adopted by
the dynasty which united Egypt from its
base at Thebes. The other gods of rival
leaders were assimilated by the figure of
Amon, including the great sun and creator-
god RA, to give the composite all-
embracing deity Amon-Ra. Amon was at
first depicted as a ram, which animal was
sacred to him. He appears in that form in
multiple at his great temple at Thebes, now
known as Karnak, which also testifies to the
power and wealth of his adoptive kings. As
primal creator-god he was sometimes
represented as a priest-figure with tall
plumed head-dress, bearing the sun disc
formerly associated with Ra, and his
creative faculty also gave him the identity
of god of the wind, a function previously
held by the god SHU, in which capacity he
was worshipped at the other main Theban
temple at what is now Luxor. In one story
of his origin he rested above the aboriginal
flood on a mound, where he hatched from
a self-generated egg. In his more specific
dynasty form he was thought (like other
major gods before him) to be embodied as
the reigning pharaoh's father, at the time of
his conception, and thus to be the actual
physical father of the king, making each
king into a god. The name of one of the
most famous pharaohs, Tutankamen (or
Tutankhamon), means 'Tut-life-Amon' or
'Tut whose life is from Amon'.

## AMPHITRITE

In Greek mythology, she is the wife of
POSEIDON, the sea god, and is herself the
daughter of OCEANUS (or in some accounts
NEREUS), an older marine deity. She is
notable for having silently suffered her
husband's frequent infidelities.

OPPOSITE: *A Tibetan tangka, probably 18th-century, showing Amoghasiddhi, one of five meditation Buddhas of Mahayana Buddhism, surrounded by 202 other figures of Amoghasiddhi.*

LEFT: *Amon, sometimes referred to as the King of the Gods, in whose honour grandiose temples were errected at Thebes. 18th Dynasty.*

## AMPHITRYON

The mortal husband of ALCMENA a figure of
Greek mythology, whom ZEUS seduced,
with the result that she gave birth to twins,
one human, one divine.

## AN

A Mesopotamian deity, the Sumerian version of Babylonian ANU.

## ANAHIT

The chief goddess of the mythology of ancient Armenia, a divinity of fertility and also the goddess of wisdom, identified in the later Armenian tradition with the Greek goddess APHRODITE. The figure comes from the adoption by Iranians of an Assyro-Babylonian goddess to whom they gave the title *Anahita*, which means 'Immaculate'. Further adopted by the Armenians, she was known as 'the mother of all knowledge', and said to be the daughter of their god ARAMAZD.

## ANANDA

In the Buddhist religion of India, he was the half-brother and loyal boyhood and adult friend of the Buddha.

## ANANSI

In West African tradition, the name of the spider, originally a man and the agent of God, seen as being a great trickster, and the subject of many popular folk tales.

## ANAT

Or Anath. A Syrian deity: a goddess, sister to the great god BAAL.

## ANCHANCHO

A number of evil spirits connected with

RIGHT: *A wooden headdress from Cameroon of hornlike forms probably representing the chameleon who, according to West African myths, was tricked by the spider figure who in some parts of West Africa is known as Anansi.*

LEFT: *A Sassanian silver dish depicting at its centre the goddess Anahita, a later version of Anahit, a divinity of fertility and wisdom in the mythology of ancient Armenia.*

illness and debility, still regarded as a powerful danger by the Andean Indians of Peru.

## ANDROGEOS
In Greek myth he was the son of King MINOS of Crete. The crucial point of his story was that he died in violent circumstances while visiting Attica, with the result that Minos thereafter exacted from the Athenians a tribute of seven boys and seven maidens every three years. See THESEUS.

## ANDROMACHE
Wife of the Trojan hero HECTOR, a figure of Greek myth occurring in the story of the war of the Greeks against Troy.
HOMER: *Iliad*

## ANDROMEDA
A heroine occurring in the mythology of the Greeks. Essentially a maiden-in-distress in a typical heroic rescue story, she was saved by PERSEUS from the clutches of a sea-monster, and later became his wife.

## ANDVARI
A dwarf, occurring in the stories of Scandinavia. He was the possessor of a

hoard of gold and a magic ring. Both were stolen from him by the gods, but the ring was cursed by Andvari with the property of bringing disaster to whoever owned it. The story is more familiar in its German version (in which the dwarf is named ALBERICH) through Wagner's Ring Cycle. See NIBELUNG, SIEGFRIED, SIGURD. Dwarfs played an important part in Scandinavian and Germanic myth, in which they figure as a type of elf.
SNORRI STURLUSON: *Prose Edda*

## ANGRA MAINYU
The Hostile Spirit, the representative of evil and the enemy of AHURA MAZDA in the Zoroastrian religion of Iran. He was more developed in his later form of AHRIMAN.

## ANHUR
An Egyptian deity. Originally he was a local god of the area of Abydos. He had connections with the sun, but was more popular as a war-god, in which capacity the Greeks identified him with ARES.

## ANINGAN
The name of the moon in the tradition of a northern group of the Eskimo of the North American continent, unusually viewed by them as being a male figure and the brother of the female sun. He is seen as chasing her continually across the sky, and himself is thought of as a great hunter.

## ANNAN
In Irish Celtic mythology, she was the mother of the gods, best known as the eponym of twin hills near Killarney, the Paps of Annan.

## ANTAEUS
Offspring of POSEIDON and the Earth, in the myths of the ancient Greeks. He consistently defeated passing strangers in a wrestling match, drawing renewed strength by contact with the ground, thus reviving whenever apparently defeated. HERACLES overcame him by lifting him clear of this source of renewal, and crushed him to death in the air.

BELOW: *A bronze of the Egyptian god Anhur represented as a warrior. 25th Dynasty, 700 BC.*

**ANTIGONE**

A figure of Greek mythology. She was the daughter of OEDIPUS, king of Thebes. Her main action was one of defiance of a decree of CREON's, her uncle, forbidding burial of her brother POLYNICES, for which defiance she was put to death.

SOPHOCLES: *Antigone*

**ANTIOPE**

Queen of the Amazons (a nation of female warriors regarded as living on the Black Sea), in the myths of Greece. She was carried off by THESEUS, and in due course bore his son HIPPOLYTUS.

**ANTUM**

In Mesopotamian tradition, she occurs as the wife of ANU.

**ANU**

God of the sky in the Babylonian beliefs of ancient Mesopotamia, occurring as AN in Sumerian. A father-figure among the gods,

he coupled with the earth (Sumerian KI) and their offspring was ENLIL, the god of the air. Anu is himself remote, and he became supplanted by Enlil as the supreme deity. He was however worshipped at the great temple at Uruk, along with his daughter ISHTAR.

*Epic of Gilgamesh*

**ANUBIS**

Son of the Egyptian god OSIRIS, sometimes portrayed as a black jackal, an animal associated with death both from its carrion habits and from its mournful howling in the desert on the sunset side of the Nile, thought to be the home of the dead. Anubis officiated at the funeral rites of OSIRIS, the formula for ritual human burials, and hence was thought of as the conductor of human souls to their destination. He also acted as the soul's judge. Sometimes represented as a dog- or jackal-headed man, his portrait occurs in the decoration of many tombs.

*The jackal-headed figure of the Egyptian god Anubis, who presided over the embalming of the dead, shown in a wall-painting from the necropolis at Thebes, preparing a mummy. 20th Dynasty.*

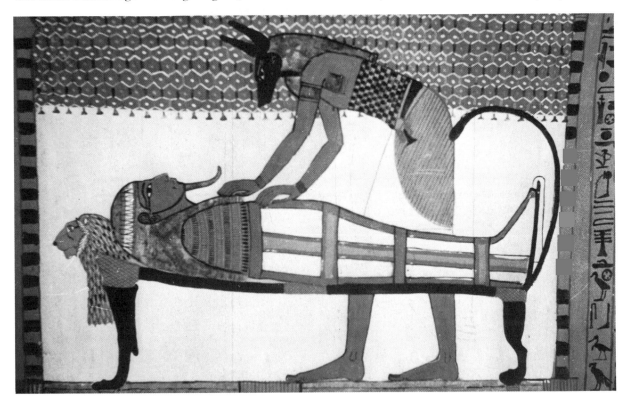

**ANUKET**

Or Anukis. A female river divinity of ancient Egypt, centred on the area of what is now Aswan. She became connected with fertility (through the providing effects of the Nile floods) and hence with licentiousness.

**AO CHIN**

In the Chinese pantheon of spiritual beings, he is one of the four great 'dragon kings', who are regarded jointly as rulers of the sea and the gods of rain. AO KUANG, AO SHUN and AO JUN are the other three. They live in palaces in the sea, attended by sea creatures. Each area, however, has its own local dragon-king, who (as bringers of rain) are connected with wells and water-courses. The dragon-kings are petitioned in times of drought.

**AO JUN**

One of the four great 'dragon kings' in Chinese mythology. See AO CHIN.

**AO KUANG**

One of the four great 'dragon kings' in Chinese mythology. See AO CHIN.

**AO SHUN**

One of the four great 'dragon kings' in Chinese mythology. See AO CHIN.

**APEP**

In Egyptian myth a serpent, the enemy of the god RA; he lived in the heavenly version of the Nile, and attempted to prevent the sun-god's boat taking its daily journey. In bad weather it seemed that he had a momentary victory, but Ra in the end overcame him and cut off his head.

**APHRODITE**

Goddess of love in the central Greek pantheon. The name is possibly connected with *aphros*, 'foam', and the goddess was said to have been born of the foam which arose in the sea when CRONUS severed the genitals of his father URANUS. The sea they fell into was alternatively off the southern Peloponnese, where the goddess drifted ashore on the island of Cythera, or off the island of Cyprus. She was married to the unattractive smith-god HEPHAESTUS, but had affairs with several of the major gods. Her winning of the beauty-contest judged by PARIS was a primary cause of the Trojan War. She personified chiefly unmarried love, and her influence is seen mainly in adulterous affairs. In Roman mythology the goddess VENUS came to represent the same character.

*A marble statuette of Aphrodite, the Greek goddess of pure and ideal love as well as of lustful passion.*

## APIS

An Egyptian deity, the bull-god of Memphis, on the lower Nile. He was worshipped in the physical form of a black bull, killed at the end of each period of twenty-five years, when a new incarnation (recognized by Apis' priesthood by certain markings) was born somewhere in Egypt, eventually discovered and brought to Memphis. The god-bulls were embalmed and buried, and their huge sarcophagi may still be seen near Saqqara. See BUCHIS, MNEVIS.

## APOLLO

Son of ZEUS and LETO and a major god in the Greek pantheon. Chiefly a god of prophecy, in which capacity he succeeded an older goddess-cult at Delphi, Apollo had several different functions. He was a huntsman, a healer, a musician, and as a shepherd the guardian of flocks; originally he may have been a sun-god, or god of light. He and his twin sister ARTEMIS were born on the island of Delos, another centre of his worship, to which his mother had retreated to escape the anger of HERA, Zeus' legitimate wife. He is shown in the mythology as being in conflict with the gods of goat-cults, DIONYSUS and PAN, and with HERMES, who has cattle-herding associations, indicating probably the occurrence of rivalry between mobile pastoral groups. There are many fine statues of the god as a good-looking and rather proud young man, the best example perhaps being that in the museum at Olympia, where it formed part of the west pediment of the temple of Zeus.

## APOPHIS

Another name for APEP, the serpent enemy of the Egyptian sun-god RA.

## APSU

In Mesopotamian cosmogony, he was the male element in the primordial pair, representing the sweet water, which merged with the salt water of the sea to produce the first beings. See TIAMAT.

*Epic of Creation*

## APU PUNCHAU

An Inca god of Peru. See INTI.

## AQHAT

A figure of Syrian tradition, the son of King DANEL. His story tells how he was presented by the gods with a bow, which the goddess ANAT coveted; she offered to exchange for it the gift of immortality. The story is probably one of death and rebirth.

## ARAM

Son of SHEM, in the traditional early history of the Hebrews as recorded in the Old Testament. The tribe he founded was known after him as the Arameans. *Genesis*

LEFT: *A detail from the coffin of a priest of Amon dating from approximately 1000 BC depicting Apis, the bull-god of Memphis.*

*Apollo, one of the major gods of ancient Greece, is frequently portrayed as a handsome young man of proud bearing.*

*The Argonauts, the band of Greek heroes who accompanied Jason in his quest for the Golden Fleece, gather under the protection of Athene.*

**ARAMAZD**

The Armenian version of Zoroastrian AHURA MAZDA, equated by the Armenians with the Greek god ZEUS.

**ARANDA**

A gigantic snake, in the beliefs of the Australian aborigines, occurring in the area of Emianga. In the past it was said to have swallowed human beings, and it is thought to be still present, lurking deep below the water.

**ARANRHOD**

Also Arianrhod. A figure in the Celtic mythology of Britain. She is a powerful mother-figure occurring in the tale *Math son of Mathonwy*, in which she struggles to outwit her brother, the wizard GWYDION. She gave her name to the *corona borealis* (known in Welsh as *Caer Aranrhod*, 'Aranrhod's Castle'), and may therefore be related to the Greek heroine ARIADNE. *Mabinogion*

**ARAWN**

In British Celtic myth, the king of the otherworld. His story tells how he changed places for a year with PWYLL, Prince of Dyfed, who defeated a rival for Arawn's land. *Mabinogion*

**ARAWOTYA**

In the stories of the aboriginal Wonkamala people of the Lake Eyre district of South Australia, he is a being who lives in the sky. At one period he was said to have lived on earth, where he was responsible for producing the springs which occur unexpectedly in the arid lands of South Australia and western Queensland.

**ARES**

The Greek god of war. Compare MARS in Roman mythology. Son of ZEUS and HERA, Ares is little characterized apart from his military aspects of rage and violence. He did however have a love-affair with APHRODITE, in which he was caught by her husband HEPHAESTUS, who trapped the lovers in a net. He is generally portrayed as being unpopular among the gods, perhaps representing to the Greeks the less heroic and more unpleasant aspects of warfare. (Compare ATHENA).

**ARGONAUTS**

In the Greek story of the hero JASON these are the prominent hero-figures whom he gathers together to man his ship, the Argo, at the start of his expedition in quest of the Golden Fleece.

*Arjuna, the third of the five Pandava princes whom Krishna helped in their struggle against their cousins, the Kurus. This miniature from an* illustrated Mahabharata *(1761-3) shows a battle between Arjuna and Bhaga-datta.*

## ARGUS

A giant with a hundred eyes, occurring in the stories of Greek myth as the custodian of Io, who had been committed to him by HERA because ZEUS was in love with her. Argus was killed by HERMES, who was sent to rescue Io.

## ARIADNE

In Greek mythology, the daughter of King MINOS of Crete. She enabled THESEUS to escape from the Minotaur's labyrinth (see ASTERION) by providing him with a ball of string: unwinding it on entering he was able to retrace his steps by winding it up again. He fled from Crete with her, but abandoned her on the island of Naxos, where she was comforted by the god DIONYSUS, whom she later married. Part of her wedding regalia became a constellation, the Corona Borealis.

## ARISTAEUS

A somewhat minor god of Greece. Son of APOLLO, like his father he was a pastoral god, his function being that of guardian of flocks and hives. He was responsible for the death of ORPHEUS' wife EURIDICE, who trod on a poisonous snake when he tried to rape her.

## ARJUNA

A figure of the mythology of India. The son of KUNTI by the god INDRA, he became a principal character in the work known as the *Bhagavad-Gita*. He is a member of the PANDAVA family who seek KRISHNA's help in their struggle against their hostile cousins. Krishna becomes Arjuna's charioteer when the former attends, but will not participate in, the final battle, and it is to Arjuna that the divine hero delivers his wisdom.

*Mahabharata*

## ARMAITI

A spirit in the Zoroastrian religion of Iran. Sometimes Spenta (Bounteous) Armaiti; he is one of the AMESHA SPENTAS, translated as Right-mindedness or Devotion, the element of pious worship inherent in man's relation to God, and connected with the humble but providing earth, sometimes identified with that.

## ART

A hero of Celtic Irish story best known for having made a voyage of strange adventures, not unlike that of ODYSSEUS.

## ARTAVAZD

An early king of the Armenians, said in the mythology to have been imprisoned by demons while out hunting. Two dogs perpetually gnaw at his chains, where he is held captive in a cave, but the Armenian blacksmiths symbolically renew them at New Year because it is believed that when he is released the world will end.

## ARTEMIS

In the Greek pantheon the goddess of hunting. In the mythology she is contrasted with APHRODITE, goddess of love, and stories often treat of a rivalry between the two. Twin sister of APOLLO, born on the island of Delos, she is also like him a figure connected with light, in her case with the moon. Emphasis is placed on her chastity, a quality which as a consequence became associated with the moon. See DIANA in Roman mythology. She never married, and spurned domestic life and amorous affairs. She is seen spending her time out of doors in the mountains of Arcadia, with her hounds and her company of maidens – a rather unfeminine figure, usually wearing severely practical clothes.

*A gold pectoral plaque depicting the Greek goddess Artemis. From Camirus, Rhodes, 7th century* BC.

## ARTHUR

This best-known and most enduring figure of Celtic British mythology also has the most complex roots. Early historians treated Arthur as a historical figure of the post-Roman period, while continuing to attribute to him supernatural qualities which indicate a possible origin as an early god. Geoffrey of Monmouth took up this amalgam and made Arthur a national emblem of British independence, at the same time helping to set up his later image as a chivalrous medieval monarch. The earlier Welsh tales however portray a cruder and more primitive figure. Much subsequent literature uses Geoffrey as its model, and the Arthurian theme was taken up in France where it came to form a cycle of stories equivalent to those centred on Charlemagne. In the process the independent matter of the Holy Grail (see PERCEVAL, GALAHAD) came to be associated with Arthur, as did the independent figure of MERLIN. Much additional material also became embedded in the Arthurian tradition, but an early feature which survived throughout is his rivalry with his nephew MORDRED, which led to both their deaths at the battle of Camlan. See also LANCELOT, GUENEVER.

GEOFFREY OF MONMOUTH: *History of the Kings of Britain;* MALORY: *Morte d'Arthur*

## ARUBANI

The queen of the god HALDI, a high god of Armenia.

## ARURU

The Babylonian goddess of creation, she was the maker of ENKIDU in the story of GILGAMESH. *Epic of Gilgamesh*

## ARYAMAN

A sky-god, in the beliefs of India, associated with VARUNA. He was also a god of hospitality. *Rig Veda*

*In Malory's version of the stories of Arthur, the King's last companion, Sir Bedevere, twice failed before returning, as commanded, his master's magic sword to the lake from which it came. This early 14th-century French miniature shows the Lady of the Lake retrieving the sword as the mortally wounded Arthur waits to die.*

*A cylinder seal dating from 990 to 600 BC depicts two winged figures, two streams of water running from heaven to earth and the symbol of Ashur the principal god of Assyria.*

### ASA

Sometimes Asa Vahista. A spirit occurring in the Zoroastrian religion of Iran. One of the **AMESHA SPENTAS**, translated as Order or Rightness, he was connected with the regularity and stability of the sun.

### ASAG

A demon, one who brings illness, in the beliefs of ancient Mesopotamia.

### ASCLEPIUS

A Greek god (correctly a demigod) of healing, son of **APOLLO** by a mortal princess. He learnt his arts from the centaur **CHEIRON**. Asclepius is portrayed as a gentle figure, living a life of peace and wisdom. In the practice of his skill he succeeded in bringing the dead back to life, and this revolt against nature angered **HADES**, god of the dead. He complained to his brother **ZEUS**, who struck Asclepius himself dead with a thunderbolt. To the Romans the same god was known as **AESCULAPIUS**; he was worshipped as a protector, after supposedly saving the city from a plague in 293 BC.

### ASDIWAL

Or Asiwa, Asi-hwil. A great hunter, in the mythology of the Tsimshian Indians of North America, remarkable for having climbed a ladder into heaven and married the daughter of the sun. Himself the son of an Indian woman by a supernatural being, he showed signs of his extraordinary nature from early childhood, and later successfully achieved a series of apparently impossible tasks, success being a pre-condition of being permitted to marry his celestial bride. Compare African **KINTU**, **NAMBI**.

### ASHUR

Also spelt Asshur. The chief god of Assyria, after whom the capital city of the Assyrian empire was named.

### ASHVINS

Figures of the Sanskrit tradition of India, in modern Hindi, Aswins. A pair of male twins, sons of the sun, great horsemen who feature extensively in the *Rig Veda* as heroic interveners on behalf of mankind.

*Rig Veda*

33

*The birth of the Greek goddess Athena, fully grown and armed, from the head of Zeus, which Haphaestus has split with his axe. Detail of an Athenian cup, 560-550 BC.*

### ASK
The first man, in Scandinavian tradition. The word means Ash-tree, the reference being to the story of how the human race was made by the gods out of trees.

SNORRI STURLUSON: *Prose Edda*

### ASTARTE, ASHTORETH
Principal goddess of the Phoenicians and Canaanites, responsible for fertility, akin to ISHTAR of Mesopotamia. In Egyptian mythology, occurring as the queen of Byblos who received the goddess ISIS as nurse for her newborn son, in the course of Isis' search for her dead husband OSIRIS. The goddess in due course revealed her divine nature and was granted the pillar enclosing the chest which contained her husband's corpse.

### ASTERION
The name of the Minotaur, a figure of Greek mythology. Born of MINOS' wife PASIPHAE after her sexual encounter with a bull sent for sacrifice by POSEIDON (see MINOS), Asterion is seen as being part man, part bull. He lived in a labyrinth constructed for the purpose by DAEDALUS, where he devoured victims sent there by the king.

OVID: *Metamorphoses*

### ASURAS
A group of early gods of India, including VARUNA, who became reduced in importance with the emergence of new religious focuses until they sank to the status of demons. See Zoroastrian AHURAS and compare DEVAS.

### ATAENTSIC
In the mythology of the Iroquois and Huron Indians of North America, thought to have been a woman of the sky people who came to earth, who is viewed as being the ultimate ancestor of the human race. She is the equivalent of the Navajo 'first woman', and her daughter likewise conceived twins, by the Lord of the Winds,

of whom a story is told similar to that of
NAGENATZANI and THOBADESTCHIN. See
IOSKEHA, TAWISKARE.

## ATAR

The sacred fire in the Zoroastrian religions
of Iran, the god embodied in this element
being said in later tradition to be the son of
AHURA MAZDA, but a very ancient principle
in Iranian religion. Zoroastrianism is still
based on attention to the sacred flame, and
from early times it has been addressed as a
deity itself, provider, sustainer, an element
in the original creation.

## ATEN

Or Aton. In Egyptian tradition, a rival god
to AMON among the pharaohs, adopted by
Amenhoten IV, who changed his name to
Akhenaten ('it pleases Aten') and instituted
an interlude of non-conformity in an
otherwise Amon-dominated epoch. He was
in fact an early sun-god, but as developed
by Akhenaten, in an attempt at monotheism,
he was viewed as the supreme all-
embracing deity and the originator of life.

## ATHENA

The Greek goddess of wisdom, and patron
goddess of Athens, also known as Pallas
Athena, or Athene. Though not as overtly
masculine in character as ARTEMIS, she
nevertheless represents one of the non-
sexual aspects of womanhood. One of the
terms used to describe her is *parthenos*,
the maid – hence the name of her temple
on the Acropolis, the Parthenon. Compare
also HERA, APHRODITE. Her story tells that
she was born from the head of ZEUS fully-
armed, and she is normally shown as a
warrior figure, with shield and helmet. In
this aspect she is the patron of the Greeks
in battle, bringing to the fray a
characteristic tendency towards political
intrigue, rather than mere violence.

## ATIRA

In the tradition of the Pawnee Indians of
North America, she is the wife of TIRAWA,
the supreme god and governor of heaven
and earth.

*A statuette of the Greek goddess Athena, who is typically represented as a warrior.*

*Atlas and Prometheus endure their punishment for offending the new gods of Olympus. While Atlas was compelled to hold the skies on his shoulder, Prometheus was chained to a rock, where an eagle tore at his liver. Kylix from Sparta, c. 550 BC.*

## ATLAS

One of the Titans, or early gods of Greece. Seen as a giant, he led the Titans in an unsuccessful war against the new gods of Olympus, and was punished by being condemned to hold up the sky on his shoulders. The supposed site of this ordeal was the mountain range called after him, the Atlas mountains of north-west Africa, the story being a figurative way of saying that they themselves are so high that they appear to support the sky.

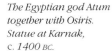

*The Egyptian god Atum together with Osiris. Statue at Karnak, c. 1400 BC.*

## ATRAHASIS

In an Old Babylonian story of the Great Flood, the hero who survived to propagate mankind. See UTNAPISHTIM, ZIUSUDRA, and compare DEUCALION, NOAH.

## ATREUS

King of Mycenae, father of AGAMEMNON, in one of the central stories of Greek mythology. He was the son of PELOPS and hence grandson of TANTALUS. Atreus brought a curse on the dynasty of Mycenae and Argos by serving his brother's children to him at a feast. See THYESTES. Evidently monarch of a pastoral people, he possessed the golden fleece of a lamb sent for sacrifice by ARTEMIS.

## ATROPOS

In Greek myth, one of the three Fates. See CLOTHO.

## ATTIS

Sometimes spelt Atys. A hero of Phrygia whose story relates him closely to the Greek ADONIS and to the Mesopotamian TAMMUZ. Attis was loved by CYBELE, the Asiatic mother-goddess adopted by the Greeks. In some accounts he castrated himself and bled to death under a pine, and was himself changed into a tree. A great spring festival of mourning and revival was held in his honour.

## ATUM

An Egyptian deity, the local god of Heliopolis, on the lower Nile, connected with the sun and hence absorbed into the figure of RA as Ra-Atum. Becoming universalized as creator of all things, he is shown wearing the double-crown of the 'kings of the two lands', Upper and Lower Egypt. He was said originally to have mated with himself to create the first gods.

## AUGEAS

A figure in Greek myth, in which he is the king of Elis, in the north-west Peloponnese. He occurs solely as the subject of one of the labours of HERACLES, who was obliged to clear the dung of his

*A bronze figure of Avalokiteshvara, the Bodhisattva whose task it was to convert Tibet to Buddhism.*

many cattle from Augeas' stables, and who went to war with the king when he failed to keep his part of the bargain.

## AUTOLYCUS

A character of Greek myth, a figure of an utterly scurrilous nature. He was a rustler and bandit inhabiting the wild slopes of Mount Parnassus. Sometimes he is said to be the son of HERMES (who also has connections with thieving). According to Homer ODYSSEUS was the son of Autolycus' daughter.

## AVALOKITESHVARA

In the Tibetan Buddhist religion, and in Mahayana or northern Buddhism generally, a Bodhisattva (meaning an 'enlightenment-being') who was given the task of converting Tibet to Buddhism, which he did with the assistance of a monkey which he created and taught for the purpose, and through whose agency he populated Tibet with human beings. Known as 'The Lord of Compassion', he is the tutelary spirit of Tibet, often represented as a four-armed figure, much worshipped and greatly respected in the popular religion. The name is Sanskrit, meaning 'Lord who looks down with compassion', and his local Tibetan name is Chenresi. The same figure occurs in Chinese (in this case however as female) as GUAN YIN, and in Japan as KWANNON.

## AWONAWILONA

The pre-existent and creative spirit in the cosmogony of the Pueblo Indians of North America. He is regarded as having made the world in gradual progression from inside himself. The female earth and the male sky which he created then mated to produce the first living beings.

## AYA

A Mesopotamian deity, the wife of the sun-god SHAMASH, and goddess of the dawn.
*Epic of Gilgamesh*

## AYAR CACHI

One of the legendary founders of the Inca race of Peru, he was a member of a family of brothers and sisters who emerged from a cave. He incurred the envy of his brothers, who attempted to destroy him but were pursued by his spirit. He is the subject of a local cult, in which it is thought he was turned into a piece of stone.

# B

## BA

The Chinese goddess of drought, sometimes said to be the daughter of HUANG DI. When she was called to earth to assist the latter in his war against his rival CHIYU, she overdid her part in resisting his weapons of rain and fog by bringing on a great drought, and her continuing presence threatened the complete destruction of the earth. This threat still occasionally occurs, although Huang Di was obliged to drive her into exile.

## BAAL

The main god of ancient Syria, a fertility and storm god seen as having a long-running conflict with YAM, the sea-god. Baal is the son of EL, and is often referred to as the Rider on the Clouds. He is also sometimes assimilated with the storm-god HADAD. The name (the sense of which is 'Lord') was adopted by many separate tribes as that of their major god, and for the Hebrews entering Canaan it represented the main non-Judaic deity, hence it occurs in the Bible as the paradigm of a false god.

## BABA-YAGA

In Slavonic tradition, a monstrous witch, seen as a man-eating hag living in a compound fenced with human bones. She is of huge size, and in some versions it is said that her mouth (an explanation of earth-cracks such as chasms and ravines) stretches from earth to hell.

## BACABS

Four gods who support the four corners of the sky, in the mythological system of the Maya Indians of Mexico.

## BACCHUS

The Greek god of wine and drunkenness. Compare DIONYSUS. Bacchus replaced

ABOVE: *A stele from Ras Shamrah representing Baal, in the mythology of ancient Syria a fertility and storm god generally depicted as a triumphant warrior.*

RIGHT: *In this bas-relief from Herculaneum Bacchus, the god of wine and drunkenness, whose cult in Roman times displaced that of the Greek god Dionysus, is shown as a young man.*

Dionysus in that capacity in the mythology which the Romans adopted from the Greeks. He was originally represented as a bearded man, later as a youth. The name, possibly derived from a word indicating noisiness, may have started as a title of Dionysus, connected with the rowdy behaviour of his followers. The Roman feast in his honour, the Bacchanalia, exhibited this quality of disorder.

## BACHUE

A goddess of the American Indians of Colombia, believed by them to be the originator of the human race.

## BALAAM

In Hebrew tradition as recorded in the Old Testament, he was a prophet who was instructed by the king of Moab (BALAK) to curse the invading Israelites. In a famous story the ass he rode on refused to pass an angel sent by God to obstruct him, and miraculously spoke to him, remonstrating with him when he struck it to urge it on.
*Numbers*

## BALAK

According to the Hebrew tradition, a king of Moab. The story tells how he attempted to use the prophet **BALAAM** to counter the advance of the Israelites with a curse.

*Numbers*

## BALAM-ACAB

One of the four 'first men' in the cosmogony of the Maya Indians of Mexico. See **BALAM-QUITZE** and **GUCUMATZ**.

*Popol Vub*

## BALAM-QUITZE

One of the four 'first men' in the cosmogony of the Maya Indians of Mexico. They were possessed of great intelligence and had all-seeing vision, and so at once grew omniscient. This displeased their creators (see **GUCUMATZ**) who decided to restrict their sight. As a result they were from then on inferior to the gods.

*Popol Vub*

## BALARAMA

Elder brother of **KRISHNA**, in the Hindu mythology of India, and also the partial avatar of **VISHNU**.

## BALDER

A Scandinavian god, the son of **ODIN** and **FRIGG**, he is firmly distinguished by his beauty and total goodness. So great were these qualities, in fact, that a light shone around him. Anyone who saw him at once loved him. He spread a mood of goodwill and harmony. The irony of his story is that in spite of the effort of the gods to protect him he nevertheless came to grief. Having presentiments of danger, in the form of disturbing dreams, he sought advice of the gods, and as a precaution his mother demanded of all things an assurance that they would not harm Balder. Secure in this universal promise the gods played a game, throwing things at Balder knowing that none could hurt him. There is among the gods one dedicated to evil, the god **LOKI**, who was envious of Balder and resented the merriment he heard. He discovers that one item has been left out of the oath-

taking, as being too innocuous to bother with: the mistletoe. Loki puts a twig of this into the hand of the blind god **HOD**, directs his aim at Balder, and to the immense consternation of the gods Balder dies. An attempt, thwarted by Loki, is made to retrieve him from the realm of the death-goddess **HEL**, who makes it a condition that all the world should weep for Balder – an expression of the dripping thaw of the northern spring. In the end Loki is punished, and Balder reborn into the new order of gods in a new world, after the cataclysm of Ragnarök. His name itself possibly means 'lord', like the Greek **ADONIS**, and his glow and goodness may identify him as originally a god of light.

SNORRI STURLUSON: *Prose Edda*

*Despite his radiant beauty and goodness and the goodwill of the other gods, Balder fell victim to the evil of Loki. In this episode of the Scandinavian myth, Hermod, one of Odin's sons, assails the gates of the underworld in an attempt to fetch Balder back. From an illustrated manuscript of* The Prose Edda, *1760.*

## BALOR

Also spelt Balar. A figure of Irish Celtic myth, the king of a race of giants. He forms a primitive and formidable background figure in the Irish stories of the displacement of the older order by new peoples. He possessed a single evil eye, which could destroy whole armies, and he terrorized the heroes of Ireland until defeated by LUGH.

## BAST

The cat goddess of the ancient Egyptians, the cat being a creature domesticated very early in Egypt and honoured as protector against snakes and guardian of grain. She is shown as a woman with a cat's head. In her myth she became viewed as related to RA, and was said to come to his help in his perpetual struggle with the serpent APEP.

## BATHSHEBA

Wife of DAVID, in the Hebrew stories preserved in the Old Testament, taken by him from her husband, URIAH, whom he arranged to be killed in battle, an act which provoked God's displeasure. She became the mother of David's son SOLOMON.

*2 Samuel*

*A bronze figure of the Egyptian goddess Bast, whose sacred animal was the cat and who is generally represented as a woman with a cat's head.*

## BAUCIS

A figure of Greek mythology, in which she is the wife of PHILEMON. A model of humble rectitude, she and her husband modestly accommodated ZEUS and HERMES travelling disguised, for which they were duly rewarded by the gods.

OVID: *Metamorphoses*

## BAUGI

He occurs in Scandinavian mythology as the giant who possessed, along with his brother SUTTUNG, the mead of inspiration. See also ODIN.

SNORRI STURLUSON: *Prose Edda*

## BEDEVERE

In British Celtic myth, an Arthurian knight, originally, as Bedwyr, one of the heroes of ARTHUR's war-band, later his cup-bearer, and finally the companion who went with him at his request when he was fatally wounded.

GEOFFREY OF MONMOUTH: *History of the Kings of Britain;* MALORY: *Morte d'Arthur*

## BEELZEBUB

A figure of Hebrew tradition. Originally Beelzebul, a derivative of Baalzebul, he was an aspect of the multiple god BAAL, worshipped in Canaan at the time of the Hebrews' invasion, and hence taken by them to be the representative of false religion. From this origin the word has come to be sometimes used as the name of the devil, the leader of the forces of evil.

## BEL

A Babylonian word for God, and one of the titles of MARDUK and of ENLIL.

## BELENUS

The Latinization of the Celtic god BELI.

## BELI

One of the main gods of the continental Celts at the time of the Roman occupation of Gaul; identified by the Romans with APOLLO and therefore perhaps bearing associations with flock or with music. He occurs in British myth as Beli the Great, who ruled Britain before or at the time of the Roman invasion. He probably gave his name to the Celtic spring festival, Beltane, and one of the gates of the city of London was called after him, now corrupted to Billingsgate.

## BELINUS

According to Geoffrey of Monmouth, in his collection of Celtic British stories, an early king of Britain. The figure is however clearly based on the name of the Celtic god BELI.

GEOFFREY OF MONMOUTH: *History of the Kings of Britain*

## BELIT-SHERI

A Mesopotamian god of the underworld, and the recorder among the gods.

*Epic of Gilgamesh*

*The Greek hero Bellerophon, astride Pegasus, attacking the Chimaera, described in the Iliad as 'in front a lion, behind a serpent, in the middle a goat.' Terracotta relief from Melos, c. 450 BC.*

### BELLEROPHON

Typical of those Greek heroes destined, as a test or a penance, to destroy dangerous monsters, Bellerophon is particularly noted for the assistance he acquired from the winged horse PEGASUS, which he caught and tamed. This however finally brought about his downfall when, in a fine display of hubris, he attempted to ride heavenward to Olympus, the home of the gods. ZEUS sent a gadfly to sting the flying horse and throw him, and he ended his days friendless and exiled.

HOMER: *Iliad*

### BELSHAZZAR

Son of NEBUCHADNEZAR, in Hebrew tradition, and his successor as king of Babylon. A historical figure, he occurs as ruler of Babylon during the exile there of the prophet DANIEL. At a banquet which he held a hand appeared and wrote on the wall some words which Daniel interpreted as predicting the fall of Babylon.

*Daniel*

### BELTESHAZZAR

The Babylonian name given to the Hebrew prophet DANIEL during his exile there.

*Daniel*

### BENJAMIN

Younger brother to JOSEPH in the Hebrew tradition as recorded in the Old Testament. During the famine in which the latter rose to dominance over Egypt, Benjamin was kept at home while Joseph's brothers went to Egypt to seek food. Knowing this, Joseph obliged them to send him, and took advantage of their protectiveness to Benjamin as part of his scheme for revenge on his brothers.

*Genesis*

### BENKEI

In the tradition of Japan, he is the companion of the hero **YOSHITSHUNE**. He himself was said to have been conceived by a demon (a **TENGU**) and was born after a thirteen-month pregnancy, whereupon he quickly grew to great stature and to possess extraordinary strength. At the first encounter of the two heroes Benkei was defeated by Yoshitsune. He then became the latter's servant and the pair then set out to conquer enemies in many adventures.

### BENTEN

Chiefly a Japanese sea-goddess, she is often shown riding on a sea-dragon. She is however also a goddess of the arts and is herself a musician. She brings good luck in love and arranges favourable marriages for those who pray to her.

### BEOWULF

In an Anglo-Saxon story, he was the hero of a people known as the **GEATS**. He perfectly represents the monster-slaying saviour of a nation, superhuman in power and yet humanly identified enough to be sympathetic. See **GRENDEL**. Beowulf's story is told in an epic poem probably of the eighth century, surviving in a manuscript of the tenth.

### BERSERKS

In Scandinavian tradition the Berserks were warriors in the service of **ODIN** who

*Benkei, the companion of the Japanese hero Yoshitshune, depicted waiting for waves to subside in a fan print by Kuniyoshi (1797-1861).*

were said to wear the skins of bears and to howl like animals when they fought: they probably formed the model for the bodyguards of early kings, noted for their battle-frenzy. Compare Irish LUGH. The name has given us our modern English word 'berserk', as in 'going berserk'. The root form is 'bear sark' meaning 'bear coat'.

## BES

In Egyptian myth, a cheerful dwarf, the spirit of the family and the protector of married women, particularly at the time of childbirth. He is shown as ugly and deformed, but these features were positive features as they served to frighten away evil spirits.

## BHARATA

A figure of the mythology of India, in which he is an ancestral king, the deeds of whose descendants form the subject matter of the great epic poem, the *Mahabharata*.

## BIA

A river deity of the Akan tribes of Ghana, the spirit of the river of the same name, the Bia, seen as a rival to TANO, and said to be the elder and preferred son of God. In their story, Tano gained by a trick the more fertile lands intended for Bia, who was left with the more arid areas.

## BIHEKO

The name used by the Kiga tribe of Liganda in Africa for God, as the supreme being. It means 'the one who carries everyone on his back', an image drawn from the means of transporting African babies, which suggests a female, mothering role for God.

## BISHAMON

A god of Japanese Buddhism derived from the Chinese Buddhist tradition, in which he is the bringer of wealth. Normally depicted as a warrior, he also has attributes of religious devotion symbolized by an emblem of a pagoda which he carries in his hand.

## BLADUD

A king of Britain in Geoffrey of Monmouth's compilation and according to him the founder of Bath. The story tells how he died, like ICARUS, in an attempt to fly.

GEOFFREY OF MONMOUTH: *History of the Kings of Britain*

*The Japanese god Bishamon, typically represented as a warrior. Gilt wood statuette, 1760.*

43

## BLODEUEDD

In a British Celtic story, she was a woman made out of flowers by the wizards GWYDION and MATH to be a wife for LLEU LLAW GYFFES, who had been cursed by his mother ARANRHOD with never having a wife of any existing race. A character of both charm and treachery, she eventually deceived him with a lover, lured him to his death. For this she was turned by Gwydion into an owl and in this form she is still molested by all other wild birds.

*Mabinogion*

## BOALIRI

The younger of a pair of sisters occurring in a story of origins in the mythology of the aboriginal people of Arnhem Land, in the north of Australia. See WAIMARIWI.

## BOAZ

A figure occurring in a Hebrew story recorded in the Old Testament. See RUTH.

## BOCHICA

A major god of the American Indians of Colombia who bears connections with the sun. He is also regarded as the institutor of civilisation, giving the people their laws and setting the form of their religion. According to the story he once was a man on earth (though not of a race recognizable to the Indians), and in due course he retired to heaven and reigns there still transcendent. He is embattled with his special enemy CHIBCHACUM, and he once saved mankind from destruction when the latter brought about a great flood.

## BOIUNA

Goddess of the Amazon rivers, in the beliefs of the Indians of Brazil. She is viewed as a giant serpent with shining eyes, and is much feared for her powers of magic.

## BOLON DZACAB

A god of ancestry, in the beliefs of the Maya Indians of Mexico, his name connecting him with lineage. His image appears on monuments as an attribute of people of importance.

## BOMAZI

In the beliefs of the people of the African Congo region, a white man who appeared among the early people of the Bushongo tribal area, and initiated the expansion of the people by enabling an old man and woman to reproduce.

## BOR

The father of ODIN, in Scandinavian mythology.

## BOREAS

A Greek god, the personification of the North Wind.

## BORS

In British Celtic myth, one of the knights of King ARTHUR's court, who figures prominently in Malory's telling of the Grail quest, but remains otherwise an undistinguished figure.

MALORY: *Morte d'Arthur*

## BRAGI

God of poetry, in Scandinavian mythology, the husband of IDUN.

## BRAHMA

The creator god, in the Hindu tradition of India, himself self-created and the origin of all forms. Unusually he is regarded as being fallible, and said to have made a number of mistakes, and the process of creation proceeded by advances and setbacks. His name, which is masculine, is not the same as the neuter word *Brahman*, meaning the general omnipresent World-Soul, from which the priestly caste known as Brahmins or Brahmans comes, but these, however, were among the more important creations of Brahma. Like many Hindu gods Brahma is depicted as having multiple heads, in his case usually four.

## BRAN

Also known as Bendigeidfran, 'Bran the Blessed'. A major composite figure of

Celtic British myth, undoubtedly based on an important continental Celtic god. It appears that originally his cult was in opposition to that of BELI (since tales tell of war between the two). In the early story of BRANWEN he appears as King of Britain, and undertakes an invasion of Ireland. Evidently of enormous size, he waded across, and later lay down across a river to form a bridge. He also possessed a giant cauldron in which dead warriors could be brought back to life. These connections with rivers and with vessels of rebirth recur in his later manifestation as Bran, or Bron, the fisher-king, in the Grail stories, and therefore may indicate important special attributes of the god. In the Welsh story he instructed his head to be cut off and taken to London, where it was buried on the hill of the Tower of London to form a talisman against invasion. The ravens still kept on the site may be a survival of this tradition, since Bran's name means 'crow'. As the fisher-king he lived in a castle in which mysteries took place, near a river, where he fished, and possessed a mystically curative vessel. See PERCEVAL.

*Mabinogion*

**BRANWEN**

In Celtic British myth, the tragic heroine of a tale called after her. She was married to the king of Ireland MATHOLWCH, who however treated her badly. In due course she managed to tell her brother BRAN of this, with the result that he then invaded Ireland. Such devastation was caused by the ensuing war that Branwen died of a broken heart on the way home.

*Mabinogion*

**BRENNIUS**

In Geoffrey of Monmouth's account, a British leader who led the Britons against Rome, and who is also mentioned as being in conflict with his brother BELINUS. The figure is however clearly a Latinization of the Celtic name BRAN, an ancient god. See also BELI.

GEOFFREY OF MONMOUTH: *History of the Kings of Britain*

**BRICRIU**

A chieftain of Ulster, in Irish Celtic tradition. The story tells how he gave a great feast for King CONCHOBAR and his men, with, however, treacherous intentions. In the Ulster Cycle of stories, he is the arch trouble-maker, the 'poison-tongued', and on this occasion stirs up a sequence of conflicts which result in the assembled heroes contesting each other.

**BRIGANTIA**

One of the chief goddesses of the Continental Celts, the Romanized version

*The creator-god Brahma, shown here with four heads. Brahma, Vishnu and Shiva make up the Hindu trinity.*

of the British goddess Briganti, 'the exalted one', the patron goddess of the Brigantes, a Celtic tribe which was possibly named after her.

### BRON

A figure of Celtic British mythology, in which this is the name of the Fisher-King in the medieval stories of the quest for the Holy Grail. See BRAN.

### BRYNHILD

A figure of Scandinavian mythology, in the German version known as Brunhild. She is a leading member of the VALKYRIES, the war-spirits who conduct the slain to Valhalla, and the story tells how she attracted the love of SIGURD but herself married a mortal king. In one episode attached to her she disobeyed ODIN by choosing the wrong victor in a battle, and was condemned to imprisonment within a wall of fire, from which she was rescued by SIGURD. When he died she decided to join him by burning herself to death.
SNORRI STURLUSON: *Prose Edda*

### BUCHIS

A sacred bull of the ancient Egyptians, see APIS, MNEVIS. Buchis was a local god of a cult near Thebes, a late-comer to Egyptian religion and less developed than the subjects of the other bull-cults.

### BUDDHA

A title of the founder of the Indian religion called after him, Buddhism. See SIDDHARTHA, his personal name.

### BURI

The first being, in the Scandinavian story of origins, the father of BOR and hence grandfather of ODIN. He emerged from the primal ice.   SNORRI STURLUSON: *Prose Edda*

### BUTO

In ancient Egypt, the cobra goddess depicted, on the crowns worn by the pharaohs, in the form of the symbol known as the '*uraeus*' – a forward-facing cobra with hood spread, protecting the king.

**NOTE:** In the transliteration of Greek the letter 'c' may alternatively be rendered as 'k'.

## CADMUS
The founder of the city of Thebes, in the mythology of the Greeks, the brother of **EUROPA**, and ancestor of **OEDIPUS**. He sowed the teeth of a serpent he had killed in the ground of Boeotia, from which sprang his followers, the 'Sown Men', and he thus formed for the people of that part an expression of their feeling of belonging.

## CAGN
The god of the African Bushmen. See **KAGGEN**.

## CAHA-PALUNA
In the story of origins of the Maya Indians of Mexico, one of the first women, the wife of **BALAM-QUITZE**.                    *Popol Vuh*

## CAIN
In the Hebrew creation story which forms the start of the Old Testament, he is the elder son of **ADAM** and **EVE**. His significance is that he commits the first murder by killing his brother **ABEL** when God favours the latter. He is cursed by God and sent into exile in the land of Nod, but obtains from God a sign of protection so that men will not further harm him. He then builds a city and it is his offspring who form the roots of human civilization.
*Genesis*

## CAIPORA
In the beliefs of the Indians of Brazil, a female spirit found in the forest. She is seen as protecting the animals sought by the hunter, and is consequently much feared by hunters.

## CALCHAS
A figure of Greek myth, in which he occurs as the prophet who accompanied the army which gathered under **AGAMEMNON** to launch the attack on Troy. See **IPHIGENIA**.
EURIPIDES: *Iphigenia in Aulis*

## CALLIOPE
In Greek myth, the name of one of the Muses, her particular province being epic poetry. See **CLIO**, **ERATO**, **TERPSICHORE**.

## CALLISTO
In Greek myth, a nymph whom **ZEUS** admired, and who consequently suffered the misfortune of being turned into a bear by his jealous wife **HERA**.

## CALYPSO
A figure of Greek mythology, occurring as a goddess encountered by **ODYSSEUS** on his arduous journey. She appears as a wilful and beautiful seductress, offering him immortality if he stays, and Odysseus reacts to this feeling of ensnarement with deep depression and the desire to leave.
Compare **CIRCE**.                    HOMER: *Odyssey*

*OPPOSITE: A Roman representation of the Celtic goddess Brigantia.*

*LEFT: In the Hebrew account of the descent of man Cain, the elder son of Adam and Eve, was sent into exile after murdering his brother, Abel. St Mary's Church, Addington, 16th-17th century.*

### CAQUIXAHA

One of the first women, wife of IQUI-BALAM, in the cosmogony of the Maya Indians of Mexico. *Popol Vuh*

### CARI

Said to be a pre-Incan chief of the area of Lake Titicaca in Peru, who waged a war against his rival ZAPANA and by inviting the help of the Inca king allowed the Incas to conquer the region without resistance. His story contains the interesting feature that he was said to have discovered a race of white men with beards living on an island in Lake Titicaca, but conquered and destroyed them.

### CASSANDRA

A Greek prophetess, and the princess of Troy who was brought back to Argos by AGAMEMNON after his victory over the Trojans. With an irony very typical of Greek tradition, it was her peculiar predicament that although she always accurately foretold the future she was cursed with the bitterness of never being believed.

AESCHYLUS: *Agamemnon*

### CASSIOPEIA

In Greek mythology, the mother of ANDROMEDA. She gives her name to a constellation.

### CASTOR

A Greek figure, one of a pair of twins (see POLYDEUCES and Roman POLLUX) who were the offspring of ZEUS and LEDA.

### CECROPS

A king of Athens, in the traditions of the ancient Greeks, to whose daughters ATHENA gave the infant ERICHTHONIUS.

### CELEUS

In Greek mythology he occurs as king of Eleusis at the time of the visit of DEMETER.

### CENTAURS

In Greek mythology, a race of half-human, half-equine beings living in the mountains of the Peloponnese. They are regarded ambivalently in myth, being at times wild and unruly but in certain cases exhibiting kindliness and even wisdom. See CHEIRON, PHOLUS, NESSUS.

ABOVE: *Castor and Pollux were the semi-divine twin sons of Leda, whom Zeus had visited in the form of a swan. This mosaic of Castor is from a Roman villa at Paphos in Cyprus. 3rd century AD.*

LEFT: *At the fall of Troy, Cassandra took refuge at the sanctuary of Athena. Here she is shown being dragged away from the goddess's statue by Ajax.*

### CERBERUS

A many-headed dog guarding the entrance to Hades, in the tradition of the ancient Greeks. He was brought up out of the underworld by **HERACLES** as one of the latter's labours.

### CERES

The Roman version of the Greek **DEMETER**, but a less developed figure. As the goddess of corn, she has given us the word 'cereal'.

### CERIDWEN

In Celtic British myth, a witch-goddess who possessed the prototype of the witch's cauldron, and in it set about brewing a potion which would give universal knowledge. See **GWION**. Eventually she became the mother of the prophet-bard **TALIESIN**.

### CERNUNNOS

The horned god of the continental Celts, who appears in various guises in British stories. The name appears to be descriptive, from the phrase 'the horned one', and little is known about the nature of the god himself, whose appearance however is well attested by artefacts. In some depictions he is surrounded by

*A Gallo-Roman funerary stele representing the Celtic god Cernunnos.*

animals, and so may have been a 'lord of the beasts'. See HERNE, and Hindu SIVA.

### CHACS

For the Maya Indians of Mexico, the Chacs were the rain gods, and were also responsible for thunder and lightning. They were however mainly benevolent deities.

### CHALCHIUHTLICUE

Sister and wife of TLALOC, a god of the Toltecs and Aztecs of Mexico, and herself a goddess of streams and lakes.

### CHANDAKA

A Buddhist figure of India, also known as Channa. He was the charioteer of the Buddha and his companion on the occasion of his departure from home.

### CHANDASHI

The wife of LEZA, the supreme godhead of peoples of Central Africa, by whom he is regarded as living underground and hence as being the cause of earthquakes.

### CHANG XI

Just as the people of the Shang dynasty of ancient China believed that the sky was once populated by ten suns and that a woman named XIHE was their mother, so they also saw the heavens as originally possessing ten moons, and Chang Xi was the mother of these. As Xihe bathed the suns, she also bathed them regularly, in a pool at the foot of a tree.

### CHARON

In Greek mythology, the ferryman who conveys the souls of the dead across the river Styx into Hades, the land of the dead.

### CHARYBDIS

A figure occurring in Greek myth as a monster taking the form of a whirlpool, which ODYSSEUS had to negotiate at the same time as the hazard of the rock-dwelling monster SCYLLA.

HOMER: *Odyssey*

*Chalchiuhtlicue, the sister and wife of the Mexican god Tlaloc, was believed to protect new-born children and marriages.*

### CHEIRON

Also spelt Chiron. In Greek myth, a leader of the CENTAURS, half-human, half-equine creatures living in the hills of the Peloponnese. Cheiron is portrayed as a being of great wisdom and feeling, a teacher and a figure of peace, and it is a poignant feature of the myth that he chose to die (though immortal) when unable to bear the pain resulting from being struck by accident by one of HERACLES's poisoned arrows. See also PHOLUS.

### CHENG-HUANG

An earthly god in the ancient Chinese pantheon, derived from the primitive god of the soil. He was responsible for the land and its use in each district, and was prayed to by the local ruler as a safeguard against damage to the harvest. He also acted as a check to the activities of YEN-LO, the god of the dead, in making sure that the latter carried out his collection of the souls of mortals correctly and did not take away those not yet destined to go. In this respect Cheng-huang himself became in part a judge of the dead. From being to some extent transcendent in these ways, he became envisaged very much on the model of the human political figure of the district administrator.

### CHENRESI

A figure of Tibetan Buddhism, better known by the Sanskrit name AVALOKITESHVARA.

### CHERUBIM

Heavenly beings, in the Hebrew tradition recorded in the Old Testament, in which they are the servants and attendants of God, being thought of as winged beings with otherwise human attributes.

### CHIA

Wife of the great god of the Indians of Colombia, BOCHICA. She displeased him by her attempts to prevent his imposition of order on the world, and in some stories the great flood from which he saved mankind is attributed to her. See

*An Etruscan bronze of the Chimaera, the monster defeated by the Greek hero Bellerophon.*

CHIBCHACUM. Her husband sent her from him, and she was transformed into the moon.

### CHIABOS
In the mythology of the Algonquin North American Indians, the Wolf, the younger brother of NANABUSH. The latter restored him to life after he had been killed by their enemies, the Underground Panthers, and thereafter he rules the land of souls, the destination of the dead.

### CHIBCHACUM
A god in the beliefs of the Indians of Colombia who regarded him as being responsible for an attempt to destroy

mankind by a flood, which catastrophe was prevented by the chief god BOCHICA. Chibchacum thereafter became an underworld deity whose task was the holding up of the world (compare ATLAS). When he moves his burden from one shoulder to the other he sometimes bumps it, which is the cause of earthquakes (compare LOKI).

### CHIMAERA
In Greek myth, a monster with three parts, the front being the body of a lion, the middle a goat and the rear a dragon. Regarded as female, she breathed fire and caused great destruction until killed by BELLEROPHON.

## CHIMINIGAGUA
An all-encompassing primal being of the American Indians of Colombia, to whom he was the creator, a god who first spread light from within himself, and then made the world.

## CHINGICHNICH
Or Chungichnich. For a group of Californian Indians known as the Luiseño from their proximity to the mission of San Luis Rey de Francia, the main and controlling god, institutor of their religious practices and judge of their actions. As a dominant all-powerful god he is an unusual feature in North American Indian religion, which is normally diverse and animistic.

## CHI SONGZI
A character in Chinese mythology noted for bringing about the end of a terrible drought which threatened the survival of the people. He achieved this by means of sprinkling the earth with water from a bowl, using the branch of a tree to do so. He became the heavenly controller of the rain, and lived with other celestial beings in their paradise on Mount Kunlun.

## CHIYU
In the Chinese combination of religious tradition and mythical history, he was the son or other descendant of the early ruler SHENNONG. He is noted for having opposed the emperor HUANG DI and fought with him for the succession, using for that purpose the assistance of the god of rain. See BA.

## CHOMIBA
One of the first women, in the cosmogony of the Maya Indians of Mexico, the wife of BALAM-ACAB. *Popol Vuh*

## CHONG
In Chinese mythology, a being appointed to govern heaven, in an attempt to produce order from the confusion caused by the intermingling of heaven and earth. See also CHONGLI, and LI. The early emperors were said to be descended from Chong and Li.

## CHONGLI
Sometimes viewed as two separate beings, CHONG and LI: the Chinese fire god, who also took part in the process of creation, being responsible for the initial separation of heaven and earth, which were previously in close contact, and thereafter prevented movement to and fro between them.

## CHRYSEIS
A figure occurring in the myths of the ancient Greeks as the daughter of the priest of APOLLO near Troy. The story tells how she was taken captive by ACHILLES and allocated to AGAMEMNON. In due course Apollo forced him to give her back to her father. HOMER: *Iliad*

## CIRCE
A witch-like goddess in the myths of the Greeks, who seduced ODYSSEUS on his voyage. Circe's dangerous power and seductive enchantment infatuates Odysseus, and his men for once have to remind him of their goal. She first turned his men into swine, but when overcome by a counterspell provided by HERMES she relented and feasted them all for a year. HOMER: *Odyssey*

## CLIO
The Muse of history in the mythology of the ancient Greeks. See ERATO, CALLIOPE, TERPSICHORE.

## CLOTHO
In Greek myth, one of the three Fates, represented as spinning the thread of destiny, which the other two Fates, LACHESIS and ATROPOS, are sometimes viewed as being able to cut at their will.

## CLYTEMNESTRA
Wife of AGAMEMNON, in a central story of the myths of the Greeks, the daughter of the king of Sparta and LEDA, and thus a

half-sister of HELEN (who was conceived by
ZEUS). She is an ambivalent figure, partly
sympathetic as a wronged mother (see
IPHIGENIA), but morally flawed by taking a
lover when her husband was away at Troy,
AEGISTHUS, with whom she conspired to
kill Agamemnon on his return. See also
ORESTES.

AESCHYLUS: *Agamemnon;* EURIPIDES:
*Iphigenia in Aulis*

## COATLICUE
A mother goddess of the Aztecs of Mexico,
identified with the earth. She gave birth to
the warrior god HUITZILOPOCHTLI after
conceiving through swallowing a ball of
hummingbird feathers.

## COEUS
In Greek mythology, one of the Titans, the
older order of gods, and the father of LETO
and thus grandfather of APOLLO and
ARTEMIS.

## CON
Or Coniraya. A figure in the traditions of
the Indians of Peru. He is sometimes
amalgamated with one of the aspects of
VIRACOCHA. A supreme deity of the Indians
of the coastal area of Peru, he was said to
be the offspring of the sun and to have
supernatural powers. In some versions he
is also the creator god.

## CONAIRE
Conaire Mor, a king of Ireland in the
tradition of the Irish Celts; forbidden by a
portent to perform a number of specific acts,
he breaks these taboos one by one in the
course of events which lead dramatically to
his death, thus illustrating in intense form
the theme of the inevitability of fate.

## CONCHOBAR
King of Ulster, the central figure of a heroic
cycle of Celtic Irish material, the 'Ulster
Cycle', which has CUCHULAINN as its main
protagonist. Conchobar's function is
largely to play the part of a focal point, his
court providing the base for the deeds of
his followers.

## CONN
In Celtic Irish myth, the king of Connacht
(which was called after him), who held his
court at Tara. He is mainly a background
figure in the stories of other heroes, the
figure of the king whose court provides a
setting for adventures.

*The fearsome Aztec
goddess Coatlicue,
mother of the war-god
Huitzilopochtli,
represented in a
massive sculpture
found at the centre of
Tenochtitlan.*

## CORDELIA
A figure of British myth. See CREIDDYLAD.

## CORINEUS
In Geoffrey of Monmouth's collection of Celtic British material, a refugee leader of the Trojans who settled in Cornwall, and there combated the giants which were at the time a trouble to Britain. He wrestled with their leader GOGMAGOG in single combat, and managed to throw him into the sea. There have been no giants in Britain since then.
GEOFFREY OF MONMOUTH: *History of the Kings of Britain*

## CORMAC
King of Connacht, in Irish Celtic myth, and grandson of CONN. He is a more developed character than his ancestor, and stories tell of his experiences at Tara, their seat. These bear an air of mysticism, and one of Cormac's possessions, a golden cup which can distinguish truth from falsehood, makes him probably one of the prototypes of the owner of the Holy Grail.

## CORONIS
In Greek myth, a princess seduced by APOLLO by whom she bore ASCLEPIUS.
PINDAR: *Pythian Odes*

## CREIDDYLAD
A British Celtic figure more familiar in the Anglicized form Cordelia. She figures in early Welsh tales as the daughter of King LLUDD, and is developed by Geoffrey of Monmouth in the form known to us from Shakespeare's *King Lear.*
*Mabinogion;* GEOFFREY OF MONMOUTH: *History of the Kings of Britain*

## CREON
A figure occurring in Greek myth as the brother of JOCASTA and hence uncle to OEDIPUS. In the story of ANTIGONE he features in a position of typical paradox, being torn between his duty to uphold the rule of law and his natural feelings of kinship. See POLYNICES.
SOPHOCLES: *Theban Plays*

*Cupid, the Roman equivalent of Eros and the subject of much light-hearted statuary and painting.*

## CRONUS

One of the Titans, the ancestral gods, in the pantheon of the Greeks. He was leader of the children of URANUS, and set the theme of feud and guilt which runs through Greek myth by the primal crime of castrating his father, and thus supplanting him. The name is associated with the similar Greek word for 'time', which would be more correctly transliterated as Chronos, and although the identification was originally accidental, a linguistic coincidence, Cronus nevertheless became thought of by the ancient Greeks as the personification of time, or eternity, itself.

HESIOD: *Theogony*

## CUCHULAINN

The major hero of the collection of Irish Celtic stories known as the 'Ulster Cycle'. He embodies many of the archetypal heroic qualities: a prodigious childhood, an early proof of his special quality, the carrying out of extraordinary deeds and undertaking of exploits in defence of his people, and a prophesied, tragic, and unavoidable death. The son of LUGH and a member of the family of CONCHOBAR, he went through a long and symbolic series of initiations before becoming his people's champion. His adult exploits are profuse both in variety and in vividness of imagery, and he is one of the very few heroes outside Greek mythology who can justifiably be compared in stature to the super-hero HERACLES. Moreover he is unusually well characterized. Described as being normally inoffensive in appearance, his most notable characteristic is the onset of his battle frenzy, which transforms him into a terrifying ghoul. In a most poignant episode he unwittingly kills his son in the process of carrying out his martial duty. The sequence leading to his death is highly charged with portents of doom and beset with the snares of moral dilemma. In finally fighting to a desperate end he fulfils the heroic task of acknowledging the supremacy of mortality. In the end even this extreme hero, we feel, cannot win the unequal struggle.

## CULHWCH

This hero of a single ancient tale in British Celtic mythology, *Culhwch and Olwen*, embodies a primitive theme of heroism, that of the need to carry out seemingly impossible tasks in the course of gaining the hand of a woman, in this case OLWEN, the daughter of the giant YSBADDADEN. With the help of his cousin ARTHUR and the latter's war-band he achieves most of the tasks, and between them, like so many primitive heroes, they destroy the giant.

*Mabinogion*

## CUMHAU

God of death for the Maya Indians of Mexico, in their beliefs he ruled over one of the grim underworlds.

## CUPID

The Roman equivalent of the Greek EROS, but more developed than him in story, since the main Greek love-deity was female (see APHRODITE).

## CYBELE

The Greek version of the Asiatic mother-goddess.

## CYCLOPS

In Greek myth, the monstrous giant man-eating inhabitants of one of the islands visited by ODYSSEUS. See POLYPHEMUS.

HOMER: *Odyssey*

*The Greek hero Odysseus and his companions blinding the cyclops Polythemus. Amphora decorated by the painter Menelaos.*

## DAEDALUS

A craftsman employed by King Minos at Knossos in Crete, in a set of stories in the mythology of the Greeks. See also THESEUS. He was imprisoned, after a disagreement with the king, together with his son ICARUS, with whom he escaped by the ingenious construction of wings for them both, thus becoming the first man to fly.

OVID: *Metamorphoses*

## DAEVAS

False gods or devils, in the beliefs of the Zoroastrian religion of Iran, the product of wrong thinking and now active in the world obstructing the good works of AHURA MAZDA and his spirit-ministers the AMESHA SPENTAS. Compare Hindu DEVAS.

## DAGDA

The Dagda, so known, is a powerful Irish god envisaged as a figure of giant proportions, whose name means 'the good god'. Much connected with magic and wisdom, he became the god of druidism. Originally he appears as the leader of the Tuatha de Danann in their battles against previous inhabitants of Ireland. In common with other heroes of might and physical superiority such as HERACLES his weapon and characteristic possession was a club, but he also possessed a specifically Celtic item, a cauldron of plenty, which could feed a whole army. As was the case with a figure of similar attributes, the Scandinavian god THOR, stories about the Dagda often make him look slightly ridiculous.

## DAHAK

A dragon, featuring in the body of beliefs of ancient Iran, embodiment of the demon of lies (a supreme evil in Zoroastrian thought). Defeated by the hero Thraetona,

he was not killed but imprisoned in a mountain, from where he will break loose to add to the havoc of the final cataclysm. Compare Scandinavian FENRIR.

## DAIKOKU

One of the Japanese gods of good luck (of whom there are seven), in this case the god of wealth (compare HOTEI). He is traditionally shown as a contented man accompanied by rice bales and a sack of possessions.

## DAKSHA

In the Hindu beliefs of India, the male principle of creation, said to be the offspring of BRAHMA. His daughter became the wife of SHIVA The waning of the moon is sometimes attributed to a curse Daksha uttered.                    *Rig Veda*

## DANAË

A figure in the myths of the Greeks. Imprisoned by her father because of a prophecy that his grandson would kill him, she was seduced by ZEUS in the form of a shower of gold, and conceived PERSEUS.

*An 11th-century mosaic from Greece showing Daniel in the den of lions.*

**DANANN**

Also Danu – see DON. A goddess of Celtic Irish myth. The ancestral mother of the magical race called after her, the Tuatha de Danann, the 'people of the goddess Danann', who feature in Celtic Irish mythology as one of the early nations of Ireland.

**DANAUS**

He occurs in Greek myth as the father of fifty daughters, who were mainly remarkable for being seduced (in some versions in one night) by the hero HERACLES.

**DANEL**

The Syrian version of the Hebrew DANIEL. However the character appears to be quite unconnected with the story of that Hebrew prophet. The Syrian Danel figures most prominently as the king who was the father of AQHAT.

**DANIEL**

In the Hebrew stories collected in the Old Testament, he occurs as a prisoner of the Babylonian king NEBUCHADNEZZAR, in which role he is the hero of a story of how he and three companions resist attempts to induce them to worship heathen gods. The other three survive the 'fiery furnace', being rendered immune to the heat by God. Daniel rose to occupy governmental posts at the Babylonian court, and made a reputation for interpreting dreams and visions. He further survived the persecution of a later heathen king in which he was thrown into a den of lions. His invulnerability converted the kings to his religion. See BELSHAZZAR. *Daniel*

**DANU**

See DON. A Celtic goddess.

**DANU**

In the Hindu beliefs of India she was regarded as the mother of demons, particularly of the demon VRITRA, an enemy to INDRA.

**DAPHNE**

A character of Greek myth, a woman who was wooed by APOLLO. The story tells that she evaded his attentions by being turned into a laurel tree (still called *daphne* in Greek). OVID: *Metamorphoses*

**DARAMULUN**

Sky-dwelling creator figure of the eastern coast of Australia, known in neighbouring areas by other names, representative of a belief in an originator who fashioned the landscape and added human beings, their artefacts, and their social systems.

**DARIUS**

Known as Darius the Mede, he is named in the Hebrew stories preserved in the Old Testament as the successor to BELSHAZZAR, king of the Chaldeans. He does not appear to be a historical figure and his occurrence in an otherwise semi-historical context remains something of a mystery. There were several Persian emperors of that name, but Belshazzar was succeeded by Cyrus. *Daniel*

**DAVID**

One of the leading heroes of the Hebrew material collected in the Old Testament. He is the archetype of the young and precocious hero, rising to prominence as the protégé of SAUL, king of the Israelites, at a time when they were at war with the Philistines. He came from a sheep-herding family of the town of Bethlehem, the youngest of eight brothers, the others taking towards him a scornful and hostile attitude. Chosen by God to be Saul's successor, he was anointed as king by the prophet SAMUEL. He came to Saul's court as a harpist at a time when the king, in a troubled mental state, required comfort. Saul took to him and made him his armour-bearer. He then distinguished himself by accepting the challenge of the Philistine champion GOLIATH, whom he defeated miraculously with no weapons other than a sling. Later he became a close friend of Saul's son JONATHAN, who however died along with his father in battle, causing David to lament his loss in a famous passage of mourning. Compare GILGAMESH, ENKIDU. Much of David's early career is taken up by his need to avoid the increasingly violent hostility of Saul. In due course in his turn he became king of Israel, led the people in great victories, and established the kingdom at Jerusalem, where the citadel of Mount Zion became known as the City of David. He survived many setbacks and rebellions, to appoint his son SOLOMON as his successor. To David was attributed the writing of the Old Testament Book of Psalms.

*1 & 2 Samuel, 1 Kings*

### DAZHBOG

The Slavonic god of the sun, the son of SVAROGU. A later but authentic source records a tradition that the Russians were his descendants.

### DDUNDA

In the Uganda area of Africa, the Baganda people's name for God. The word means 'Pastor' and thus indicates the idea of God as shepherd of his people.

### DEIANEIRA

In Greek myth she is the devoted wife of HERACLES. The story tells how she unwittingly caused his death by applying corroding poison, which she thought to be a love potion that would ensure her husband's fidelity (see NESSUS), to his shirt.

### DEIRDRE

A tragic heroine of a tale of elopement in Celtic Irish mythology. She was prophesied from birth to be the cause of trouble to her people, the men of Ulster.

### DELGETH

The North American Navajo Indians viewed this creature as a fearsome man-eating antelope. In their stories he occurs mainly as the monster killed by the primal twins NAGENATZANI and THOBADESTCHIN, in the course of their ridding the world of dangerous beings.

### DELILAH

In the Old Testament Hebrew material, she appears as the seductress who was bribed with money by the Philistines to betray the Hebrew hero SAMSON, whose strength was lost when she cut off his hair. *Judges*

### DEMETER

One of the strongest figures in Greek myth, in which she occurs as the mourning mother of PERSEPHONE, abducted by HADES. Demeter is inconsolable and shuns the court of the gods when ZEUS declines to help her, causing a general barrenness of the earth by this disorder. She went to live among men, and was taken in as a nurse by the royal family of Eleusis. Eventually the famine threatened to destroy the human race, and a compromise was arranged by which Persephone could return for part of the year. This symbolism of the seasonal changes, together with Demeter's connection with agriculture, makes her a deeply basic figure of mythology, and indeed her name itself comes from the Indo-European root-word 'meter' which gives many languages their word for 'mother'.

*Delilah, shearing the locks of the Hebrew hero Samson. Woodcut from the Luther Bible, 1534.*

**DEMOPHON**

In Greek mythology, the infant son of the royal family at Eleusis, given to DEMETER to nurse. He grew so fast under the divine care that they came to suspect her real nature.

**DENG**

Ancestor of the Dinkas, an African tribe of Sudan; he is associated with storm and thunder, and thought to be the cause of lightning and the giver of human births.

**DEUCALION**

The equivalent in Greek myth of NOAH, he survived a flood by being warned in time to construct a boat, in which he and his wife floated above the drowned world until they came to rest on the top of a mountain. See also UTNAPISHTIM, MANU.

**DEVADATTA**

Boyhood companion, cousin, and lifelong rival of the Buddha, as described in the traditional biography contained in the material of the religion of India based on the latter's life.

**DEVANA**

A central Slavonic deity, Dziewona in Polish and in Serbian Diiwica. A goddess of the hunt, she is the Slavonic version of DIANA. She was viewed as riding through the great forests of Europe accompanied by her hounds.

**DEVAS**

The group of Aryan gods of both India and Iran who are led by INDRA. They became dominant in Indian religion, supplanting the ASURAS. In the related religion of Zoroastrianism, however, they became reduced to the status of demons.

**DEVI**

A goddess in the Hindu religion of India, the goddess most closely connected with the great god SHIVA, as his spouse. In this capacity she takes different forms which go under separate names. See DURGA, KALI, PARVATI, SATI.

**DHARMA**

An element of the beliefs of India, originally an abstract principle, the means of acquiring merit by obedience to the rule of right living, by observance of the proper rituals and laws. Dharma became a god in later Hindu religion, being seen as one of the aspects of YAMA.

**DHRITARASHTRA**

According to the mythological tradition of India, the uncle and foster-father of the PANDAVAS. His kindness to them provoked the envy of his own son DURYODHANA. Dhritarashtra had been blind from birth, due to his mother's having closed her eyes when she conceived him.     *Mahabharata*

**DI**

A supreme deity in Chinese belief. See SHANG DI, his full name.

**DIANA**

The Roman version of the Greek goddess ARTEMIS, but originally possessing more connections with light, and hence with the moon, than with hunting.

LEFT: *Demeter whose mourning for her daughter Persephone brought barrenness to the world which was only alleviated by the daughter's seasonal return.*

BELOW: *Diana, the virgin huntress, a Roman goddess identified with the Greek goddess Artemis.*

59

*A mosaic, dating from the 4th century AD, showing Dido, Queen of Carthage (left), and Aeneas (centre), who in Virgil's account stayed at Carthage after escaping from Troy.*

### DIARMAID

A figure of Celtic Irish myth, occurring as a younger hero in the tales of **FINN** and best known for the episode of his elopement with **GRAINNE**, Finn's fiancée. The lovers are pursued by Finn throughout Ireland. Eventually reconciled with his leader, Diarmaid lives happily with Grainne until fatally wounded by a magic boar (compare **ADONIS**) which was his foster-brother in animal form. Finn could heal him, but jealousy makes him hesitate, and Diarmaid dies.

### DIDO

In Roman tradition, the daughter of the king of Tyre. The story tells how when her uncle (who was also her husband) was murdered by her brother (**PYGMALION**) she fled to Africa and there founded Carthage. Forced to accept a marriage against her will she committed suicide, building her own funeral pyre. In Virgil's version she fell in love with **AENEAS** and killed herself when he abandoned her to fulfil his destiny in Italy.                VIRGIL: *Aeneid*

### DI JUN

Husband of **XIHE**, in Chinese beliefs of the time of the Shang dynasty, and also the husband of **CHANG XI**.

### DIOMEDES

One of the Greek heroes in the story of the Trojan War.                HOMER: *Iliad*

### DIONE

One of the female Titans, the primal gods of ancient Greek mythology. She was loved by **ZEUS** and in some versions became the mother of **APHRODITE** (but see **URANUS**).

### DIONYSUS

A pastoral god in Greek mythology (compare **APOLLO**), in this case connected with goat-herding, and also the god of wine, in which character he merges with the lesser-developed wine god **BACCHUS**. The uncontrolled nature of his worship is in contrast to the ordered character of Apollo, and the two cults were in a state of rivalry at Delphi.

### DIS

A Roman god of death and of the underworld, usually known as Dis Pater, Father Dis. The name indicates wealth. See **PLUTO**.

### DIYA

Also Dimu, meaning Earthmother. In the creation myth of the ancient Chinese, she is the female half of the primal pair from whose coupling mankind and all other things are derived.

### DJABO

The 'spotted cat man', a figure of the beliefs of the aboriginal people inhabiting western Arnhem Land, on the north coast of Australia. He was one of a pair of primal

*The Djanggau sisters, according to the aboriginal people of coastal Arnhem Land in Australia, gave birth to the first human beings. The second panel down in this bark painting by Malawan shows this act of creation.*

men (the other being Yakul, a 'pigeon man') who had the option of imitating the moon by coming to life again when dead, but declined it, and hence introduced death from which there is no return as a condition of mankind.

## DJANGGAUS

Also Dianggawuls. A pair of sisters who were responsible (in the beliefs of the aboriginal people of Australia) for populating the northern coastal area of Arnhem Land.

## DOMOVOI

Gods of the home in Russian mythology: Domovik in Ukrainian. They are partly derived from previous tribal ancestral spirits, and are worshipped at small shrines set up in a part of the house, often being thought to live near the stove. The name comes from the word *dom* meaning 'house'. In some versions of their origin the Domovoi were said to be fallen divinities, the spirits cast to earth after they had rebelled in heaven. Though they were thought to be only very exceptionally seen, they were sometimes visualized as being of human form, but covered in hair. The Domovoi were generally considered benevolent, giving warning of impending dangers and domestic difficulties.

## DON

In Celtic British mythology, the parent (presumably father) of GWYDION and ARANRHOD, but originally a female figure. The same personage as the Irish goddess DANANN, evidently an ancestor in a matrilinear pedigree. Since there seem to be several rivers called after her, including the Danube and the Russian Don, it may be that this otherwise uncharacterized figure was a major deity of the continental Celts.

*Mabinogion*

## DONGO

A spirit in the beliefs of the Songhay of West Africa, who is thought by them to cause the thunderflash by throwing his axe. Compare SHANGO.

**DONG WANG GONG**

In Chinese mythology he was the male counterpart of XI WANG MU, the 'Queen Mother of the West', and himself resident in the east. The annual meeting between them was seen as the conjunction of opposites, representing the union of the contrary principles of YIN and YANG.

**DONG-YO DA-DI**

Chief minister of YU-HUANG, in Chinese mythology, he was known as the Ruler of the Eastern Peak, and connected with the other male figure representative of the eastern direction, DON WANG GONG. To Dong-yo Da-di fell the organization of all earthly matters, under the presiding dominance of Yu-Huang, the governing of the lives of men and other animals, and also the supervision of those lesser deities who were involved in the same sphere.

**DRAUPADI**

Occurring in the myths of India, she is a princess wooed by many, including the family of the PANDAVAS. Their most prominent member, ARJUNA, succeeded in an archery contest set by her father as a test of the suitors. She became the wife of all the brothers, due to a stipulation by their mother KUNTI that Arjuna should share his prize (of which she did not know the nature) between them equally.

*Mahabharata*

**DUAMUTEF**

Son of HORUS. In the elaborate symbolism surrounding the burial of the Egyptian god OSIRIS, which formed the prototype for the rituals of human burials, Duamutef was a jackal-headed god who stood at the east corner of the sarcophagus and protected the canopic jar containing the stomach of the embalmed deceased. The four gods who performed this function (see IMSET, HAPY, QEBEHSENUF) were the four sons of Horus, usually thought of as being by his wife ISIS. Sometimes the four are represented in the form of their heads as lids of the canopic jars themselves.

**DUMUZI**

The Sumerian form of the Babylonian TAMMUZ.

**DURGA**

A goddess of the mythology of India, the fierce form taken by the wife of SHIVA, worshipped as the active element in his makeup, and as a supreme mother goddess. In this capacity she is seen as a demanding influence not easily placated. She was said to have been born fully formed, like the Greek ATHENA.

**DURYODHANA**

In the myths of India, he is the cousin, foster-brother and jealous enemy of the PANDAVAS. He plotted to kill them by setting fire to their house, but warned by an uncle they escaped to the forest and lived there disguised as Brahmins. His enmity pursued them, and in the war

*A late 19th-century folk painting of Durga, the fearsome goddess in Indian mythology who was the wife of Shiva.*

*The mother and wife of the Hindu figure Duryodhana mourning over his body. Miniature from an illustrated* Mahabharata, *1761-3.*

which breaks out between the parties both claim the assistance of **KRISHNA**. See **ARJUNA**.                    *Mahabharata*

**DXUI**

For the African Bushmen the first spirit, metamorphosed in various forms before becoming the first man. Among the Bushmen of part of the Kalahari this figure is the equivalent of the spirit **KAGGEN** for other groups. According to some reports Dxui is a more introverted, less worldly-active force than Kaggen.

**DYAUS**

An early creator god in the cosmogony of India, who became god of the sky. The name in fact is connected with the Aryan word for the bright, daytime sky, and eventually led both to the name for the Greek father-god **ZEUS** and to the Latin word for 'day', *dies*. Dyaus formed a union with **PRITHIVI**, the female earth, and they gave birth to **INDRA**, the great god of storms and rain who became representative of the new order of gods.

*Rig Veda*

## EA

A Mesopotamian deity, the god of wisdom, and of the sweet waters with their fertilizing power. He was benevolent and peace-loving, but also occasionally a trickster. One of his functions was patronage of the arts, and he also played a role in the creation of men. His temple was at Eridu, on the Persian Gulf.

*Epic of Gilgamesh*

## EBISU

One of the seven gods of good luck in the developed mythology of Japan. In this case he is a patron of fishermen and traders and also a promoter of hard work.

## ECHO

In Greek mythology, a nymph who aided ZEUS' amorous sport with the other nymphs by keeping his consort HERA engaged in chatter, and when found out was condemned by the goddess to speak only in reply. She fell in love with NARCISSUS, was spurned by him, and sadly faded away until only her voice remained. Hence her identity is largely a fanciful explanation of the natural phenomenon to which she gives her name.

OVID: *Metamorphoses*

## EDOM

In the Hebrew material preserved in the Old Testament, this was a name given to ESAU, and hence the eponym of his descendants. *Genesis, Numbers*

## EFÉ

The first man, in the beliefs of the Pygmy people of Africa, and a representative of

*An impression from a seal of the 3rd millennium BC shows the Mesopotamian god Ea seated on his throne, which is surrounded by water.*

the idea that at one time God and the earth were more closely connected.

## EHECATL

A Mexican wind god, depicted as a monster with an animal's nose and bulging eyes.

## EITHINOHA

In the mythology of the Iroquois Indians of North America, 'Our Mother', the earth.

## EK CHUAH

For the Maya Indians of Mexico, he was the patron deity of merchants and also of the growers of cacao.

## EKKEKKO

For the Indians of Peru, he is thought of as a benevolent spirit, and the bringer of good fortune. Ekkekko is depicted as a small fat man in statuettes often found in a household context, in which he is often shown as bearing in miniature items desired by the family. He belongs to a very ancient tradition which is still current.

## EL

A Syrian deity, the high god of the Canaanites, and one of the titles of the Hebrew YAHWEH. El is regarded as the father of the gods.

## ELAINE

In the material derived from Celtic British tradition, she was the daughter of the king of Astolat, a maiden in love with Sir LANCELOT in Malory's developed form of the tales of King ARTHUR. The story mainly tells how she died of a broken heart when rejected. By some confusion another Elaine (no doubt originally the same) appears as the daughter of King PELLES in the Grail stories of the same collection, in which she seduces Lancelot and becomes the mother of his son GALAHAD.

MALORY: *Morte d'Arthur*

## ELECTRA

A figure of Greek myth, in which she occurs as the daughter of AGAMEMNON and CLYTEMNESTRA. In the most notable

ABOVE: *Bronze figure of El, the chief god of the Canaanite Kingdom which flourished in northern Syria between 1500 and 1000 BC.*

RIGHT: *A print by Kunisada of Ebisu, one of the seven gods of good luck in Japanese mythology.*

episode of her story she joined with her brother ORESTES in plotting the murder of their mother and her lover AEGISTHUS.
AESCHYLUS: *The Libation Bearers;* EURIPIDES: *Electra*

## ELFFIN

A Celtic British character, best known for his misfortunes, a figure rather of bitterness than heroism. The son of a king whose land suffered inundation by the sea, Prince Elffin had one solitary piece of good luck. In the weir which he unsuccessfully fished he found washed up the cast-out child TALIESIN, who developed into a powerful spellbinder and prophetic bard. In a fairly late story his misfortunes continue when the two come to the court of the historical king Maelgwn, said to be his uncle, where he is cast into a dungeon until rescued by the power of Taliesin.

## ELIJAH

An early historical prophet of the Hebrews endowed with strong mythic qualities: in contest with the priests of BAAL he miraculously produces fire; in meditation in the wilderness he receives a message from the voice of God; most notably he does not die, but is received into heaven accompanied by a fiery chariot and a whirlwind. It is believed that he will return to herald the apocalypse.     *1 & 2 Kings*

## ELISHA

Follower of and successor to ELIJAH. On the latter's ascension to heaven his mantle fell, to be received by Elisha.     *1 & 2 Kings*

## EMBLA

The first woman, in the pre-Christian beliefs of Scandinavia. She was created along with her partner ASK from two trees by the three sons of BOR, the first of whom gave them life, the second understanding and movement, and the third the senses.
SNORRI STURLUSON: *Prose Edda*

## EMMA-O

In the mythology of Japan, he is an underworld deity and a judge of the dead.

## EMRYS

The Celtic British form of the semi-historical sub-Roman figure **AMBROSIUS**. His story tells how, when he was about to be sacrificed by **VORTIGERN** to overcome his failure to build a castle, he revealed the cause: under the spot was a pair of buried dragons, a white and a red. These fought when released, and he foretold that the red one, apparently losing, would eventually win – thus initiating a piece of familiar symbolism, the red dragon of Wales. The hill, near Snowdon, is still known by his name.

## ENDUKUGGA

A Sumerian god of the underworld, together with **NINDUKUGGA** the parent of **ENLIL**. *Epic of Gilgamesh*

## ENDYMION

A handsome youth occurring in a minor episode of Greek mythology. He had the habit of sleeping on a mountain, where he attracted the attention of the moon, who fell in love with him.

## EN-KAI

A Kenyan African deity, also transliterated as 'Ngai. The name given by the Masai for both God and rain, indicating an equivalence between the two, rain being the sustainer and provider of life. Compare **OWO**, **TANUKUJEN**.

## ENKI

The Sumerian version of the Akkadian **EA**.

## ENKIDU

A major character of Mesopotamian myth. Formed by the gods out of clay to provide a companion and counterpart to **GILGAMESH**, he provides one of the strongest, and strangest, images in any mythology: partly natural, wild, uninhibited and free of the taints of civilization, but also partly vulnerable, open to corruption, touchingly moved by friendship and, ultimately, mortal. Brought up in the wilds with animals, he loses his innocence when seduced by a harlot sent from the city to trap him. She brings him back with her to Uruk, where, in his new state of weakness, he meets the king, the semi-divine Gilgamesh. Their friendship, initiated by a wrestling bout, forms a main theme of the epic. The illness and death of Enkidu bring home to Gilgamesh the error of having taken him from his natural state, equivalent to a fall from grace, and the tragedy inherent in the curse of mortality. 'My brother,' Enkidu cries, 'though you are so dear to me, yet they will take me from you.' It is his refusal to accept complacently this bitter state of affairs that drives Gilgamesh thereafter in a desperate quest to find immortality. *Epic of Gilgamesh*

## ENLIL

God of the air, in the mythology of Mesopotamia. Seen in one story as dwelling on earth at the town of Nippur before the creation of men, he was thought of as being himself a creator god and the great leader among the gods. Having connections with storm and wind, he became viewed as embodied in breath, the 'spirit of the word', a type of sacred influence at work in the world. *Epic of Gilgamesh*

## ENNUGI

A Mesopotamian god of water-ways and irrigation, 'the canal inspector'. *Epic of Gilgamesh*

## ENOCH

Father of **METHUSELAH**, in the Hebrew tradition recorded in the Old Testament. He is described as having 'walked with God' for three hundred years, indicating a close devotional relationship with the deity, and it is implied that he was translated directly to heaven rather than dying. *Genesis*

## EPIMETHEUS

A character in Greek myth, in which he is the brother and counterpart of **PROMETHEUS**, himself being seen as a figure of lustful greed who accepted the first woman, **PANDORA**, as a gift from **ZEUS**.

**EPONA**

The horse-goddess of the continental Celts, depicted in statuettes as a lady on a horse. Her name comes from the Celtic word 'epos' meaning horse, and so may have been a title or description. Probably she occurs in the stories in the person of RHIANNON.

**ERATO**

The Muse of love poetry in the mythology of the Greeks. See CALLIOPE, CLIO, TERPSICHORE.

**ERECHTHEUS**

He occurs in Greek myth as an early king of Athens, who was supposed to have succeeded CECROPS. His temple, the Erechtheon, stands on the Acropolis at the spot where ATHENA was said to have had a contest with POSEIDON for the control of Attica.

**ERESHKIGAL**

A Mesopotamian deity, the sister of ISHTAR, and herself the queen of the underworld. She is seen as a fearsome figure.

*Epic of Gilgamesh*

**ERICHTHONIUS**

In an episode of Greek mythology, Erichthonius was the offspring of the earth of Attica which had been fertilized by the sperm of HEPHAESTUS which fell there when he attempted to violate the maiden ATHENA. Athena collected the infant and brought it in a basket to the Acropolis, warning the daughters of CECROPS to whom she gave it not to look inside. When of course they did so they went mad at what they saw and leapt from the Acropolis: Erichthonius had a serpent's tail.

**ERIS**

In Greek myth the goddess of discord, she was the original cause of the Trojan War by her act of throwing down before the goddesses assembled at the wedding of PELEUS and THETIS a golden apple inscribed 'To the fairest'. ZEUS decided that a mortal, PARIS, should make the judgment.

**EROS**

A Greek god, the son and companion of APHRODITE, developed by the Romans as the god CUPID. Eros is the god of the disturbances, rather than the romantic emotions, brought by love: he is seen as irresponsibly firing his affecting arrows, as being winged and playful, having his eyes covered and therefore shooting at random.

**ESAU**

In the Hebrew material as recorded in the Old Testament, the son of ISAAC and REBECCA, and the twin brother of JACOB. Esau grew up to be a hunter, while his brother farmed the plains. They were also physically distinguished by Esau's being hirsute, Jacob smooth-skinned. Under persuasion from Jacob Esau sold him his

OPPOSITE: *The Celtic horse-goddess Epona, here represented in a Gallo-Roman stone carved relief.*

BELOW: *Eros, the Greek god of love, developed in Roman times as Cupid. He is frequently depicted as the companion of his mother, Aphrodite. In this detail of a Roman mosaic from Cyprus he is shown with Amymone, who was seduced by Poseidon.*

share of the inheritance in exchange for a meal. Isaac however favoured Esau, and a popular story tells how in his old age he sought to bless him but was tricked by Jacob into blessing him first, thus giving him permanent precedence, although it was Esau who had actually been born first.

*Genesis*

## ESHU
For the Yoruba people of Nigeria in West Africa, Eshu is a mischievous spirit who spreads trouble among people, but may also protect them. He is known to other tribes of West Africa as LEGBA.

## ESTANATLEHI
In the tradition of the North American Navajo Indians, she was a girl child found by the 'first woman', who developed supernaturally and in due course had an amorous encounter with the sun in human form, from which she gave birth to twin brothers named NAGENATZANI and THOBADESTCHIN. She re-created the race of men after it had undergone near-extinction, by making models out of flour. The Navajo regarded her as the source of all good things, and revered her as a great benevolent deity.

## ETANA
In Mesopotamian mythology, the first king of men, after the great flood which destroyed all the human race except for its one survivor. In one episode of his story he flew to heaven on the back of an eagle.

## ETEOCLES
One of the sons of OEDIPUS in a principal story of Greek myth. See also POLYNICES.

AESCHYLUS: *Seven Against Thebes*

## EUMENIDES
Figures of ancient Greek myth, in which they are a group of female spirits also known as the Furies, whose particular function was the pursuit of unpunished crimes of violence against kin. The name itself is a euphemism designed to placate them, meaning 'the kind ones'. They are

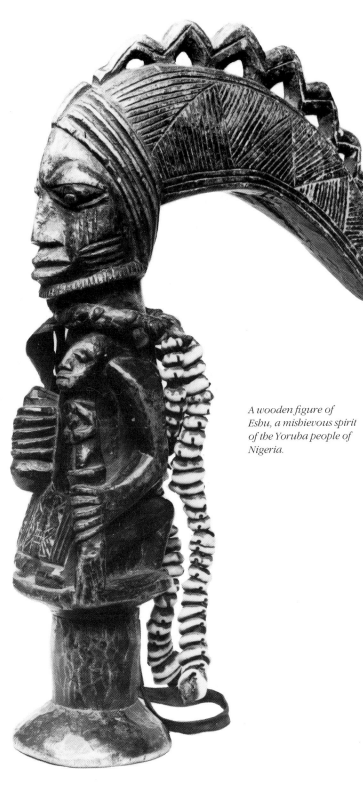

*A wooden figure of Eshu, a mischievous spirit of the Yoruba people of Nigeria.*

*Zeus in the form of a bull carrying off Europa, a narrative vividly brought to life in Ovid's* Metamorphoses. *Metope from a temple at Selinunte,* c. 550 BC.

seen as old and ugly dog-faced women, and haunt those who will not face them. See ORESTES.    AESCHYLUS: *The Eumenides*

### EURIDICE
The wife of ORPHEUS, in the myths of the Greeks, and one of the few mortals to be allowed to return from Hades. Orpheus used the power of his music to free her, but the one condition, that he should not look back at her when leading her out, is broken, and she has to go back.
OVID: *Metamorphoses*

### EUROPA
In a story of Greek mythology, she was a Phoenician princess loved by ZEUS. She was seduced by him in the form of a bull,

borne across the sea to Crete, and gave birth to three sons, MINOS (later king of Crete), RHADAMANTYS, and SARPEDON.
OVID: *Metamorphoses*

### EURYNOME
A Greek sea-goddess, one of the many wives of ZEUS.

### EURYSTHEUS
A character of Greek myth, in which he occurs as the ruler of Tiryns and cousin to HERACLES. When Heracles sought the verdict of the Delphic oracle as to how he should expiate the murder of his children during his madness, he was sent to be subject to his cousin Eurystheus for twelve years, and thus began his twelve labours.

## EVE

The first woman, in the Hebrew creation story with which the Old Testament begins, in which she was said to be formed from a rib taken from her husband **ADAM**. She was tempted by a serpent to partake of the one fruit forbidden to them by God, and was joined in this transgression by her husband. Expelled from paradise, they gave issue to two sons, **CAIN** and **ABEL**. The name 'Eve' means 'life' or 'life-giving'.

*Genesis*

*In the Hebrew account of Creation, Eve, the first woman, was formed from one of Adam's ribs. Stained-glass from Königsfelden, Switzerland, 14th century.*

# F

## FA

The great oracular spirit of the Benin people of West Africa. He can see all that goes on, and is even able to look into the future. He is said to live in a heavenly palm tree, and diviners operating through him interpret his messages by throwing palm nuts. The name is an abbreviation of the Yoruba IFA.

## FAFNIR

In Scandinavian mythology the dragon who guarded the gold treasure (which included a ring which created wealth but brought bad luck, see ANDVARI) eventually acquired by SIGURD, who killed the dragon and roasted its heart. Sigurd burnt his finger on the heart while cooking it, sucked it and thus imbibed universal knowledge (compare FINN, GWION). Although ending thus as a defeated monster Fafnir was the son of HREIDMAR, who briefly possessed the fateful treasure.

SNORRI STURLUSON: *Prose Edda*

## FENG BO

Or Feng Po, in the older variant of spelling. Also known as Fei Lien. The Governor of the Winds, in the mythological system of China, sometimes visualized as an old man, but in other versions as a woman known as Feng Popo, literally 'Mrs Wind'. The winds are stored in a goatskin bag in his possession.

## FENRIR

A fearsome wolf, in ancient Scandinavian tradition, the first child of the evil god LOKI by a giantess. It grew so fast that the gods became concerned for their safety and bound it by an unbreakable cord which the elves made out of apparently non-existent things (such as the sound of a cat moving, the beard of a woman, the breath of a fish, and so on). Fenrir howls and drools in his captivity until Ragnarök, the ending of the old order, when he breaks loose among the chaos of that apocalypse. See ODIN.

SNORRI STURLUSON: *Prose Edda*

## FERGUS

Fergus mac Roich, a figure of Celtic Irish story, in which he is one of the younger heroes (along with the more prominent CUCHULAINN) at the court of King CONCHOBAR of Ulster.

*Fafnir, the great dragon of Scandinavian mythology, slain by the hero Sigurd. Stone carving from Sweden.*

*OPPOSITE: A seated portrait of Fuxi, one of 'three sovereigns' who ruled over the remote stages of China's civilization. Portrait by Ma Lin, Sung Dynasty.*

## FINGAL

A Scottish Celtic character, whose name is also spelt Fingel. See **FINN**, **OSSIAN**.

## FINN

A major name in the Celtic Irish material. Known as Finn (or Fionn) mac Cumhaill, he forms the centre of a collection of stories known after him as the 'Fenian Cycle', in which he led a band of heroes called the Fiana, and in his exploits and his position as a national leader he has much in common with the figure of King **ARTHUR**. Characterized as being human and down-to-earth in his attitudes, he led a rural and itinerant life in close contact with wild nature, hunting and warring over the whole surface of Ireland. From an early episode in which he was set to cook the Salmon of Knowledge and burnt his thumb on it, he could acquire instant omniscience by sucking his thumb. (Compare **GWION**). In the form of **FINGEL** or **FINGAL** he occurs in a similar role in Scottish tradition. Although himself the hero of a typically prodigious biography he gradually becomes, like King Arthur, the provider of a setting for the adventures of a younger set of heroes. See **DIARMAID**.

## FLORA

The Roman goddess of the spring.

## FORSETI

A Scandinavian character, the son of **BALDER**. He lived in a golden hall where he acted as judge and arbitrator to gods and men.        SNORRI STURLUSON: *Prose Edda*

## FREYJA

Sister of **FREYR**, one of the family of ancient Scandinavian gods known as the **VANIR**, deities particularly connected with fertility; she was much desired by the gods and the giants, and also had a connection with death and battle.
        SNORRI STURLUSON: *Prose Edda*

## FREYR

Sometimes spelt Frey, a deity in the pre-Christian system of beliefs of Scandinavia.

*Freyr, a Scandinavian god of fertility and weather. Bronze figurine from Sweden, 11th century.*

A god of fertility and of the weather, his connection with abundance made him one of the leading gods of the Vikings, for whom he also had associations with horses.
        SNORRI STURLUSON: *Prose Edda*

## FRIGG

A major Scandinavian goddess, the wife of **ODIN** and therefore queen of the gods. She presided over the court of Asgard where her husband Odin ruled. See German **FRIJA**.
        SNORRI STURLUSON: *Prose Edda*

## FRIJA

An ancient German goddess, the wife of **WODEN**, and so the German equivalent of the Scandinavian **FRIGG**. Apart from the connection with child-bearing and fertility which these wife goddesses possess (compare Greek **HERA**, Roman **JUNO**), they are not greatly personalized. The day of the week Friday is called after her.

## FUKUROKUJU

Or Fukurokujin. A character occurring in the developed mythology of Japan. A god of good luck, one of the seven bringers of good fortune, in this case the source of both long life and of wisdom (compare **JUROJIN**). He is highly characterized physically as a long-headed man with a small body. It is probable that the figure is ultimately derived from Chinese tradition.

## FUXI

Or Fu-hsi, in the former type of spelling. The first of the 'three sovereigns' who ruled over the remotest stages of the development of Chinese civilization. He is depicted along with his wife **NUGUA** as having a dragon's tail. His province is the earth, hers the sky, and together they represent the conjunction of opposite principles, the **YIN** and the **YANG**. Compare **DONG WANG GONG** and **XI WANG MU**.

## FUXING

Or Fu-hsing, in the former convention of spelling. The Chinese god of happiness, along with **SHOULAO** and **LUXING** forming a triad of gods of good fortune.

# G

## GABRIEL

An Archangel, in the beliefs of the Hebrews as recorded in the Old Testament, one of the highest ministers of God. Only two angels are mentioned in the Bible (other than in the Apocrypha) by name. See also MICHAEL. *Daniel*

## GAEA

In Greek cosmogony, the first deity, the mother of CRONUS and of his father URANUS. She is the origin of all things, the personification of the earth itself. To the primitive Greeks she was in all probability the great deity. HESIOD: *Theogony*

## GALAHAD

A figure of French and British Celtic material, the hero who seeks and attains the Holy Grail. In his developed medieval form Galahad represents the ideal purity and rectitude towards which Christian heroes should strive, by contrast with which all his companions fail in the quest for the Grail through human weakness. He is the son of LANCELOT and ELAINE, a latecomer to King ARTHUR's court both in the story and in the literature, in which he replaces the previous main Grail-seeker PERCEVAL, no longer pure enough for the

*'Sir Galahad', appropriately represented here in a watercolour by the Pre-Raphaelite Dante Gabriel Rossetti, was the only knight of King Arthur's court pure enough to enter the presence of the Holy Grail.*

achievement. Galahad is too good to be true, and in the stories shows only brief and slight touches of humanity and contact with reality. His resulting privilege of being the only knight permitted into the presence of the Holy Grail is a striking spiritual apotheosis which raises the whole matter onto a high mystical level.

ANON: *The Quest of the Holy Grail*: MALORY: *Morte d'Arthur*

## GANESHA

A wise and clever god, in the Hindu tradition of India, said to have been the first scribe of the *Mahabharata*. Depicted as short and fat, and with the head of an elephant, he has a reputation for having a great appetite.

## GANGA

A deity of India, the goddess of the sacred river Ganges.

## GANGLERI

The name taken by King **GYLFI** as a disguise in the compilation *The Prose Edda* by Snorri Sturluson, a collection of the traditional material of ancient Scandinavia.

## GANYMEDE

A handsome youth from Troy, carried to Mount Olympus by **ZEUS**' emblematic bird, the eagle, and made immortal as the cup-bearer of Zeus.

## GAOH

In the beliefs of the Iroquois Indians of North America, he was a giant who controlled the winds.

## GAOYAO

In Chinese mythological history, he is the last in the line of the 'five emperors' who presided over the formative stages of the development of early Chinese civilization, following on from the 'three sovereigns'. He was himself said to be a great judge and became the personification of justice. As his mascot he had a mythical creature, the Chinese equivalent of a unicorn, part deer, part horse and ox, with a single horn.

*Ganga, who in Hindu mythology personifies the sacred river Ganges. Red sandstone figure from the Khajuraho region, 10th century* AD.

## GARANG

For the Dinka people of Sudan in Africa, the first man, by whom men can also become possessed. He is also connected with a brown-and-white snake, and with those colours. See ABUK.

## GARUDA

A bird-god, in the mythological system of India, the protector against snakes and devourer of all evil things. The god VISHNU rides on him.

## GATSWOKWIRE

The Wiyot North American Indian equivalent of the Yurok figure WOHPEKUMEN.

## GAUTAMA

The family name of the founder of the Buddhist religion of India. See also SIDDHARTHA.

## GAWAIN

In the Celtic British material, one of the knights of King ARTHUR's court, and later said to be his nephew. He figures as an independent hero in his own tale, the medieval 'Sir Gawain and the Green Knight', in which he appears as the epitome of courtly virtue and courage. Even as this stage however there is a distinct touch of humanity, and therefore potential weakness, and he later becomes notably fallible and human. In Malory, he quarrels fatally with the king, and his refusal to be reconciled brings about their downfall.               MALORY: *Morte d'Arthur*

## GAYOMARD

In the Zoroastrian religion of Iran, the primeval man, at first immortal and self-sufficient, who lived in the unspoilt world with the other primal creature, a bull, until the world was attacked by AHRIMAN, spirit of evil. He and the bull then died, but in doing so they sowed their seed of perpetual growth and increase. See MASYA.

## GBOROGBORO

The first man, in the creation story of the Lugbara tribe of Central Africa. See MEME.

## GEATS

The people of the Anglo-Saxon hero BEOWULF, a Baltic tribe of historical origin inhabiting what is now southern Sweden.
                                    ANON: *Beowulf*

## GEB

In the ancient Egyptian religious system's story of origins, the deity representing the earth, son of SHU and TEFNUT, brother of NUT, the sky, with whom he coupled to produce the god OSIRIS and other divinities. At the end of a long reign over the earth he divided his kingdom between Osiris and SET, a partition which gave rise to a struggle between these gods. The ideogram of his name is a goose and in depictions of him this bird sometimes features surmounting his head.

### GEIROD

A powerful giant who occurs in Scandinavian tradition in an encounter with the god THOR, who eventually slew him.  SNORRI STURLUSON: *Prose Edda*

### GERD

A beautiful goddess of Scandinavian mythology, whose story tells how she caught the attention of the god FREYR, who wooed her and in due course became her husband.  SNORRI STURLUSON: *Prose Edda*

### GERYON

A three-bodied giant killed by HERACLES as one of his labours, in the heroic saga which forms a major element in Greek mythology.

### GE-SAR

In Tibetan tradition, a legendary early king, born after prophecies of conflict as a scourge of demons. He was himself the offspring of a god and of a divine serpent. Possibly the name Ge-sar is an echo of Caesar, and some of his exploits have a clear European origin. The character's early biography follows that of many mythic heroes: a reigning king attempts to destroy him as a prophesied successor, but he escapes; he spends a period in exile before returning to fulfil his mission; he takes up his role as his people's champion, and victoriously combats the supernatural forces of evil. In the end he is absorbed into heaven.

### GIDEON

A Hebrew figure, a leader and judge of the Israelites, at a time of their domination by the Midianites, from whom he liberated them at God's insistence.  *Judges*

## GIDJA

A male creator figure identified with the moon in the beliefs of the aboriginal people of northern Queensland, Australia. After creating the first woman he was destroyed by a rival but instead of dying he became the moon.

## GIKUYU

Occurring in the traditions of the people of Kenya in Africa, he was one of the sons of God, the ancestral founder of the people called after him 'the Gikuyu', now more generally known as the Kikuyu. God provided him and his descendants with the fine country below Mount Kenya.

## GILGAMESH

The main hero of Mesopotamian mythology. Born of the goddess NINSUN, and hence half-human, half-divine, he is the king of the city of Uruk and the hero of a cycle of poems recovered on clay tablets during excavations in the last century at the sites of the ancient cities of Nineveh and Nippur. The hero is based on a historical king of Uruk, who lived during the third millennium BC. In the epic however he is a powerfully portrayed figure, strong, good-looking, forceful, the essence of a mythic hero. He has, however, the one weakness inherited with his human blood, the curse of mortality, and it is this which forms the driving force of the epic. In the story Gilgamesh rules with wild restlessness, lacking the companionship of any equal, until the gods decide to make a counterpart being to form a foil for his energy, and construct the wild man ENKIDU. The two become heartfelt friends, and set off together on a journey of adventure to the great cedar forest and the borders of the world, their purpose being to combat evil, which they overcome in the person of HUMBABA the monstrous guardian of the forest. In the course of these undertakings, however, Enkidu dies, reinforcing the preoccupation which perpetually dogs Gilgamesh, the knowledge that 'only the gods live for ever in the glory of Shamash; as for mankind,

their days are numbered'. He then goes on alone to seek the disproof of this, the one man, UTNAPISHTIM, who has been granted immortality. He crosses mountains and oceans, and combats monsters, and at last reaches paradise. Yet in the end he returns, and dies as he must, leaving only the memory of his name. *Epic of Gilgamesh*

## GITCHI MANITOU

A character occurring in the tradition of the North American Algonquin Indians. See MANITOU.

## GLISPA

To the North American Navajo Indians she was a girl who visited an otherworld where she learnt one of the tribe's great chants, which she eventually taught to her brother and hence bequeathed to the Navajo. The chants of the Navajo people still form an important part of their cultural ritual, accompaniments to their famous symbolic sand-paintings.

## GLUSKAP

Creator god of the Algonquin Indians of North America. He is responsible for the good things of the world, competing with and finally outwitting his evil counterpart, MALSUM. He left the earth by sailing away towards the east, but it is said that he may some day come back.

## GOG

Originally GOGMAGOG, the name given by Geoffrey of Monmouth, in his collection of Celtic British traditional material, to a giant living in Cornwall (see CORINEUS). The name first appears in the Bible as a representative of evil, but came to be divided both in the Bible and in British lore into Gog and Magog (*Ezekiel* 38), in which form two giants are represented in statues in the Guildhall, London.

## GOGMAGOG

A Celtic British figure. See GOG.

## GOLIATH

In the Hebrew stories collected in the

*A bronze head of one of the three Gorgons, female monsters of Greek mythology. 6th-5th century BC.*

books of the Old Testament, a champion of the Philistine army at a time of war against the Israelites; he was eleven feet nine inches tall. The young hero **DAVID** accepted the challenge to combat him, which to their shame all other Israelite leaders had feared to do, and succeeded in concussing him with a sling stone, whereupon he cut off Goliath's head.             *1 Samuel*

### GONG-GONG
In Chinese mythology, a monster with a great horn, the enemy of the early emperor **YAO**, which caused a disastrous flood by impaling on its horn Mount Buzhou, disturbing the balance of the earth and making the rivers overflow their banks. The monster further ripped a hole in the sky, disturbing the course of the sun, and is in general an explanatory feature of irregularities of light and the weather.

### GORGONS
Three female monsters, occurring in the myths of Greece, whose hair was composed of venomous snakes. See **MEDUSA**, **PERSEUS**.

### GRAIAI
Three old women in the mythology of the Greeks who possessed between them one tooth and one eye.

*Wrought-iron sculpture of Gu, honoured in West Africa as the god of metal.*

## GRAINNE

A figure of Celtic Irish myth, anglicized as Grania. She is the heroine of an elopement story, for details of which see DIARMAID.

## GRANI

In Scandinavian mythology, the name of a horse given to SIGURD by ODIN, which would move only for Sigurd, and on which he rode the wall of flames to gain the hand of BRYNHILD for GUNNAR.

SNORRI STURLUSON: *Prose Edda*

## GRENDEL

The name of the monster which besieged the hall of the King of the Danes, and was eventually defeated by the hero BEOWULF in the Anglo-Saxon story of the latters' deeds. Grendel is a curiously personalized evil presence in the epic poem. Condemned to live miserably in the waste lands at the borders of the inhabited country, he is tormented by the sound of revelry from the Danish king's hall, and is driven to creep from his swamp to spoil their merriment by seizing and carrying off many Danes. ANON: *Beowulf*

## GSHEN-RAB

A figure of the Bon-po religion of Tibet, the legendary founder of that pre-Buddhist religion. He was said to have come into the world with a series of mystical effects and to have carried out remarkable feats in childhood which distinguished him as a great teacher and spiritual leader. At length he came to Tibet, where he combated demons and set a religious example by becoming a possessionless monk.

## GU

In West Africa, the Abomey tribe's name for the god of metal. See OGUN.

## GUAN DI

The Chinese god of war, a deity much venerated in historic times. He was originally a hero with possibly historic roots, and his cult consequently combines the attitudes of earthly heroic respect with a more religious worship.

*Guan Di, in Chinese mythology the god of war.*

## GUAN YIN

Formerly spelt Kuan-yin, or Kwanyin. A goddess in the ancient Chinese religion who introduced mankind to the cultivation of rice, which she made wholesome for the purpose by filling it with her own milk. The figure is derived from the Chinese Buddhist tradition, and was much venerated by women in a household context, being known as the 'lady giver of children'. The figure is equivalent to the male deity of Tibet and other Mahayana Buddhism, AVALOKITESHVARA, and occurs again in Japan as KWANNON.

## GUCUMATZ

A god of the Quiche-Maya people of Mexico, perhaps identified with the feathered serpent god QUETZALCOATL or KUKULCAN. He is said to have taken part in the creation of the world, the animals, and finally mankind, the latter however involving several unsuccessful attempts resulting in failed species which were destroyed, some by flood, others becoming monkeys. He and his companion TEPEU wished to make man because none of their previous creations was able to praise them and provide for them.                                     *Popul Vuh*

## GUDATRIGAKWITL

A figure exclusive to the beliefs of the Wiyot Indians of North America, a pre-existent being who created the earth, made the first man and his successor species and also made many other objects of the world. All this he achieved by mental effort, without the use of implements.

## GUDRUN

Wife of SIGURD and sister of GUNNAR, in the pre-Christian tradition of Scandinavia.
SNORRI STURLUSON: *Prose Edda*

## GUENEVER

Originally Gwenhwyfar, later Guinevere, a major figure of the Celtic British materials. In early Welsh tales she was said to be the daughter of a giant, perhaps originally a minor goddess. She became important in the tradition as the wife of King ARTHUR, in developed form the subject of the poignant triangular love-affair in which she deceived him with his most trusted knight, Sir LANCELOT. Guenever does not emerge from the tales as entirely blameless, but comes over as being trapped and led by human frailty and crushed by the dilemma of her two loves. Her tragedy is further compounded by her nobility, since in the stories she remains a regal figure throughout her humilation and suffering.
MALORY: *Morte d'Arthur*

## GUINECHEN

The chief deity of the Araucanian Indians of Chile. He was the creator god and the giver of life, the upholder of the order of nature. He saved mankind from a flood sent by the forces of evil to destroy the human race. Compare BOCHICA.

## GULU

For the people of Buganda in Africa, the king of heaven, and the father of NAMBI. See also KINTU.

## GUN

In the mythology of China, he occurs as a hero called in by the early emperor YAO to advise on the means of saving the world from inundation in a great flood which was rising as high as the mountains. He at first attempted but failed to stem it by building dams. At length he made use of the aid of some magic earth, which grew in size under its own power (compare North American WISAGATCAK). This, however, he first had to steal from its owner, said to be the early emperor HUANG DI, and his successful use of it caused the latter to send his agent JURONG, the fire spirit, to destroy the unfortunate Gun.

## GUNNAR

In the ancient Scandinavian stories he occurs as the suitor of BRYNHILD, whom SIGURD acquired for him by riding through the wall of fire which guarded her, which Gunnar failed to do.
SNORRI STURLUSON: *Prose Edda*

*The Chinese goddess Guan Yin taught mankind the cultivation of rice and, according to popular belief, it was her milk that filled the rice ears.* Blanc-de-chine *figurine,* c. 1760.

### GWION

A figure of Celtic British myth, Gwion bach, 'little Gwion', was set by the witch CERIDWEN to stir her cauldron of knowledge. Some drops flew out of the mixture onto his thumb, which he sucked, as once becoming omniscient. He then becomes part of a shape-changing tale, being pursued by Ceridwen in various forms until he is swallowed as a grain of wheat by her as a hen. She becomes pregnant, and he is reborn as the all-knowing prophet-bard TALIESIN.

### GWYDION

One of the most imposing figures in Celtic British myth, the prototype wizard-figure, a powerful magician dominating the court of the king of Gwynedd and embroiling his country and himself in both personal and political conflicts. See also ARANRHOD, BLODEUEDD, LLEU LLAW GYFFES.

### GWYN

A Celtic British figure known as Gwyn ap NUDD, he is one of the figures connected with the 'wild hunt', in which capacity he also functions as the collector of souls. He held an annually-repeated contest against a rival, and was said to have his court on the summit of Glastonbury Tor.

### GYLFI

The character used by the compiler and story-teller Snorri Sturluson to tell the tales of the pre-Christian Scandinavian gods in his collection known as *Prose Edda*. The stories unfold as King Gylfi of Sweden questions the gods about their nature, deeds and history.

*Gunnar (Gunther, in the* Nibelungenlied*) is the suitor of Brynhild but it is through the heroism of Sigurd (Siegfried) that Gunnar wins her hand. This wood carving from a 12th-century church at Hylestad, Norway, shows the dying Gunnar in a snake pit playing the harp with his toes.*

# HACHIMAN

A god of war in the mythology of Japan. Originally he was the deification of the emperor Ojin, and has developed into a very popular deity in the Shinto religion, having thousands of temples. Paradoxically he is also a god of peace, and is regarded as a protector of Buddhism and himself thought to be a Bosatu (the Japanese form of a Bodhisattva).

# HADAD

A storm-god of Syria, and one of the aspects of BAAL. Compare Babylonian ADAD.

# HADES

According to the story of the beginning of order as contained in Greek mythology, when the three sons of CRONUS divided the world between them, ZEUS ruled the sky, POSEIDON the sea, and Hades became lord of the underworld, which was populated by the spirits of the dead. His kingdom is usually known by the same name. In later Greek tradition he is known as PLUTO, originally one of his titles, meaning wealthy.

# HAEMON

A figure of Greek myth, in which he is the son of CREON (King of Thebes after the exile of OEDIPUS) and betrothed to Oedipus' daughter ANTIGONE. Haemon is part of the classic struggle of contradictory moral forces to which both Creon and Antigone are subjected. SOPHOCLES: *Antigone*

# HAGAR

In the Hebrew material contained in the Old Testament, she served as as a maid to ABRAHAM's wife SARAH. In this capacity she bore Abraham a son, ISHMAEL, at a time when it seems that Sarah's barrenness would produce no heirs. *Genesis*

## HAIO HWA THA

A figure in the lore of the North American Mowhawk Indians. See HIAWATHA, by which name he is better known.

## HANISH

A Mesopotamian deity, a herald of the gods, whose function is to warn of stormy weather. *Epic of Gilgamesh*

## HANUMAN

In the mythology of India, he is the monkey-god, a character connected with RAMA (one of the incarnations of VISHNU). A popular god among the country people, he is regarded as clever and resourceful, and as a faithful servant to Rama, whom he aids in times of difficulty. On this account there is a resistance to killing monkeys, in spite of the agricultural damage they do.

*Ramayana*

## HAOMA

The god of the plant of the same name, the juices of which were used to make an intoxicating liquor (the same as that of SOMA in India) which is an important element in the religious rituals of the Zoroastrian religion of Iran. Haoma as a god is regarded as the son of AHURA MAZDA, and his incorporation in the ritual is seen as the sacrifice of the son offered to the father. The partakers of this communion imbibe with the mixture the immortality of the god.

## HAPI

An Egyptian deity, a god of the Nile floods on which Egyptian agriculture has always depended. He is consequently seen as a god of fertility and as of extreme importance. In the religious system he had connections with many other gods, but specifically was regarded as living on an island in the Nile's First Cataract. He was represented as a man with heavy female breasts.

## HAPY

A figure of Egyptian religious ritual. Shown as an ape-headed god, one of the sons of

OPPOSITE: *Hachiman, who, in the Shinto religion of Japan, is the god of war, originated from the deification of the Emperor Ojin.*

LEFT: *In Hindu mythology Hanuman is the chief of the monkey people who helped Rama find his wife Sita when she had been abducted by the demon Ravana. Bronze statuette dating from before the 15th century.*

HORUS, his function was funerary, as guardian of the jar which contained the lungs in the rituals of embalmment.

## HARAKHTE

In Egyptian mythology, one of the forms of HORUS, as a god of light, and subsequently absorbed into the person of RA, the sun god, one of whose titles was Ra-Harakhte.

*Hathor, the Egyptian goddess associated with joy and celebration, licks the arm of a man who is about to enter the other world. Detail from a papyrus, 18th Dynasty.*

## HARMONIA
Daughter of ARES, the Greek god of war, and wife to CADMUS, the legendary founder of Thebes.

## HATHOR
A sky goddess in the Egyptian pantheon, sometimes shown as having a cow's head, and generally connected with that animal and viewed as a nursing mother-goddess. Although her role changed several times, she became mainly a figure associated with joviality and celebrations. When depicted as a woman she is normally shown wearing on her head the solar disc, enclosed by tall horns. This headdress was however later adopted by the goddess ISIS, who absorbed many features of other mother goddesses.

## HAUMEA
A creator deity in the beliefs of the people of Hawaii, a mother-goddess whose functions included that of the goddess of childbirth, which she was responsible for introducing. She was an ambiguous figure capable of occasional malevolence. As a goddess of provision she controlled the supply of edible vegetation, and this function connects her with HAUMIA, the Maori god of edible plants. She was also seen as the mother of PELE, a fire goddess of Hawaii particularly associated with volcanoes.

## HAUMIA-TIKE-TIKE
One of the main family of gods in the beliefs of the Maori, a son of RANGI and PAPA, the original pair of sky and earth. He was the god of the fern root, which is representative of uncultivated edible vegetables, especially root food (compare RONGO).

## HAURVATAT
An element of the Zoroastrian religion of Iran, being one of the AMESHA SPENTAS, benevolent spirits who act as the agents of

*Priam and Hecuba watch while the Greek hero Hector puts on his armour.*

God. The name Haurvatat is translated as 'Well-being' or 'Wholeness'.

## HAYK

In Armenian mythology, a supposedly historical figure who was the ancestor of the Armenians. He was said to have been descended from JAPHETH, one of the sons of NOAH, and to have returned to the area of Mount Ararat after a dispute with the leaders of the religion of the Babylonian god BEL.

## HEBE

A figure of Greek myth, being the daughter of ZEUS and his legitimate wife HERA. She was given as a wife to HERACLES when he was finally rescued from his self-imposed funeral pyre and elevated to the company of the gods.                    HOMER: *Iliad*

## HECABE

See HECUBA, the more common form for this figure of Greek myth.

## HECATE

Originally one of the Titans, the family of early gods of Greece, she became a goddess of the underworld and thus associated with PERSEPHONE, but also retained connections with the moon and with magic. Regarded as a figure of horror, she haunted tombs and crossroads, always accompanied by her howling dogs.

## HECTOR

Champion of the Trojan forces in the Greek story of the Trojan War. He was the son of King PRIAM, and was eventually defeated by the supreme Greek hero ACHILLES, though not before wreaking much damage on the Greeks.  HOMER: *Iliad*

## HECUBA

The common Latinization of the more authentic Greek form Hecabe. Queen of Troy, wife of PRIAM and mother of HECTOR, PARIS and CASSANDRA. When Troy fell she was carried off by the Greeks.  HOMER: *Iliad*

*The cause of the Trojan War was the abduction by Paris of Helen, wife of Menelaus. Her former suitors, who had sworn to come to the aid of the man who successfully won her, took arms under Agamemnon and laid siege to the city of Troy.*

### HEH
In Egyptian mythology, one of the aspects of NUN, the name Heh signifying Eternity. He was depicted in the form of a man, with the emblems of life and good fortune.

### HEIMDALL
In Scandinavian myth, the guardian of the approach to Asgard, the citadel of the gods, which was vulnerable to attack by their enemies the giants. Known as the White God, he had miraculous sight and hearing. Nonetheless, Loki managed to steal his sword. Heimdall bore the great horn which would warn the gods of the coming of Ragnarök, the cataclysmic end of their rule.

### HEL
A Scandinavian goddess, the daughter of the wicked god LOKI and herself of exceptionally unpleasant appearance; she ruled the underworld, the abode of the (unheroic) dead where she lived in a vast hall, the counterpart to Valhalla, the home of dead heroes. Our word 'hell' comes from this source.

SNORRI STURLUSON: *Prose Edda*

### HELEN
A Greek heroine, the daughter of ZEUS and LEDA, and princess of Sparta, the kingdom which MENELAUS gained by marrying her. Her love was offered to PARIS, Prince of Troy, by APHRODITE, the goddess of love, as a bribe in the contest between the three leading goddesses which he adjudicated. (See ERIS, PARIS). It had been agreed between the many suitors for Helen's hand that if her eventual husband needed them they would all come to his assistance; hence when Paris and Helen eloped a large league gathered in support of Menelaus to launch the Trojan War. Helen is thus placed in the position of illustrating the dangers and bitterness innate in what

appears to be an ideal romantic affair, and through no fault of her own caused much tragedy.

## HELIOS
The personification of the sun, in the pantheon of the ancient Greeks.

## HENG
The name of the spirit of thunder in the tradition of the Huron Indians of North America. He is said to be energetic but clumsy, and on that account thought to have been rejected by his family.

## HENG BO
Or Ho Po. A river god in the mythology of the Chinese, also known by the name of Bingyi. His specific realm was the great Yellow River, and like the river itself he occupied an important position in Chinese culture and custom. He formed the object of placatory ritual sacrifice, for a long period the sacrifice of human beings. He was said to have originally been a man on earth, who committed ritual suicide by throwing himself, weighted with stones, into the river.

## HENGIST
Almost certainly a historical figure of early British history, the leader of a group of Saxons who established a settlement in Kent; he was however elevated by Geoffrey of Monmouth into the mythic enemy of the Britons. In the story he arrives in Britain with his brother HORSA, befriends the king, VORTIGERN, but later exploits the king's friendship and betrays him.
GEOFFREY OF MONMOUTH: *History of the Kings of Britain*

## HENG-O
Sometimes called Chang-o. In Chinese mythology, the wife of YI the archer. She stole from him the elixir of immortality which he himself had obtained from XI WANG MU, and when she had done so she retreated with it to the moon, with which she is connected either as its goddess or as its mother.

*A terra cotta statue of the Chinese goddess of the moon, Heng-o.*

*Heracles, shown here engaged in typically valiant struggle, was the prime example of the Greek hero who through strength and prowess overcame formidable obstacles and achieved immortality. Bronze statuette, 2nd-3rd century AD.*

## HENO

Or Hino, Hinu. The god of thunder for the Iroquois Indians of North America, and said to be the ruler of the sky.

## HEPHAESTUS

The blacksmith god in the central Greek pantheon (see Roman VULCAN). Athough portrayed as lame and ugly he received generally favourable treatment in myth, and was married to the loveliest of the goddesses, APHRODITE. Kindly and generally peaceful, he was evidently admired by the Greeks as a skilled craftsman.

## HERA

The principal goddess of Greek mythology. Wife of ZEUS, she was the representative of the marital side of the female role. Characteristically the Greeks saw the husband as being avidly unfaithful, and the wife is therefore mainly expressive of possessiveness and jealousy. Hence in many stories Hera plays a rather bitter and vengeful role. Compare Roman JUNO.

## HERACLES

A central figure of Greek mythology; in the Roman version HERCULES. Heracles is the epitome of the mythical hero, the representative of the superhuman elements in the makeup of myth: the monster-slayer, the traveller on extraordinary journeys, giant in strength and stature, invincible, yet predestined to suffer great ordeals and to undergo a tragic death. Oddly, however, for Greek myth, he is not highly personalized in human terms, unlike the wilful ACHILLES or the wily OEDIPUS. The brute force which he wields is certainly governed by intelligence and skill, but still the heroic dominates the human. Son of ZEUS by a daughter of the High-King of Mycenae, he would have become the ruler of the Peloponnese had not Zeus boasted that a son born that day into the house of PERSEUS would become High-King. Jealous of his infidelity, Zeus' wife HERA arranged for Heracles' cousin EURYSTHEUS to be born first, and thus his fate was to be a subject rather than a ruler. His life was spent under this shadow of Hera's hostility. She caused the madness which led him to kill his children, which in turn led to his subjection to the labours imposed by Eurystheus. It was Hera too who sent the Hydra, a many-headed water-monster, to be his downfall. The blood of a centaur (see NESSUS) killed by an arrow poisoned with the Hydra's blood was mistakenly used by his wife as a love-potion, causing him such pain that (though offered immortality) he chose to die. (See DEIANEIRA). Thus just as his life bears the aspirations of humanity to be superhuman, so in the end he fulfils the hero's other supreme task of expressing an unavoidable destiny. In Greek and Roman art, Heracles, often shown leaning on a heavy club, is a mature man of powerful build.

### HERCULES

A hero of Roman myth. See Greek **HERACLES**.

### HERMES

A Greek god. Like **APOLLO** he was a god of flocks and of music, the son of **ZEUS**, and connected mainly with Arcadia in the Peloponnese. Hermes is differentiated by a connection with theft and trickery, and his function extended to make him the god who guides travellers and the messenger and companion to the deities on their journeys. Thus he became the conductor of souls to the underworld. His general need for speed led him to be viewed as having wings on his heels, which in turn made him a god of athletes. He remained connected with dishonesty, being the patron of thieves and father of the bandit **AUTOLYCUS**. See also Roman **MERCURY**. A fine statue of the god by the classical sculptor Praxiteles is in the museum at Olympia, where it was discovered in the temple of Hera. It shows him carrying the god **DIONYSUS** as an infant.

### HERMOD

**ODIN**'s heroic son, in Scandinavian myth. In his most famous exploit he rode Odin's horse **SLEIPNIR** to the realm of **HEL** to ask for the return of **BALDER** from the dead. He is thus one of the few heroes of mythology to have made a visit to the underworld and then returned.

SNORRI STURLUSON: *Prose Edda*

### HERNE

A figure of Celtic British tradition, known as Herne the Hunter, a horned figure riding out of the woods on a black horse with a pack of hounds, which associations connect him with major mythic figures such as **ODIN**, **GWYN**, the horned god **CERNUNNOS** and the wild hunter of European medieval legend.

### HERO

A heroine of Greek myth. She was a priestess of **APHRODITE** at a temple on the European shore of the Hellespont; visited every night by her lover **LEANDER**, who swam to her from the Asian side. She killed herself when he drowned one night in a storm.

### HESIONE

In Greek myth, the sister of King **PRIAM** of Troy. She was abducted to Greece at a period before the Trojan War.

### HESTIA

In the Greek tradition of the early gods, she was one of the children of **CRONUS** and **RHEA**.

ABOVE: *Among the roles of the Greek god Hermes was that appointed by Zeus, to act as messenger of the gods to the kingdom of Hades.*

RIGHT: *Longfellow's Hiawatha was a historical figure to whom he attached a number of Algonquin legends and folk-tales.*

### HIAWATHA

Correctly **HAIO HWA THA**. A figure occurring in the lore of the North American Mowhawk Indians, he was in fact a great chief who brought about a federation of five Indian nations. To the name of this historical character the nineteenth-century American poet Henry Longfellow incorrectly attached the set of Algonquin legends and folk-tales now best known from his long poem *The Song of Hiawatha*.

*A carved door lintel from a Maori meeting-house said to depict Maui being destroyed by Hine-Ahuone as he tries to enter her in an attempt to gain immortality for man.*

**HINE-AHUONE**
Or Hine-ahu-one. In the beliefs of the Maoris, the first woman of the human race, created by TANE by modelling a figure out of red earth and breathing life into it. Her name means 'Earth-formed Maid'. Tane then mated with her to produce a daughter, HINE-TITAMA.

**HINE-NUI-TE-PO**
The Maori goddess of death, the 'Lady of Darkness'. See HINE-TITAMA.

**HINE-RAU-WHARANGI**
In Maori stories of origins, the daughter of the god TANE and his daughter HINE-TITAMA, the 'Dawn Maid'. She represented the growth of vegetation. She is also sometimes known as Hine-titamauri.

**HINE-TITAMA**
A figure in the creation stories of the Maori, the daughter of the first woman (HINE-AHUONE) by the creator god TANE. Her name means the 'Dawn Maid'. The term *Hine*, 'Maid', is also often applied with a suffix to the forces of nature, such as the power of natural growth, and the elements of thunder and lightning. In due course Hine-titama left her husband and father Tane and went to dwell in the underworld, where she became the 'Lady of Darkness', HINE-NUI-TE-PO, the goddess of death and the protector of the dead.

**HIPPODAEMIA**
In the stories of Greek mythology, the daughter of the King of Elis, wooed by PELOPS, her hand being only attainable by the winner of a chariot race. The name itself suggests a connection with horses.

**HIPPOLYTUS**
A Greek hero, son of THESEUS. Portrayed as worshipping ARTEMIS and neglecting APHRODITE, in that he was more interested in riding than in love, he aroused the rivalry of the two goddesses. The injured Aphrodite caused his stepmother PHAEDRA to fall fatally in love with him. His father, in jealous fury, brought about his death (through the agency of POSEIDON) in a chariot accident as he drove along the seashore, and he thus died by means of the horses he was so devoted to.
EURIPIDES: *Hippolytus*

**HOD**
A Scandinavian god, also known as Hoder or Hodr. A blind god noted for his great

strength, he features prominently in the story of **BALDER** as the unwitting slayer of that good and beautiful god.

SNORRI STURLUSON: *Prose Edda*

## HOENIR

A Scandinavian god who occasionally accompanied **ODIN**, but otherwise appears as incidental and not highly differentiated.

SNORRI STURLUSON: *Prose Edda*

## HORSA

In the traditional early history of Britain he was said by Bede and Geoffrey of Monmouth to be the brother of **HENGIST**, the invading Saxon leader. However he bears less evidence of historical reality and in the mythology of Britain plays only a supporting role.

GEOFFREY OF MONMOUTH: *History of the Kings of Britain*

## HORUS

A major Egyptian god, in origin partly an ancient sky-god, portrayed with a falcon's head. Like **RA** he absorbed some of the characteristics of many associated deities. In the form of Haroeris, Horus the Elder – a distinct personage said to be either the son or the husband of **HATHOR** – the figure is that of a god of light, whose eyes were the sun and the moon; as Harmakhis, Horus on the horizon, he is the god of the dawn and it is this deity that is represented by the great sphinx at Giza, made in his own likeness on the instructions of the pharaoh Khephren, in the third millennium BC. In his developed form in the mythology however he is the son of **ISIS** and **OSIRIS**, and his story takes a common mythic form. He narrowly avoided destruction in infancy at the hand of his uncle **SET**, and disputed the leadership of the gods with Set in his adult life, being favoured by the other gods as the successor to Ra, whose powers were waning. Although Ra favoured Set, Horus inherited his father's position, with the backing of Isis and the shade of Osiris, and eventually defeated his father's murderer. In effect he became the main god of

*A Japanese ivory figure of Hotei, the god of wealth.*

Egyptian religion, and the patron deity of the pharaohs. The confusion of the early falcon-headed sky-god with a later more personalized deity led to a diversity of interpretations of Horus.

## HOTEI

A god of good fortune, one of the seven such in the mythology of Japan. He is traditionally portrayed as a fat-bellied and smiling man carrying a bundle of treasure, a figure much influenced by Buddhist tradition.

## HREIDMAR

In Scandinavian tradition, he was a farmer who played an important part in the epic story of the treasure and the magic ring (see **ANDVARI**). It was the need to pay a ransom by covering with treasure an otter-skin which brought the ring into the possession of Hreidmar and then of his son **FAFNIR**, who was destined to be killed by the hero **SIGURD**.

SNORRI STURLUSON: *Prose Edda*

## HRUNGNIR

A giant in Scandinavian mythology who competed with the gods, and ended with a mighty duel with **THOR**, in which he was finally slain.

SNORRI STURLUSON: *Prose Edda*

*Huacas were spirits of the Inca religion of Peru. A sacrifice to the spirit of the River Vilcanota. Illustration by Guaman Poma de Ayala, c. 1613.*

## HU

In the Chinese explanation of the beginnings of the world, it was said that towards the end of the period of chaos there lived two beings, Hu, the Emperor of the Northern Sea, and his counterpart SHU, the Emperor of the Southern Sea. They used occasionally to visit each other on the territory of the Emperor of the central sphere, HUNDUN. The story of their repayment of the latter's hospitality is that of the ending of chaos and the beginning of order and structure. See HUNDUN.

## HUACAS

Spirits in general in the Inca religion of Peru, and also the names for the temples or shrines at which they are worshipped.

## HUANG DI

Or Shi Huang Di, in the older form of transliteration spelt Huang Ti. Known as the 'Yellow Emperor', he was one of the remote 'five emperors' of Chinese mythical history. He occurs chiefly in the stories of GUN's and YU's attempts to stem a great all-threatening flood, his role being that of the possessor of the magical earth which they needed to complete their task.

## HUEHUETCOTL

A Mexican Indian deity. See XIUHTECUTLI.

## HUGIN

In Scandinavian myth, one of the pair of ravens which sit on ODIN's shoulders and report to him all that goes on. He sends them out at daybreak to fly over all the world, and they come back with the morning news, having questioned the living and the dead. See also MUNIN. The names mean respectively 'Thought' and 'Memory'. SNORRI STURLUSON: *Prose Edda*

## HUITACA

A goddess of the Colombian Indians, viewed as a beautiful woman, and connected with debauchery.

## HUITZILOPOCHTLI

A war-god and storm-god in the beliefs of the Aztecs of Mexico, allocated the south quarter of the compass. At first a figure of fear, he later became sun-god and patron of the Aztec empire. In his mythic biography he was said to have been born fully-armed (compare TEZCATLIPOCA) from the belly of COATLICUE, the earth-goddess. His cult was centred on his temple at Tenochtitlan, and involved human sacrifice.

## HUMBABA

In the main story of Mesopotamian mythology, he occurs as the guardian of the great cedar forest which formed the object of the initial adventure of GILGAMESH with his friend ENKIDU. Perhaps a Syrian nature god in origin, he is depicted in the story as an angry giant and a representative of evil whom the two heroes overcome.
*Epic of Gilgamesh*

## HUNAB KU

The one transcendent God for the Maya Indians of Mexico, thought of as being unlimited and omnipresent.

## HUNAHPU

A creator god, in the beliefs of the Maya Indians of Mexico. Also known as Hunahpu-Vuch, god of the dawn, *vuch* being the brief time of pre-dawn half-light. In some aspects the figure is regarded as female, and identified with a she-fox or coyote. The name is also that of a youthful hero, who together with his companion and twin brother XBALANQUE defeated the arrogant VUCUB-CAQUIX and his sons. The heroic twin brothers feature in many folk tales. *Popol Vuh*

## HUNDUN

Or Hun-tun, in the older form of spelling. Literally meaning Chaos, Hundun occurs as a passive figure in Chinese cosmogony, a mythical emperor of the central ground on which the northern emperor HU and the southern emperor SHU come together for their periodic meetings. In effect the story tells in an anthropomorphized form how chaos ended, when the two opposed principles of north and south operated upon it. Hundun had the peculiarity that his body lacked the essential openings of mouth, ears, eyes and nose. As a way of marking their gratitude for his receiving them on his territory, the story says, the two emperors who met there made the required holes in Hundun, which unfortunately caused his destruction. It was when he died as a result of this that the ordered world came into being out of the previous state of chaos.

## HURACAN

An element in the cosmogony of the Maya Indians of Mexico. Known as 'the Heart of Heaven', he is one of the first largely abstract principles in creation, becoming viewed as one of the chief gods, along with GUCUMATZ and TEPEU, who however pre-existed him. He is associated with thunder-storms and his name is the root of our word hurricane. *Popul Vuh*

## HYACINTHUS

A hero of Greek myth. A prince of Sparta noted for his unusual beauty, he attracted the love of the god APOLLO and also that of the West Wind, and died tragically when the latter, in jealousy, threw back at him the discus which Apollo was teaching him to use. He gives his name to the hyacinth flower, which is said to bear his initials.

OVID: *Metamorphoses*

## HYMIR

In Scandinavian mythology, a giant encountered by THOR; he fished in the sea, and the god in disguise went fishing with him and dismayed the giant by catching the World Serpent.

SNORRI STURLUSON: *Prose Edda*

## HYPERION

A figure of Greek myth, in which he is the god of the sun. There is a clear overlap with the character of HELIOS, said to be Hyperion's son. Hyperion, who is himself the son of URANUS and GAEA and occurs as the sun-god in Homer, is evidently an older deity. HOMER: *Odyssey*

*A miniature mask of obsidian, thought to represent Ixtilton, the lieutenant of the Aztec war- and storm-god Huitzilopochtli.*

## IACCHUS

In Greek tradition, the god of the festivities of Eleusis, a god of revelry later confused with DIONYSUS.

## ICARUS

A hero of Greek myth, the son of DAEDALUS. His story begins with his being imprisoned with his father in Crete after the latter had fallen out of favour with King MINOS. When they escaped with wings made of wax and feathers, his father warned him not to fly too near to the sun, which would melt the wax. By failing to heed this advice Icarus endures as an image of impetuosity; inevitably he soared and fell, drowning in the Aegean.

OVID: *Metamorphoses*

## IDOMENEUS

In the Greek story, the leader of the Cretan forces at the Trojan War. Through the main event of his biography he expresses the bitter irony of fate which the Greeks habitually projected onto their mythic characters. Having sworn to POSEIDON when caught in a storm that if saved he would sacrifice the first person he met on land, he is of course greeted on arrival by his own son. A pestilence broke out when he attempted to fulfil his vow and he was then forced by his people to leave Crete for Italy where he settled in Calabria.

HOMER: *Iliad*

## IDUN

Wife of the god BRAGI in the pantheon of ancient Scandinavia, she is noted for her guardianship of the gods' rejuvenating golden apples. The trickster LOKI enticed her, with her apples, out of Asgard, the fortress of the gods, and she fell into the power of the giants.

SNORRI STURLUSON: *Prose Edda*

## IFA

A major element in the religious system of the Yoruba people of Nigeria in West Africa. Centred on the town of Ile-Ife, which is regarded as the centre of the world, Ifa is the spirit expressed by the great oracle of the Yorubas. He is also regarded as a god of healing, as are oracular gods elsewhere. See also ORUNMILA. Ifa is seen by the Yorubas as a saviour figure sent from heaven to help man in his difficulties. His priesthood operates its oracular function in all Yoruba communities.

*A divination board used in the Ifa cult of the Yoruba people of Nigeria.*

## IHY

Son of HATHOR, in ancient Egyptian religion, by a sacred bull. His function was that of a god of music, and he was depicted as a young man wearing the double crown of the two kingdoms of Egypt.

## ILYAPA

Also spelt Illapa. For the Incas of Peru, the god of storms, and of the weather. He was responsible for thunder and lightning which he brought about with his personal weapon, the sling and slingstone. In the Catholicized period following the conquest of Peru he has been identified with Santiago (St James).

*The most famous of the supermen, or bogatyrs, of medieval Russian mythology is Ilya Muromets. This folk hero is shown here attempting to rescue another bogatyr, Sviatogor, from a coffin. Print by I. Bilibine.*

## ILYA MUROMETS

A Russian mythical hero, a figure of supernatural ability whose function is the protection of his people. Though he was the son of a peasant, he possessed miraculous qualities, such as a horse which he rode through the air and a supernaturally powerful arrow. Some of his attributes connect him with PERUN, the Slavonic god of war and of lightning.

## IMAYMANA VIRACOCHA

Son of the great creator god of the Incas of Peru, and along with his brother TOCAPO VIRACOCHA the instructor of the human race, at God's direction, in the use of edible plants and of their medicinal virtues. They also gave all things names.

## IMSET

One of the four sons of HORUS, and together with his brothers DUAMUTEF, HAPY and QEBEHSENUF one of the four guardians of the sarcophagus of the dead, and the canopic jars in which the viscera of the dead were contained following embalmment. Imset was represented in human form, unlike the other three who had the heads of animals. His function was to stand on guard at the north corner of the tomb and to watch over the jar containing the liver. The four gods were important elements in these rites based on the story of the death and rebirth of OSIRIS, and were regarded as the sons of Horus by his wife ISIS. It is also said that on RA's orders SEBEK caught them in a net.

### INANNA

The Sumerian form of the Semitic ISHTAR.

### INARI

God or goddess of rice, in the mythology of Japan. The character is sometimes thought of as a fox, and in other contexts as a man with a beard who dwells in the mountains, the fox then being viewed as the god's messenger. Images of foxes, painted red, are found at all Inari shrines, being made of stone or other materials.

Inari's functions also include the protection of swordsmiths, and the god is prayed to for good harvests and for any other blessings.

### INDRA

One of the principal gods of India. A god of storms, like so many major deities (compare ZEUS, THOR, SHANGO), Indra was thought to control the thunder and to ride through the heavens in a chariot. Indra was also worshipped as the god who provided rain. In the mythology his story includes elements common to the biographies of supernatural beings, including the theme of infant prodigy, in which he proves his exceptional ability and nature immediately on being born. He represents a challenge to the old order, and in due course becomes himself the leading established deity, supplanting VARUNA. Indra is particularly connected with the soma, an intoxicating drink with sacred qualities used in religious rituals, which it is said gave him his special powers. His role in the myths is mainly as destroyer of demons, and he battled continually with his evil counterpart VRITRA. In the course of absorbing Varuna's functions he became a fertility god and a god of creation, and at a later stage of his development was viewed as a divine monarch, reigning in a luxurious heaven, Swarga, on the sacred mountain, Mount Meru, though he retained his fearful aspect as god of thunder. He is often depicted as riding on a white elephant. *Rig Veda*

### INTI

Creator god, in the beliefs of the Incas of Peru, for whom he was the maker of mankind, identified with the sun and hence the focus of the Inca's sun-religion. Also known as APU-PUNCHAU. He has a general celestial function, regulating the stars, and is represented by a sun-disc with projecting rays and the face of a man. To the Incas Inti was not only the supreme deity but their own great ancestor. They held him in very great awe; eclipses of the sun were a sign of his anger.

*An illustration by Guaman Poma de Ayala, c. 1613, showing the Aztec sungod Inti and a festival of the sun.*

DEZIEMBRE
CAPACINTIRAIMI

lagran pasçua
solene del sol

## IO

In Greek myth, the subject of one of the many love-affairs of ZEUS. As a result she was put by his jealous wife HERA into the custody of the hundred-eyed ARGUS, and eventually rescued from him by HERMES.

## IOLE

A heroine of Greek mythology, the princess of a kingdom defeated by HERACLES, who fell in love with her and brought her home, causing the fatal attentions of his wife. See DEIANEIRA.

## IOSKEHA

Also known as Tsentsa. In the cosmogony of the Iroquois and Huron Indians of North America, he was the constructive member of a pair of twins born to the daughter of ATAENTSIC. Compare NAGENATZANI, THOBADESTCHIN. He overcame destructive powers and created animals and mankind.

## IPHIGENIA

Eldest daughter of AGAMEMNON in the central story of Greek mythology, in which she was the subject of an agonizing dilemma on his part between public and private moral duty. CALCHAS the prophet had foretold that the windbound fleet could not sail for Troy unless Agamemnon sacrificed his daughter to ARTEMIS. He did so, and as a result the fleet sailed, but the consequences continued in his personal life. See CLYTEMNESTRA.

EURIPIDES: *Iphigenia in Aulis*

## IQUI-BALAM

One of the four 'first men', in the cosmogony of the Maya Indians of Mexico. See BALAM-QUITZE. *Popol Vuh*

## IRDLIRVIRISSONG

For the Eskimo of North America she was a female demon, related to the moon.

## ISAAC

An important figure in the early history of the Hebrews, as conveyed to us by the books of the Old Testament. He was the son of ABRAHAM, born to him and his wife SARAH in their old age by God's intervention. His role was to be the progenitor of the tribes of Israel through his son JACOB, and his story tells how narrowly this was achieved. Tested by God, his father Abraham was prepared to put him to death when God appeared to demand it, but Isaac was saved by a ram being provided as a substitute at the last minute. When in due course he married, his wife RÉBECCA remained barren for twenty years, but after an appeal to God she gave birth to two sons. See ESAU, JACOB.

*Genesis*

*In the Old Testament Isaac was one of the ancient patriarchs of Israel. In the episode illustrated in this Hispano-Moresque Haggadah of about 1300, Abraham, Isaac's father, is about to sacrifice his son in the belief that it is God's will.*

### ISHMAEL

A figure in the Hebrew tradition as
recorded in the Old Testament. Son of
ABRAHAM by his wife's maid, HAGAR, he was
a wild man and outlaw who later became
favoured by God on Abraham's
intervention. He is said to be the ancestor
of the Arabs, and an Islamic legend places
him instead of ISAAC as being nearly
sacrificed when God tested the devotion of
Abraham.                    *Genesis*

### ISHTAR

The Mesopotamian goddess of love, and
the queen of heaven; she also has a more
fearsome aspect as a type of war-goddess.
She was worshipped together with her
father ANU at the major temple at Uruk.
Married to TAMMUZ, she mourned and
sought for him when he died, his death
and her mourning being a symbol of the
retreat of vegetation. Compare Greek
DEMETER and Egyptian ISIS.

*Epic of Gilgamesh*

### ISHULLANA

Gardener to ANU, in a Mesopotamian story,
he is wooed by Anu's daughter ISHTAR, but
rejects her. As a punishment she turns him
into a mole, or something similar.

*Epic of Gilgamesh*

### ISIS

A major figure of Egyptian mythology. The
daughter of GEB and NUT, she married her
brother OSIRIS by whom she had a son
HORUS. Isis embodies many of the major
features of female divinities, being viewed
on the one hand as a great magician, and
also as a mother-goddess, in which
capacity she is often depicted suckling the
infant Horus. But her main characteristic is
her mourning for her dead husband
Osiris, killed by his brother SET, her search
for his body, and her institution of the
funerary and embalming rites of the
Egyptians in the process of giving him
rebirth and immortality. See OSIRIS, SET.
Her mourning was thought in some areas

LEFT: *A bronze figurine of the Egyptian mother-goddess Isis with Horus, her son by her husband (and brother), Osiris.*

**ISMENE**

A heroine of Greek myth, one of the daughters of **OEDIPUS**. She plays a lesser role in the story than her sister **ANTIGONE**.

**ISOUD**

Also spelt Iseult, Essyllt, Isolt etc. A heroine of Celtic British myth. Daughter of the King of Ireland, the betrothed of King **MARK** of Cornwall, she eloped with his nephew **TRISTAN**.          MALORY: *Morte d'Arthur*

**ISRAEL**

'He who wrestles with God', a name originally applied to the patriarch Jacob who wrestled with an angel. Later it was applied to the northern Hebrew kingdom destroyed by the Assyrians. Then it became the generic name of the Jewish people.
*Genesis*

**ISSUN BOSHI**

A diminutive figure occurring in the traditional stories of Japan. Literally 'Little One-Inch', in spite of his tiny stature he became a great hero and attacker of demons. Eventually he gained a wish and became of normal size, continuing his life thereafter as a samurai.

**ITZAMNA**

Literally 'Lizard House'; the supreme deity of the Maya Indians of Mexico, portrayed as an old man. He was said to be the inventor of writing and to be generally concerned with knowledge. Together with his wife **IX CHEL** he was the parent of the gods.

**IX CHEL**

'Rainbow Lady', wife of **ITZAMNA**, the chief god of the Maya Indians of Mexico. She is seen as an old woman, and her concerns are the aspects of the female marital role, such as childbirth and weaving and the arts of healing. Her portrayal as having claws on her hands and feet connects her with the Aztec mother goddess **COATLICUE**.

**IX CH'UP**

'The Woman', goddess of the moon, in the mythological system of the Mexican Maya.

to be the cause of the Nile floods. Her conception of Horus was sometimes said to have taken place, by means of her magic, after the death of Osiris. With the infant she fled and hid from the pursuing hostility of Set, since she regarded the child as destined to avenge his father's murder. Like the Greek **DEMETER** she lived as a woman among mankind; and on one occasion vegetation and life itself was threatened when Horus ailed (as with Demeter's mourning) and **RA** had to intervene. The cult and worship of this great goddess persisted from early to late times, and was still practised at her magnificent temple at Philae near Aswan as late as the sixth century AD. She is often depicted wearing as a headdress the horns and sun-disc which were originally the symbols of the goddess **HATHOR**, whose role she to some extent absorbed.

## IZANAGI

In the Japanese cosmogony, a primal male deity who descended to earth and was responsible for forming the first land of Japan. He then married his sister IZANAMI and they produced gods and creatures. When his wife died after giving birth to the god of fire KAGUTSUCHI he followed her to the underworld, and only narrowly escaped to return to the world. There, after ritual purification to remove the influence of the underworld, he set about creating further gods. See AMATERASU, SUSANO, TSUKUYOMI.

## IZANAMI

The primal female deity in the cosmogony of Japan, the sister and wife of IZANAGI.

*Izanami and Izanagi, in Japanese mythology two of the prime male and female deities, standing on the 'Floating Bridge of Heaven'.*

# JACOB

Ancestral head of Hebrew tribes which occupied the land of Canaan, homeland of the Jews. Divinely instructed, he took the name ISRAEL, which became the generic name of the Jewish people. He is represented as cunning and capable, not above trickery. See ESAU. Having obtained preferential inheritance to his elder brother he was then obliged to flee from his resentment, and in doing so Jacob experienced a vision of God in the form of a ladder stretching from earth to heaven, a message of his special destiny. Jacob married twice, see LEAH, RACHEL, and also had offspring by Rachel's maid when she was still barren (compare HAGAR), producing altogether twelve surviving sons who became the founders of the twelve tribes of Israel: six by Leah (see REUBEN, LEVI, JUDAH); two by Rachel (see JOSEPH, BENJAMIN); two by Bilhah the maid and another two sons by Leah's maid Zilpah.

*Genesis*

# JAMBAVAN

In the myths of India, the king of the bears, a god, and son of the great god VISHNU. The story tells how he led an army of bears in support of RAMA. He was eventually killed by KRISHNA, Rama's successor as incarnation of Vishnu.

*A miniature from the Golden Haggadah, c. 1300, showing Jacob, the founder of the people of Israel, wrestling with the angel.*

## JANUS

A god peculiar to Roman mythology, the god of all doors, gates and entrances, and hence of travel and of all beginnings, with further connections with war and peace. He is normally represented with two faces, looking to the past and the future. He was honoured on the first day of each month and the first month bears his name.

## JAPHETH

Son of NOAH, in the Hebrew stories of origins as conveyed by the books of the Old Testament. He was the founder of the group of tribes known after him as Iapetic, the 'sons of Japheth' who occupied part of Asia Minor, one of the twelve tribes of Israel. *Genesis*

## JARAPIRI

The name of a snake-man, in the beliefs of the Australian aborigines, who occurred in the area of Wimbaraka, north-west of Alice Springs, and later became part of the terrain, the explanation of a natural feature.

## JASON

A major Greek hero. Sent on an impossible mission to recover the golden fleece, he had a ship, the *Argo*, built for the purpose, and collected the best young men of Greece to be the crew. After a voyage of many adventures not unlike that of ODYSSEUS, he returned with the fleece and with the enchantress MEDEA. Jason's exploits are very much those of the folk-tale hero, and he met a typically ironic death on his return when a piece of his great boat fell on his head.
PINDAR: *Pythian Odes;* OVID: *Metamorphoses*

## JEHOVAH

An inauthentic variant of the Hebrew name for God, possibly formed from the combination of 'Adonai', 'my Lord', with the letters JHWH. See YAHWEH.

## JEHU

Occurring in the Hebrew tradition preserved in the Old Testament, he was a military leader of the Israelites, who was proclaimed and anointed king in succession to the unpopular AHAB. It was at his instruction that Ahab's widow JEZEBEL was put to death. He rid the country of the foreign cults introduced by Ahab and Jezebel, particularly from Phoenicia, and founded a new dynasty. *2 Kings*

## JEROBOAM

In the Hebrew traditional history as recorded in the Old Testament, he was a protégé of SOLOMON's who stirred up rebellion against that king and was obliged to flee into exile. He lapsed into idolatry and thus angered God, but nevertheless eventually became king of Israel. Probably a historical figure of the tenth century BC. *1 Kings*

OPPOSITE: *An episode from the saga of the Greek hero Jason who had been sent on a dangerous mission to recover the golden fleece. Athena watches as the dragon spits him out; the golden fleece hangs on a tree behind.*

*A bronze coin of standard Republican type, depicting the two-headed Roman god Janus. Probably 2nd century BC.*

## JESSE

Grandson of **BOAZ** and **RUTH**, in a Hebrew story of the Old Testament, a resident of Bethlehem and father of a family of eight brothers, the youngest of whom was **DAVID**. The prophet **SAMUEL** came to him, directed by God, to anoint David as the future king of Israel.          *1 Samuel*

## JETHRO

In early Hebrew traditional history, father-in-law of **MOSES**, a priest of Midian who welcomed and assisted Moses during his exile from Egypt. He is also known as Reuel and Hobab.          *Exodus*

## JEZEBEL

A figure of Hebrew tradition contained in the Old Testament. The wife of **AHAB**, she was known as a woman of loose morals and a schemer, and presented as wilful and dominating. The story tells that she promoted the worship of foreign gods which she brought with her from her home country of Phoenicia. The phrase 'painted Jezebel' comes from a reference to her painting her face. She came to a violent end at the instructions of **JEHU**, and her carcass was thrown to the dogs.
          *1 & 2 Kings*

## JIMMU TENNO

In the traditions of Japan, he was the first emperor, a legendary figure, being the grandson of **NINIGI** and hence the great-grandson of **AMATERASU**, the sun-goddess.

## JINGO

In the traditions of Japan, she was an empress who on succeeding her late husband invaded Korea, being aided in doing so by magical effects. She bore her son (later to become the emperor Ojin – see **HACHIMAN**) inside her for three years while carrying out the conquest.

## JIZO BOSATSU

The guardian of mankind, in the beliefs of Japanese Buddhism, especially the guardian of the young and of women in childbirth. His function is also that of

OPPOSITE: *A lacquered wood statue of Jizo Bosatsu, in Japanese Buddhism the guardian of mankind.*

BELOW: *In the Old Testament account, Job patiently endured the misfortunes sent him by God as a test of his devotion. In this medieval miniature God allows Satan to destroy Job's sheep.*

saving souls from hell. A popular god, he is often depicted as a Buddhist monk. The title 'Bosatsu' by which he is known is the Japanese version of the Indian 'Bodhisattva', the 'enlightenment-being' of Buddhism.

## JOB
The subject of a Hebrew story contained in the Old Testament. He was a man whose perfection and devotion to God brought about a test of his responses when God gave SATAN the chance to try him by removing his advantages and causing him disaster and ill-health. However he would not be moved to deny God's justice, in spite of all that happened. Hence he has become the paradigm of patience in adversity. In the end God restored his wealth and good fortune.

## JOCASTA
A character in Greek mythology. The mother of OEDIPUS, and (as foretold by a fateful prophecy) later his wife. Jocasta is a figure of suffering, embroiled in the conflict of forces over which she has no control.
SOPHOCLES: *Oedipus the King*

## JONAH
In a Hebrew story of the Old Testament, he was a prophet instructed by God to reprimand the wicked of the city of Nineveh. The story tells how he tried to avoid the task but was caught in a storm at sea and chosen to be sacrificed by the fearful crew, whereupon he was consumed by a 'great fish' which carried him to land. The next time God asked him, he went to Nineveh.
*Jonah*

## JONATHAN

In traditional Hebrew history as recorded in the Old Testament, the son of SAUL, the king of the Israelites, and a friend to DAVID. He died together with his father in battle, much to David's distress.    *1 Samuel*

## JOSEPH

A hero of the Hebrew material preserved in the Old Testament. He was the son of JACOB and RACHEL, and the favourite of his father among his twelve sons. Envied by his brothers, he was sold by them to merchants who took him to Egypt where he prospered. His father in the meantime being convinced, by being shown the 'coat of many colours' which he had given him, mauled and bloodstained, that he had been killed by a wild animal. He possessed the power of the interpretation of dreams (compare DANIEL), performing this oracular function as the mouthpiece of God. In this capacity he foretold a great famine, enabling the Egyptians to store reserves in readiness, and thereby gaining the governorship of Egypt. His story is one of unexpected requital, since the famine brings his treacherous brothers into his power. It is as a result of their reuniting under his patronage that the Israelites come to be in the land of Egypt. See MOSES.
*Genesis*

## JOSHUA

In the traditional early history of the Hebrew peoples, according to the books of the Old Testament, he occurs as the companion of MOSES. In due course it fell to him to take over that prophet's role as leader of the Israelites in their journey out of exile, and to bring his people into the land which God had promised them. As a warrior-leader he presided over the besieging and defeat of Jericho, achieved by the people led by their priests and emblems marching round the walls until they miraculously collapsed. On another notable occasion he used God's power to make the sun stand still, to prolong a battle until his nation achieved victory.
*Exodus, Joshua*

## JOVE

The main god of the Romans, an alternative name for JUPITER.

## JUDAH

A figure of traditional early Hebrew history, as recorded in the Old Testament. He was one of the sons of JACOB; hence his name became that of the Hebrew tribe said to be descended from him, which in turn gave its name to a territory around the city of Jerusalem.    *Genesis*

## JUGUMISHANTA

The earth, as mother and creator, in the mythology of Papua New Guinea's Eastern Highlands region. She was the creator of mankind and the giver of established order and of the form of the land.

## JUMALA

The supreme creator god of Finnish mythology, and the god of the oak tree. He was not highly personalized, but seen rather as a remote and largely abstract being. In origin he was probably a sky god.

## JUNO

The main goddess of the Roman pantheon. Although identified with the Greek goddess HERA (as being the wife of the leader of the gods), Juno was a more popular female divinity in her Roman form than was Hera in Greece. She is the goddess of the feminine role, of married life and child-bearing, and had a regal and dignified status not marred by the jealousy and spite which characterized her Greek equivalent.

## JUOK

The creator god of the Shilluk tribe of Sudan in Africa, who believed that he made men from clay, using different colours for the different races.

## JUPITER

The chief god of the Romans. God of the light sky, wielder of thunderbolts, he is the Roman equivalent of the Greek ZEUS, and shares much the same character.

OPPOSITE: *The Roman goddess Juno, shown here with her husband, Jove, was a nobler figure than her Greek equivalent, Hera.*

**JUROJIN**
God of long life in the mythology of Japan, one of the gods of luck, of whom there are seven in developed Japanese belief. He is seen as a white-bearded man carrying a scroll containing the world's wisdom.

**JURONG**
The fire spirit of Chinese mythology, whose role also includes that of avenger.

He is the agent of punishment not only of the disruptive monster GONG-GONG but also of the hero GUN, whom he killed for stealing magic earth to stem a great flood.

**JURUPARI**
A cult god of the Matto Grosso area of Brazil, worshipped as the upholder of traditional custom and regarded as intolerant of disobedience.

OPPOSITE: *In a realm outside space and time, the great Hindu god Vishnu reclines at ease on the cosmic serpent.*

LEFT: *A bronze figure of the Japanese god of good fortune Jurojin, seated on a stag beetle and holding a scroll. 18th or 19th century.*

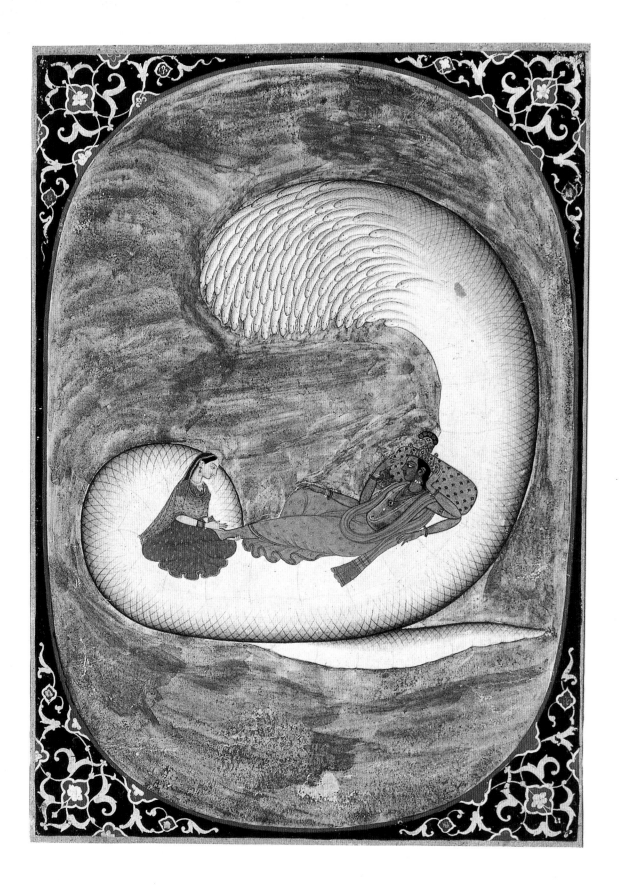

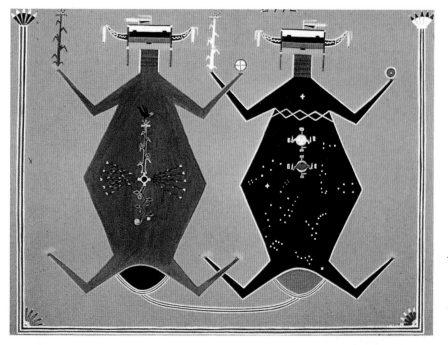

**Creation**

*The classic descriptions of creation in mythology tell of the union or conjunction of the earth and the sky, viewed for the purpose in anthropomorphized form, as in an Egyptian papyrus painting (below), showing Nut, the sky goddess, mating with Geb, the deified earth (Papyrus of Tameniu, 21st Dynasty). The same set of ideas is illustrated in a sand-painting of the North American Navajo Indians (left), which shows the Sky Father and Earth Mother. The creation of mankind and of night and day occur as episodes in many creation myths: a detail from the Golden Haggadah, c. 1320, showing, on the right, the creation of Eve (opposite, top left), and a 20th-century Australian Aboriginal bark painting (opposite, bottom left) present differing views of these episodes.*

*A late 19th-century Japanese hanging scroll, by Eitaku Kobayashi (right), shows the primal couple Izanagi and Izanami stirring the primeval waters to bring land into existence.*

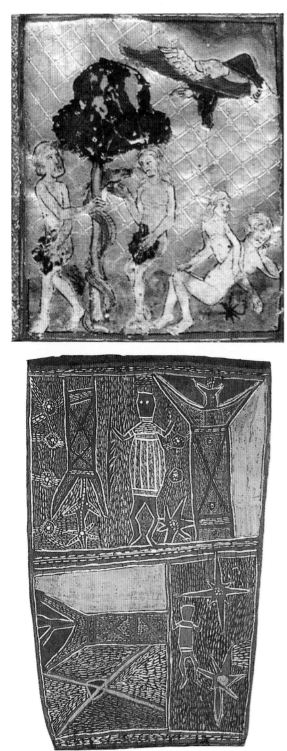

## The mythic hero

*The mythologies of all cultures contain the person of the idealized human being, victor over disorder, vanquisher of monsters and of supernatural opponents, confronted frequently by the crucial predicaments of trial and challenge, love and death. These major themes express themselves through the figure of the mythic hero, seen in classic form (above) in the person of the dragon-slaying Persian hero Rustem, as illustrated in a miniature from Firdusi's Shah-nameh, 1486. A 12th-century carving (right) from a stave church at Hyllestad, Norway, shows the confrontation of the Scandinavian hero Sigurd with his treacherous counterpart, Regin. British mythology's major hero, Lancelot, is noted for his romantic love for Guinevere, the queen of his lord and friend, King Arthur. In an illustration from an early 14th-century manuscript of the Vulgate Cycle (opposite, top left), Lancelot rescues Guinevere. A 14th-century stained-glass panel (opposite, bottom left) shows the youthful David, hero of the Old Testament, in the role of giant-killer. One of the most poignant representations of the human condition, and one of the earliest to become established in myth, was the Mesopotamian hero Gilgamesh (opposite, right). This bas-relief from Khorsabad, dating from the 8th century BC, shows him with a captured lion.*

**The task of the hero**

*Confrontation with a supernatural or specially destined opponent often forms the central task of the mythic hero. A detail of an 18th-century Indian miniature (above) shows Krishna, an incarnation of the Hindu god Vishnu, killing his predestined foe, the demon king Kamsa. The Greek demi-god Heracles, who perhaps outshines all other heroes in heroism, is seen (right) in a 6th-century BC vase painting overcoming a monstrous bull. An episode in the cycle of the Japanese hero Yorimitsu, depicted (below) in a print by Kuniyoshi (1798-1861), involves the defeat of a band of giants.*

## Forces of evil

In the background of the precariously ordered world of most mythologies there is a sinister and malevolent group of destructive forces. A scene (below) from a 14th-century Persian manuscript shows Angra Mainyu, the representative of evil in Zoroastrian mythology, tempting the first man and woman. A figure of malice and disruption in Scandinavian mythology was the trickster Loki, who is shown (bottom left), in an 18th-century manuscript of the Prose Edda, arranging the death of the good god Balder. In Hindu mythology the arch-demon Ravana was the enemy of the hero Rama. Ravana is shown (right), in a late 19th-century folk painting, struggling with Hanuman, the monkey-god who was Rama's faithful servant. One of the most fearful personifications of evil is the Hindu goddess Kali (bottom right), depicted in a Kalighat painting of about 1865, awesomely garlanded with a string of heads.

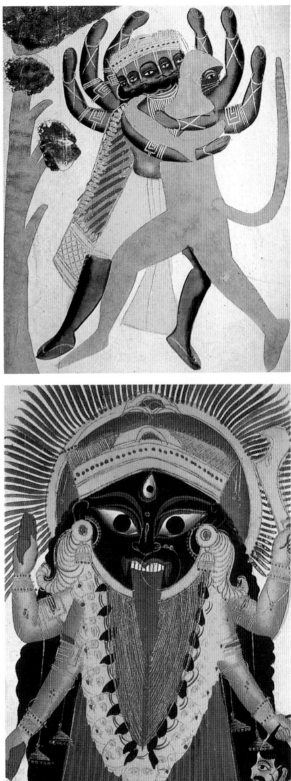

## Mother and provider

*In most mythologies the ideas of maternity and fertility are closely linked; a providing female figure, often also identified with the earth, forms an early and important element in many pantheons. Distinctive mother and child pairs occur in various parts of the world. A statuette (above left), dating from the 18th Dynasty, c. 1380, represents the Egyptian goddess Isis nursing the infant Horus; a Ming bronze (above right) shows the Chinese heavenly helper, Guan Yin, giver of rice to mankind, also in a maternal role.*

*The preoccupation of the Egyptians with the passage of death shows in a scene (right) from the Book of the Dead of Userhetmos, a papyrus of the 19th Dynasty. The goddess of child-birth, Taueret, depicted as having the head of a hippopotamus, presides at the rebirth of a dead woman.*

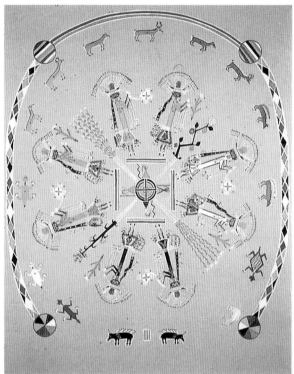

**Fertility**

*Fertility and fruitfulness are emphasized in a Greek vase painting (above left) of about 485 BC, which shows the mother goddess, Demeter, and her daughter, Persephone, teaching the mortal prince Triptolemus the principles of agriculture. A Navajo Indian sand-painting (above) presents a stylized depiction of a fertility rite in which ears of corn, maize and other plants radiate from the central fire and a circle of animals surrounds the dancing figures, sharing in the blessing. Ears of corn also feature in a 12th-century woven tapestry (left) from Skog Church, Halsingland, in Sweden. Here they are the emblem of the fertility god Freyr, who in this detail forms a trinity with the gods Odin and Thor.*

### God of the sun

As the most notable and important influence on earthly life, the sun became deified and personified in almost all mythologies. The Inca supreme god Inti (right) is shown as the golden sun in the form of a beaten gold mask, c. AD 1000. The same theme of radiance appears in a Roman mosaic (below) dating from the 1st century AD, probably representing the Greek god Apollo in the role of solar deity. The solar disc on the back of the Aztec sun-god Tonatiuh (below right) also represents the apocalyptic earthquake, which the Aztecs believed would destroy both the earth and the sun. In the mythology of the Egyptians the sun was identified with the great god Ra. He is represented (bottom) in the Book of the Dead (Papyrus of Hen-taui, 21st Dynasty) by the solar disc containing the 'Eye of Ra' symbol.

*In several cultures the god of the sun features as the driver of a chariot, advancing in a fiery course through the sky. A detail from an 18th-century Indian miniature (left) shows the progress of the Hindu sun-god Surya. An important episode in Japanese mythology tells of the sun-goddess Amaterasu taking offence and retreating to a cave. A 19th-century print by Kunisada (below) shows her being coaxed out to restore light to the world.*

## Gods of the sea

*The mythologies of all cultures have figures associated with the elements and natural features. The sea, for example, is represented by numerous gods of varied forms. In an African group depicted on a 17th-century bronze plaque from Benin (left) it seems likely that a sea god, possibly Olokun, is represented by the figure with the mud-fish legs. The sea takes a different form in the person of the Japanese 'dragon of the sea', Ryujin, shown in a netsuke (bottom left) as an old man bearing in his hand the jewel of the tide. The classic portrayal of the Roman sea god Neptune in a 2nd-century mosaic from Tunisia (below) shows him holding his identifying emblem, the trident, and riding a chariot drawn by aquatic horses.*

## Gods of storm and thunder

*In many mythologies the violence of storm is interpreted as the rage of an angry god whose temper is subject to no control other than his own whim. Such a character is Zeus, the high-king of the Greek gods, who is shown (opposite, top left) on an oil pot of the 5th century BC in the act of hurling a thunderbolt.*

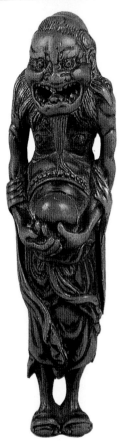

*In Indian mythology the god Indra (above), shown in a miniature of c. 1820, was a god of thunder as well as of rain and storm. A major African god of thunder is the great Yoruba god Shango, who like other gods of thunder elsewhere was said to cause the phenomenon by hurling his axe. The wooden sculpture surmounted by a double-axe symbol (far left) represents an ancestor figure associated with the Shango cult. A detail (left) of a painted silk screen by Kadanaro Gyosai (1831-89) shows the Japanese thunder god Raiden.*

### Death and the afterlife

*Coming to terms with the inevitability of death forms a motive or goal of much myth-making. A Mexican figure of Mictlantecuhtli, Lord of the Dead (left), expresses the horror and fear of death. In Egyptian mythology, as is shown in a detail (below) from the Papyrus of the scribe Ani, 19th Dynasty, c. 1250 BC, the passage from the land of the living to the land of the dead culminated in judgment, in which Anubis presided over the weighing of souls. The concept of a passage from the land of the living to the spirit world is also expressed in an Australian Aboriginal bark painting from Arnhem Land (bottom), painted by Bunia. Didjeridu players perform to aid the dead man's passage; his two wives and a spirit also help him in a long journey that begins with crossing the Great Snake and for which he sustains himself with fish killed by throwing a rock into a pool.*

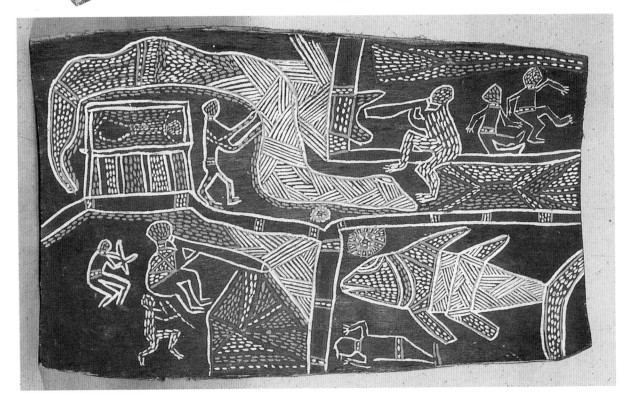

*A Japanese painting (above), probably of the late 18th century, presents an Eastern version of the weighing of souls and the damnation of sinners. In Indian mythology Soma is the ambrosia of the gods that ensures immortality to all who drink it. An 18th-century painting of the Mewar school (top right) shows it being produced by the gods and demons churning the ocean of milk, with a great snake used to turn the churning-pole and Vishnu, as his avatar the tortoise, stabilizing the violent motion. A Chinese porcelain dish of the early 18th century (bottom right) shows Xi Wang Mu, the 'Queen Mother of the West', the fruits of whose garden ensured the immortality of the gods.*

# K

NOTE: In the transliteration of Greek, some names which may be spelt with an initial C are alternatively spelt with an initial K.

## KAANG

A god of the African Bushmen. See KAGGEN.

## KACHINAS

The North American Pueblo Indian name for the multiple ancestral spirits and the spirits of other deities which pervade the world.

## KAGGEN

The main god of the Bushmen of Africa. Also spelt CAGN, or KAANG. The first creative spirit, the supreme being. The word is the same as one meaning the praying mantis, so that the god becomes in many stories and reports identified with the creature, which also occurs in many folk tales. Kaggen, as primordial spirit, is seen as a force out of the control of men, an expression of nature and climate. The eland, an important source of food for the Bushmen, is sacred to him and, therefore when it has to be killed, due reverence and care must be observed.

## KAGUTSUCHI

The Japanese god of fire. His birth caused his mother IZANAMI to fall ill and die, through being damaged by burning. See also IZANAGI.

## KAISUKI

A figure of the beliefs of the people of the Buganda region of Africa. The brother of Death, he attempts to halt the destruction of mankind through Death's vendetta with the family of KINTU and NAMBI, the first couple, but without success.

## KALERU

Also Galeru. In Australian aboriginal stories, the name of the great 'rainbow snake' of the Kimberley region. See UNGUD.

## KALI

In the mythology of India, a fearsome form taken by the wife of SHIVA, a figure whose character and identity overlap with those of DURGA, but with an even more terrible aspect: she takes the form of a black-faced, blood-covered ghoul, with a girdle of human skulls, her multiple arms bearing weapons with which she combats demons. The city of Calcutta is named after her: Kali-ghat, 'Kali's steps'.

OPPOSITE: *A 19th-century Tibetan Wheel of Life illustrates the Buddhist concept of the cycles which lead towards rebirth. In so doing it provides an image of the coming-together in a single concept of the range of concerns which underly many mythologies.*

BELOW: *A Kachina doll representing an ancestral spirit of the North American Pueblo Indians.*

## KAMA

Son of **DHARMA**, in the myths of India, also regarded as an aspect of **AGNI** and as a participant in creation, and viewed as an amorous youth, thus primarily a god of love. Like **CUPID** he bears a bow and shoots arrows of passion at random. The name means 'love' or 'desire'.

## KAMAUGARUNGA

The first woman, in the creation story of the Herero tribe of South-West Africa. See **MUKURU**.

## KAMI

A word used to describe a god or spirit in the ancient beliefs of Japan, and also to represent the spirit, in the sense of the non-material power or influence, of a natural feature. As a result of this aspect of the Shinto religion it is sometimes said that it has eight million gods, the Kami of rocks, trees and places being worshipped along with the main deities.

## KAMSA

In the mythology of India, a demon and tyrannical king, the predestined enemy of **KRISHNA**, by whom he is eventually killed.

## KAPPA

In the traditions of Japan, they are a race of monkey-like demons, small beings of a malicious nature which occasionally can be appeased and bargained with by humans. They live in ponds and rivers, from which they feed on unfortunate human beings and animals, having a particular liking for blood. A Kappa will return a low bow, losing water from his head and so power to do harm.

## KARTTIKEYA

A figure occurring in the mythology of India as the son of **SHIVA**. He is also known as **SKANDA**. A god of war, he is depicted as having six heads and six arms, and he rides on a peacock. As a war-god he conducts a campaign against the demons, but in some areas he has taken on the character of a god of fertility.

## KENOS

The first man, in the beliefs of the Ona people of Tierra del Fuego in Chile. He was sent by the supreme god **TEMAUKEN** to bring civilization to the world.

## KHEPRI

One of the forms taken by the ancient Egyptian sun-god **RA**, specifically the rising sun. Because of the belief that the scarab beetle lays an egg in its own dung, which it pushes in front of it when it moves (in fact this is a ball of collected food), the self-regenerating power of the sun was symbolized by this creature, and Khepri is therefore depicted as having the head of a scarab or simply as the beetle itself, pushing ahead of it the ball of the rising sun.

## KHNUM

In the Egyptian religious system, he was a ram-god, shown as a man with a ram's head. Khnum was an early god originally local to the area of the First Cataract of the Nile, and was said to have made the gods and men, whom he continued to create out of clay. He was responsible for the formation of children in their mothers' wombs and is depicted sculpting young pharaohs on temple bas-reliefs.

## KHONS

An Egyptian deity, sometimes known as Khonsu. He formed the son element in a trinity worshipped at the great temple of Thebes, now called Karnak, along with his father **AMON-RA** and his mother **MUT**. In his own right he was a moon-god local to Thebes, but acquired there diverse functions, such as the provision of fertility and life, and absorbed some of the qualities of **THOTH** and of **SHU**. Under the New Kingdom his cult as a healer flourished.

## KHOPUN

In Slavonic mythology, the god of rivers. He exercised moral selection in the destruction of swimmers, since he only drowned the bad.

**KHSATHRA**

The name of one of the AMESHA SPENTAS, figures in the Zoroastrian religion of Iran, benevolent spirits who act as the agents of God. The name Khsathra is translated as 'Kingdom' or 'Dominion', and the figure is a representative of strength and hence a patron of just warriors.

**KHUBA**

The wife of TEISHEBA, a god of Armenia.

**KHYAB-PA**

In the pre-Buddhist Bon-po religion of Tibet, he was a demon enemy confronting the religious leader GSHEN-RAB, making several attempts to thwart the efforts of the latter in founding the Bon-po religion. He was however eventually converted to that cause by witnessing gShen-rab's practice of monastic austerity, which set a permanent example to his followers.

**KI**

The Sumerian goddess of the earth, who mated with AN, the sky, to produce the air-god ENLIL.

**KIBUKA**

For the people of the Buganda area of Africa, a war god with associations with storms and the brother of the supreme god MUKASA.

**KILYA**

A goddess of the Incas of Peru. Also known as Mama-Kilya, she is the moon, the wife of INTI, the god of the sun, and was venerated in the Inca sun-religion second only to him. Like him she was portrayed as a disc with a human face, in her case in silver. She was regarded as a goddess of matrimony.

**KINTARO**

A hero of supernatural strength occurring in traditional Japanese stories, he was known as the 'golden boy' from the colour of his skin. In due course he became an attendant at court and the vanquisher of monsters.

*A bronze statuette, c. 1300 BC, of the Egyptian god Khnum, a god of fecundity and creation.*

## KINTU

An ancestor figure in the beliefs of the people of the Buganda area of Africa, who lived alone with his cow until the first woman arrived. See NAMBI. In an episode in his story he visited heaven where he was tested by the king of heaven to prove his worthiness to marry the king's daughter, which in due course he did.

## KIRANGA

A great spirit believed by the Barundi tribe of East Africa to be the intermediary between men and God. They approach God through him by means of sacrifices.

## KISHIJOTEN

A goddess of good fortune in the mythology of Japan.

## KITAMBA

In the tradition of the people of Angola in Africa, he was a king whose mourning for his dead wife forms the context of a story of an otherworld visit.

## KORE

A Greek goddess, another name for PERSEPHONE.

## KOSHCHEI

A figure in Slavonic mythology, known as Koshchei the Deathless from his supposed invulnerability. He is himself lean like a figure of death, and is noted for being the abductor of beautiful princesses.

## KRAK

In Polish tradition, the legendary founder of Cracow. He rescued the people from the control of a dragon by enticing it to gorge a sheepskin full of saltpetre, which eventually caused it to burst, after which he was able to start the construction of the city.

## KRISHNA

A major figure of the mythology of India. Originally he was a pastoral deity, and through association with animals conveyed the idea of a bond between the realm of nature and the world of the gods. In developed (and more familiar) form he was one of the incarnations of VISHNU, and the hero whose exploits are recounted in the long epic poem, the *Mahabharata*. Here he is prince of the Yadavas, and at war with a demon KAMSA, his predestined foe. The story of his life goes through a clear series of mythic steps, from the portentous and supernatural birth, to the prodigious, superhuman childhood, the object of repeated but unsuccessful attempts at destruction, through the youth

BELOW: *Krishna, one of the most attractive gods of the Hindu pantheon, high-spirited, amorous and heroic, shown in this 18th-century miniature with his sweetheart, Radha.*

OPPOSITE: *A grotesque wooden image from within a precinct sacred to Ku at Kailau, Hawaii.*

exiled from his people and awaiting return, to the emergence of the all-conquering hero. In this latter capacity he is a source of wisdom, and a sub-section of the *Mahabharata*, the *Bhagavad-Gita*, is devoted to his exposition of a philosophy to his friend ARJUNA at the start of the climactic battle against the demons and forces of evil. He is a popular object of worship as an infant, portrayed as chubby and mischievous; as a youth he is a figure of amorous attraction; as a developed hero he is the demon-killer, embattled (like the Egyptian RA with the serpent APEP and the Scandinavian THOR with the World Serpent) with his arch-opponent, his life's task. In this struggle of the heroic individual against the massed forces of evil he becomes (after many setbacks) eventually successful, although in the end he does not himself take part in the deciding battle, merely advising and expressing the ultimate futility of contingent action.          *Mahabharata*

## KU
A group of Hawaii war gods, the name usually being followed by a description such as in Ku-in-the-forest. As major gods the group acquired other functions such as protectors of wood-workers.

## KUBERA
In the religious system of India, this personage underwent a radical change from the role of evil spirit to that of Hindu god. He continued to be viewed as an ugly dwarf, in which capacity (like dwarfs in other mythologies, see Scandinavian ANDVARI) he is the guardian of great treasure.

## KUKULCAN
*Kukul*: 'feathered'; *can*: 'serpent'. A major character in the tradition of the Maya Indians of Mexico. God of the highest group in the social order, he is usually represented as a feathered serpent and much depicted at Maya and Toltec sites. He was said in Maya history to have been a man who arrived in the Yucatan from the

west and established a new kingdom at Chichen Itza. The same figure, also represented by a feathered serpent, is known as QUETZALCOATL, in which form he is the chief deity at the great sacred site of Teotihuacan.

## KUNAPIPI

Or Gunabibi. A figure of the mythology of aboriginal peoples in the north of the Northern Territory of Australia, and into parts of Western Australia. She is a mother goddess and goddess of fertility, known as 'the old woman', a primal figure in part an ancestress of the people, viewed as having introduced the first population. Her husband was the lightning, who is often represented in paintings as a snake.

## KUNTI

In the mythology of India, the wife of PANDU, and the mother of the PANDAVAS, whom she conceived along with her co-wife MADRI by means of worshipping various gods.                    *Mahabharata*

## KURMA

In the mythology of India, the incarnation of the god VISHNU as a tortoise.

## KVASIR

In the ancient Scandinavian pantheon, the wisest of the gods; he was made by the other gods from the spittle used as a sign of truce between the AESIR, the chief gods and the VANIR, lesser deities. Some dwarfs in due course killed him and mixed his blood with honey, thus making the mead of inspiration. See SUTTUNG, ODIN.

SNORRI STURLUSON: *Prose Edda*

## KWANNON

The goddess of mercy in the mythology of Japan. This is the Japanese form of the Chinese GUAN YIN (or Kwanyin) who in turn comes from an Indian Buddhist source. Strictly speaking the figure is not so much a deity as a Bodhisattva, an 'enlightenment-being', a Buddhist phase of spiritual development. She is referred to as the 'lady giver of children', and is a very

*A scroll depicting Kwannon, the being of mercy in the mythology of Japan. Ink on paper hanging scroll by Hakuin (1685-1768).*

popular object of worship, the protector of women and children and a compassionate saviour.

## KWAWAR

For a group of Californian Indians from the area of Los Angeles county, known as the Gabrielino after the mission of San Gabriel, the main creator deity, who having made the world stabilized it with the help of four giants who support it; it is their movements which from time to time cause earthquakes.

# LABAN
In the traditional early history of the Hebrews, as conveyed by the Old Testament, he was the brother of REBECCA and the father of RACHEL, himself a man of the city of Nahore in Mesopotamia.

*Genesis*

# LACEDAEMON
A Greek hero, the legendary founder of Sparta, which he called after his wife, the daughter of a previous king of that country.

# LACHESIS
In Greek mythology, one of the three Fates. See CLOTHO.

# LAESTRYGONIANS
According to Greek mythology as conveyed by Homer, they were the fearful man-eating inhabitants of one of the islands on which ODYSSEUS came to land, similar to but less defined than the CYCLOPS.

HOMER: *Odyssey*

# LAIUS
Father of OEDIPUS, in a main story of Greek myth, and killed by him in an encounter at a cross-roads, in the course of the inevitable unwinding of a tragic prophecy. See JOCASTA, POLYBUS.

SOPHOCLES: *Oedipus the King*

# LAKSHMI
In the religious system of India, a goddess of provision, and the wife of VISHNU, but herself not highly developed in the Hindu mythology, being mainly the companion of her husband. She came forth during the churning of the ocean of milk by which the gods were to obtain the elixir of immortality. Lakshmi has the function of a goddess of prosperity, and is worshipped at the Divali festival of lights at new year.

# LANCELOT
In the Celtic British material, the main hero of King ARTHUR's court in its developed form; a late arrival in the tradition, he became a popular romantic figure in his own right. Lancelot's humanity and amorous weakness ensure him a prominent position among fallible heroes, but deprived him in the stories of the achievement of the Holy Grail, in which he was superseded by his virginal son GALAHAD. The central story of his career and indeed of Arthurian literature tells of his adulterous love for King Arthur's queen GUENEVER, through which he brought about the downfall of all three of them and of the golden world of Camelot. The name (although invented by the medieval French poet Chrétien de Troyes) may have connections with Celtic figures, the Irish LUGH, Welsh LLEU and continental LUGUS. See also ELAINE.     MALORY: *Morte d'Arthur*

# LAOCOÖN
A figure of Greek myth, in which he is a Trojan priest, with tragic irony doomed for being right. He warned the Trojans not to take into the city the wooden horse in

*Detail from an early 14th-century manuscript, depicting, on the right, Lancelot, the hero of King Arthur's court.*

LEFT: *Lebé is one of a number of ancestor figures venerated by the Dogon people of West Africa.*

which the Greek warriors were hiding. Laocoön and his sons were strangled by two serpents which came out of the sea, a portent which the Trojans took to indicate his error. A remarkable statue of Laocoön and his two sons struggling vainly with the serpents was found in Rome in 1506 and is now in the Vatican; it is generally thought to be a Greek work of the second century BC.

### LAPITHS

Occurring in Greek mythology as the people of King **PERITHOUS**, at whose wedding the **CENTAURS** became drunk and abducted the bride and other women. They are the subject of well-known friezes both on the Parthenon and on the temple of **ZEUS** at Olympia.

### LEAH

Wife of **JACOB**, sister of his second wife **RACHEL**, in the traditional history of the Hebrews as recorded in the Old Testament. She bore Jacob six sons, but he preferred Rachel although she was barren to begin with. The twelve sons of Jacob by her and his other wives formed the ancestral founders of the twelve tribes of Israel. *Genesis*

### LEAR

A figure of Celtic British myth. See **LLYR**, **LEIR**.

### LEBÉ

An ancestor figure, occurring in the beliefs of the Dogon people of West Africa. He underwent a symbolic death and rebirth in order to instil a spirit of order and understanding in mankind.

### LEDA

In Greek mythology, the wife of King **TYNDAREUS** of Sparta. She was seduced by **ZEUS** in the form of a swan, as a result of which their daughter **HELEN** is said by some to have been hatched from an egg. Leda's children by Tyndareus are the twins **CASTOR** and **POLYDEUCES**, and also **CLYTEMNESTRA**, wife of **AGAMEMNON**.

*The feats of the hero Lemminkäinen are told in the* Kalevala, *a collection of old Finnish myths and legends assembled in the first half of the 19th century. Plaster statuette by C.A. Sjostrand, 1872.*

## LEGBA

In the beliefs of the Benin and Togo peoples of West Africa, an agent of God, responsible for acts of discord, who deflects the blame for these from the godhead. It is Legba's mischievous deeds which caused God to withdraw from the world. In the pantheon of the Dahomey of Benin he is the messenger of the gods, knowing all their languages. See ESHU.

## LEI KUNG

In Chinese mythology, the god of thunder. He is portrayed as being extremely ugly, winged like a bird and with claws on his hands. He carries drums on which he produces the roll of thunder, and his function is that of the punisher of serious violent crime. The effects of lightning, however, are caused by the activities of another deity, TIEN MU.

## LEIR

A Celtic British figure, later King Lear, originally LLYR. The name is given by Geoffrey of Monmouth to an early king of Britain, to whom he attributed the story of the king's daughters famously developed by Shakespeare.

GEOFFREY OF MONMOUTH: *History of the Kings of Britain*

## LEMMINKÄINEN

In the mythology of Finland, a youthful hero. He appears in the collection of stories known as the *Kalevala*, in which he died and was resurrected by magic practised by his mother, who pieced together his dismembered body much as ISIS did that of OSIRIS. When an infant, Lemminkäinen had been ritually bathed by his mother to ensure his wisdom and skill with song. He appears as a vigorous and cheerful character, a great wooer of women.

## LESHY

In old Slavonic beliefs, the spirit of the forest, the name coming from the word *les* meaning 'forest'. He was thought of as being of human form, though of weird

137

appearance, with green eyes and long hair. It was said that he was able to change his height according to his surroundings. Although he is not normally considered to be hostile, nevertheless it is due to his tricks that someone straying into the deep forest invariably loses his way.

## LETO

A Greek goddess. In Homer, she was an early wife of ZEUS, but in other sources one of his extramarital lovers. She was the mother by him of APOLLO and ARTEMIS.

## LEVI

In the traditional history of the Hebrews, as it appears in the Old Testament, he was the son of JACOB and LEAH. He plays a minor part in the stories surrounding the sons of Jacob (see JOSEPH), but figures most prominently as the founder of a major, priestly, tribe of the Israelite people, the Levites. *Genesis*

## LEVIATHAN

A water-dragon, in the Hebrew tradition of the Old Testament. He was a monstrous representative of evil, the enemy of YAHWEH, and was finally destroyed by him. *Psalms, Job*

## LEZA

Also spelt Lesa. A name for God, the creator and giver of life, in the beliefs of the people of Central Africa. He is also regarded as the cause of thunder and lightning, and the provider of rain, and the people pray to him when the all-important rains are late.

## LI

In Chinese mythology, a being appointed to govern earth, where his duty was to organize and order the affairs of men. Compare CHONG, and see CHONGLI. According to some sources he is seen as a fire spirit.

## LIF

According to Scandinavian mythology, at the end of the world the World Tree alone

survives, and within it shelter two human beings, Lif and LIFTHRASIR, who emerge to start the repopulation of the new world when order returns.

SNORRI STURLUSON: *Prose Edda*

## LIFTHRASIR

A figure of Scandinavian myth. See LIF.

*Li, the Chinese mythological figure governing fire and the affairs of men.*

## LIR

The Celtic Irish equivalent of the patronym LLYR in Welsh stories, occurring as the father of the Irish sea-god MANANNAN, among others.

## LISA

A male figure, in the mythological system of the Benin and Togo people of West Africa. Connected with the sun, he forms a twin with his sister and partner MAWU. The tribes believe that he was responsible for introducing mankind to the use of metal.

## LLEFELYS

A minor figure in an important Celtic British story, in which he occurs as the brother of LLUDD, an early king of Britain.

*Mabinogion*

## LLEU LLAW GYFFES

The hero of the Celtic British tale known as *Math son of Mathonwy*, in which he was fostered by his uncle GWYDION, and eventually fatally deceived by his wife BLODEUEDD. Lleu plays a rather passive part in a rich and complex story.

*Mabinogion*

## LLUDD

Son of BELI, king of Britain and hero of a Celtic British tale in which with his brother LLEFELYS he rids Britain of three pests with which it is beleaguered. The third conflict, the destruction of two dragons, is further developed in British tradition in connection with the hero EMRYS. In the story Lludd (later known as LUD) is credited with the foundation of the city of London, said to have been called after him Lundein (perhaps from Lludd-din, Lud's city).

## LLYR

An ancestor figure in Celtic British story, in which he is said to be the father of BRAN, BRANWEN and MANAWYDAN. The name became developed into LEIR and eventually into the more familiar King LEAR.

*Mabinogion*

## LOKI

An important character in Scandinavian mythology. The gods of Asgard are benevolent and order-seeking, combating the disruptive influence of the giants, but tension is generated in their world, and their stories, by the presence among them of the embodiment of deceit and trickery, in the person of Loki. Although he is one of them, and bound by their rules, he lives in a state of permanent ambivalence among them, constantly causing trouble, and as constantly having to make amends. He steals, betrays, conspires, and also when obliged to retrieves and restores. Perhaps the least forgivable of his deeds is the killing of the good god BALDER, loved by all. Loki's offspring between them form the realm of evil in these stories: the wolf FENRIR, the World Serpent, and the grim goddess HEL. Led by him they bring about the destruction known as Ragnarök, the end of the world of the gods. Loki in fact is more than the prankster of folktale; he is the devil at work in the world.

SNORRI STURLUSON: *Prose Edda*

## LOT

In the Hebrew material gathered in the Old Testament, he appears as the nephew of ABRAHAM. He and his wife and family settled in the southern Jordan valley, the area of the Dead Sea, the subsequent barren condition of which is explained by the myth, in which God destroyed the cities of Sodom and Gomorrah because of the wickedness of the people, allowing Lot and his family, residents of the former, to escape. In doing so he made the stipulation that they should not look back, and when Lot's wife does so she is turned into a pillar of salt. Compare ORPHEUS. The destruction of the 'cities of the plain', remains of which lie under the southern tip of the Dead Sea, was probably historically caused by an earthquake accompanied by eruptions taking place in about the year 2000 BC. A sequel to his story concerns Lot's drunkenness, a state which led him to have children by his two daughters.

*Genesis*

**LOXIAS**

An alternative name for APOLLO, in the mythology of the Greeks.

**LUD**

Originally a Celtic British character, derived from the British form LLUDD; King Lud, as he became, was perhaps originally a Celtic god of the same status as BELI and BRAN. In the tradition as expounded by Geoffrey of Monmouth he founded the city of London, one of the gates of which, Ludgate, was called after him.

**LUGH**

Sometimes spelt Lug. A major figure in Irish Celtic myth, in which he is the prominent young hero of the people of DANANN, who arrives at the court at Tara and at once dominates it. Truly heroic, proficient in all crafts and skills, he destroys giants and supernatural beings as well as defeating personal and national enemies. He is essentially the representative of the younger generation of heroes, the arrival of whom presents a challenge to the established order, which his forceful character eventually presses into the background. This figure is based on a popular continental Celtic god, known to the Romanized Gauls as Lugus, who gave his name to places as diverse as Lyon, Leiden and Carlisle. His feast-day on the first of August, Lughnasad, has ancient origins and is still celebrated.

**LUGULBANDA**

The hero of a set of Sumerian poems, in which he occurs as an early king of Uruk, and the patron ancestor of the Mesopotamian hero GILGAMESH (sometimes in fact spoken of as the latter's father). In one story he is credited with destroying the bird-demon ZU.

**LUGUS**

A Celtic god. See LUGH.

**LUONNOTAR**

The mother of the Finnish mythological character VÄINÄMÖINEN. In a main episode

*A late 17th-century famille verte dish on which are depicted the three Chinese gods of good fortune, Luxing, Fuxing and Shoulao.*

of her story she was responsible for creating the world, being herself pre-existent and alone. As she floated on the cosmic waters a duck laid an egg on her knee, which in due course hatched to produce the earth and all the celestial bodies.

**LUXING**

Or Lu-hsing, in the previous system of spelling. The Chinese god of salaries and officials, one of the three gods of good fortune, along with FUXING and SHOULAO. He was (like Fuxing) regarded as having been a man on earth before becoming deified, and the figure is based on a historical character of the third century BC.

**LYCOMEDES**

King of Skyros, in an episode of Greek myth in which he acts as host to THESEUS and is responsible for his death by treacherously throwing him over a cliff.

**MAAHES**

In Egyptian mythology, the son of **BAST** by **RA**. He is often shown as having a lion's head.

**MAB**

A figure of British and Irish Celtic tradition, in which she is known as the midwife of the fairies from her function of facilitating the birth of dreams, which were regarded as the progeny of the fairies. The name probably comes from the Celtic for son.

**MABON**

A character in Celtic British mythology, in which he is known as Mabon son of **MODRON**, meaning in effect the great son of the great mother. He is probably the same figure as the god **MAPONUS**.

**MACARDIT**

For the Dinka of Sudan in Africa, the divinity who causes suffering and ill luck.

**MACSEN**

A figure of Celtic British myth, he is in fact the transformation into myth of the usurping Roman emperor Magnus Maximus. In the story (which forms a sort of fanciful explanation of the Roman invasion) he falls in love with a woman in a dream, and settles in Britain after discovering her there. Eventually he has to withdraw to combat a rival emperor, a mythical parallel to the depletion of Roman troops in Britain caused by the historical Maximus' attempt to assert his rule in Europe. *Mabinogion*

**MADER-AKKA**

The female part of the primal couple believed by the Lapps to have created mankind. See **MADER-ATCHA**.

**MADER-ATCHA**

The male member of the primal couple, along with his spouse **MADER-AKKA** believed by the Lapps to have created mankind, he being responsible for the soul, she for the body. The child thus created was then placed in the womb of an earthly mother.

**MADRI**

A figure of the mythology of India. See **KUNTI**, **PANDU**.

**MADUMDA**

A sky-dwelling benevolent being believed in by the Pomo Indians of California. Though wise and powerful he allowed his younger brother, the coyote (an enterprising, ingenious trickster who occurs as a character in many North American Indian stories) to create the world and its population, while Madumda himself plays only a remote and rather abstract part in the system.

**MAFDET**

An Egyptian goddess personifying the cat, known as the 'Lady of the Castle of Life', revered in early Egyptian times as a protector against snakes.

**MAHAMAYA**

Frequently **MAYA**. The mother of the Buddha, in the tradition of the Buddhist religion of India based on his teaching. The story concerning her in the religion's background mythology tells that she dreamt that a small white elephant had entered her womb, and this was **SIDDHARTHA**, the future supreme Buddha. She gave birth to him from her side, and he at once revealed his extraordinary nature. She died shortly afterwards, and Siddhartha was reared by her sister and co-wife **PRAJAPATI**.

**MAHUCUTAH**

One of the four 'first men', in the traditional beliefs of the Maya Indians of Mexico. See **BALAM-QUITZE**.
*Popol Vuh*

141

## MAIA

In Greek mythology, a land goddess, seduced by **ZEUS**, and thus the mother of **HERMES**.                    HESIOD: *Theogony*

## MAINA

An ancestor figure occurring in a tradition of Kenya in Africa, as the son of the founder of the Luyia tribe, who introduced death into the world by refusing hospitality to a chameleon (a creature commonly given importance in African myth).

## MAKA

One of the aspects of the Egyptian crocodile god **SEBEK**, but regarded rather as a monstrous serpent and an enemy and obstructor of **RA**, in his constant journey in the boat of the sun.

## MAKEMAKE

A local deity of Easter Island in the Pacific, he became viewed as a great creator. He is connected with the bird cult which formed the central focus of Easter Island religious tradition, in which the annually chosen Bird Man was thought to represent him.

## MAKOSH

A Slavonic goddess who had connections with water, and through that agency of growth with fertility and provision also.

## MALAVA

The first woman, in the creation myth of the Vugusu people of Kenya in Africa. See **UMNGOMA**.

## MALSUM

A figure occurring in the tradition of the North American Algonquin Indians. See **GLUSKAP**, his benevolent opponent.

*A wooden figure used in the Easter Island bird cult in honour of the god Makemake.*

## MAMA OCLLO

Sister and wife of **MANCO CAPAC**, and the legendary first queen of the Incas of Peru.

## MAMANDABARI

The names of two brothers or for a father and son, in the stories of the Walbiri aboriginal people of Australia's Northern Territory. They travelled across the Walbiri homeland from the north and set the pattern for cult rituals.

## MANANNAN

Known as Manannan mac (son of) **LIR**; a Celtic Irish sea-god, he rides his wonderful horse across the waves as if they were dry land and lives in a magnificent palace in the sea, very much in the style of the Greek **POSEIDON**. He feasts his guests in great luxury there, and it was he who gave to **CORMAC** the magic golden cup. He also seems to have been a god of fertility. The Isle of Man is called after him.

## MANAWYDAN

Son of **LLYR**, the same figure in Celtic British tradition as **MANANNAN** in Irish myth, but lacking the sea dwelling and with a separate story attached to him, for which see **PRYDERI**.                    *Mabinogion*

## MANCO CAPAC

Also known as Ayar Manco. One of the legendary founding members of the Incas of Peru (see also **AYER CACHI**), he became their first ruler. He and his wife journeyed until they found fertile country, where they settled and founded the city of Cuzco. There he instituted the sun worship which became the Inca religion. From his association with the sun-god was derived the privileged position of the Incas, their dominance over other races.

## MANGI

A minor figure of Scandinavian mythology, in which he occurs as the son of **THOR**, who along with his brother **MODI** inherits Thor's great hammer, Mjollnir.

SNORRI STURLUSON: *Prose Edda*

*Manco Capac, the first ruler of the Incas and the founder of the city of Cuzco. Illustration by Guamon Poma de Ayala, c. 1613.*

## MANINGA

An evil spirit in the mythology of the Mandan tribe of North American Indians, seen as the bringer of a great flood.

## MANITOU

The Great Manitou was the supreme deity, known as Gitchi Manitou, in the mythology of the Algonquin Indians of North America. Many deities described by this name were present in the objects and phenomena of nature. Gitchi Manitou is viewed as the pre-existent father of all things.

## MANU

A figure of the mythology of India, a mortal who survived the great destruction by flood of the first created world, by being forewarned to build a boat (compare **DEUCALION**, **NOAH**), and continued, as a great sage, into the new world. As the sole ancestor of mankind he gave the species its name, and sets an example by his austerity and sacrifices, by which he gained an almost divine status and great bounty.

## MAPONUS

A Celtic god worshipped both in Britain and Gaul, the Latinization of **MABON**, a word connected with 'son', and having much the same associations with music and youth as the Greek **APOLLO**.

## MARA

In the background mythology of the Buddhist religion of India, a tempter, devil-figure, the evil spiritual force opposing the desire of the Buddha to reach enlightenment, and thereafter obstructing his mission. The name literally means 'death'.

## MARCH

A figure of Celtic British mythology. See **MARK**.

## MARDUK

The local god of Babylon, a late influence in Mesopotamian religion but one who became the leader of all the gods. He was said to be the son of **EA**, and a fertility deity mainly connected with agriculture. However as he rose to prominence, due to the conquests made by Babylon, he absorbed the characteristics of all the other deities. In this capacity he became a creator god, and one story tells how he attacked **TIAMAT**, who stood as the representative of the old order of gods, Marduk acting as the leader of the younger deities (compare **CRONUS**). By splitting Tiamat in two he formed the earth and the sky, and went on to arrange the remainder of the ordered world.

## MARK

Originally **MARCH**, a character of Celtic British myth. King of Cornwall, uncle of **TRISTAN**, he figures mainly in the latter's story as his nephew's vengeful rival.

MALORY: *Morte d'Arthur*

## MARS

The Roman god of war (compare Greek **ARES**) and hence one of the leading gods of the Romans, who were essentially a military people; he was said to be the father of **ROMULUS**, founder of Rome. His deeper origins however were mainly agricultural, and he entered early mythology as a rural deity.

## MARSYAS

A character of Greek mythology. A satyr; foolish enough to challenge **APOLLO** in a musical competition, he lost and was punished by being flayed alive.

OVID: *Metamorphoses*

## MARUTS

In the mythology of India, they are the numerous companions of the chief god **INDRA**, themselves storm-gods and warrior figures forming a glittering warband.

*Rig Veda*

## MARWÉ

In stories of the Chaga people of Kenya she occurs as a girl who pays a visit to the otherworld, and returns with riches.

## MASYA

In the background mythology of the Zoroastrian religion of Iran he was, with his consort **MASYANE**, the parent of mankind. He was said to have been born from a rhubarb plant which itself grew from the seed of **GAYOMARD**, the first primeval man. Their initial progress was marred by setbacks, and like **ADAM** and **EVE** they disobeyed God and caused him anger.

## MASYANE

A figure of the mythology of Iran. See **MASYA**.

## MATH

A Celtic British character, the king of Gwynedd, a central but background figure in the story (*Math son of Mathonwy*) which tells of the exploits of **GWYDION**, **LLEU LLAW GYFFES** and **BLODEUEDD**.

*Mabinogion*

## MATHOLWCH

A figure of Celtic British tradition, in which he occurs as the king of Ireland, featuring in the mythology solely as the husband of the heroine BRANWEN; under pressure from his people to avenge an insult he treated her humiliatingly and thus caused a war between Britain and Ireland.

*Mabinogion*

## MATI-SYRA-ZEMLYA

The earth as mother, in Russian mythology, a being dominant over evil powers and the controller of the forces of nature. She was also viewed as being a figure of justice and prophecy.

## MATRONA

A Celtic goddess. See MODRON.

## MATSYA

A figure of the mythology of India: the incarnation of the god VISHNU as a fish.

## MAUI

The great hero and magician in the mythology of the Maori, a figure intermediate between gods and men, responsible for bringing out of the water the Polynesian islands and for the introduction of fire to the world, a true culture hero. He was born by miscarriage and reared by a spiritual ancestor, being in due course returned to join his family of five brothers. He was a great trickster, and his deeds (such as a scheme to lengthen the day and an attempt to overcome death) sometimes express the heroic will of mankind to overcome its innate disadvantages. Characteristically of mythic trick-players, his pranks so irritate the gods that he has constantly to keep compensating (compare Scandinavian LOKI), and he ends up defeated, crushed in the form of a caterpillar by the goddess of the underworld during an attempt to overcome her powers and bring immortality to mankind by entering her womb, in a story about him which is peculiar to New Zealand. In general, stories about this popular hero occur not

*A carved wood wall panel from a Maori meeting house at Te Kuiti, New Zealand, said to represent the hero-god Mani snaring the sun.*

145

just in New Zealand Maori culture but throughout the Pacific islands.

**MAWU**
A figure occurring in the creation myths of the Benin and Togo people of West Africa; she was viewed as connected with the moon, and regarded as the female side of a pair of twins. See LISA.

**MAYA**
A figure of Indian Buddhism. See MAHAMAYA.

**MAYET**
Or Maat. In Egyptian mythology, the female personification of justice, and hence of general equilibrium and stability in social life. She was much revered by the pharaohs, whose rule upheld her law. As the daughter of RA and wife of THOTH she was also held in high honour by the gods, and thought to have emerged early from the primal waters in her father's ship of the sun, in which she is often depicted as riding. Her distinctive emblem is a tall ostrich feather which she wears on her head, and often the feather on its own represents her. In this form she is placed in the scales which judge the trueness of the heart of the dead, which is weighed against her in the symbolism of transition to the afterlife.

**MAZDA**
A name for the great god of the Zoroastrian religion of Iran. See AHURA MAZDA.

**MBOMBO**
Sometimes spelt Bumba. In the tradition of the Bakuba people of Zaire in Africa, the pre-existing creator god, known as the 'white god', who gave rise to all animals, men and objects by vomiting them up, following an appalling stomach pain.

**MEDB**
Queen of Connacht, in Celtic Irish tradition, seen as a strong and warmongering figure who led a raid against the people of Ulster to gain from

them a mystical bull, an episode which triggers the famous tale, 'the Cattle-Raid of Cooley'.

**MEDEA**
A figure of Greek myth, the daughter of the king of Colchis, known for her skill in magic. In a main episode of her story she helped the hero JASON obtain the golden fleece. Also a background figure in the story of THESEUS.
EURIPIDES: *Medea*
OVID: *Metamorphoses*

**MEDUSA**
A character in Greek mythology, the chief member of the three GORGONS. Like them she is depicted as having serpents for hair, and she herself had the particular quality of turning to stone those who looked in her face. PERSEUS cut off her head, using his shield as a mirror to avoid looking at her directly.

**MEGARA**
In Greek mythology she was the daughter of the king of Thebes, and first wife to HERACLES. Having killed her children in a fit of madness, he left her when he set out on his adventures.

**MELWAS**
King of the Summer Country, in the Celtic traditions of Britain, an area identified with Somerset but possibly an indication of his origin as king of summer itself. An early story tells how he abducted King ARTHUR's wife GUENEVER and secured her in Glastonbury which Arthur then besieged. He appears in the same episode in Malory's work as Sir Meliagaunt.
MALORY: *Morte d'Arthur*

**MEME**
The first woman, in the creation myth of the Lugbara tribe of Central Africa. See GBOROGBORO.

**MENELAUS**
King of Sparta, husband of HELEN, in the central saga of Greek myth. Principally cast in the unfortunate role of the deceived

husband, he was away on business when **PARIS** came and eloped with his wife to Troy. As brother to **AGAMEMNON**, he was in a position to gather a considerable force to pursue them, and hence instigated the long and fateful Trojan War.

## MEN SHEN

In Chinese custom and belief they are a pair of door gods, commonly represented one on each of the leaves of the outside doors of Chinese houses. The figures are based on mythical beings of an early tradition, but later supposed to represent two generals who achieved a heroic defence of the emperor's palace against an assault by demonic forces. Their function is that of guarding the house against the entry of evil demons.

## MENTOR

In the Greek myth as originally conveyed by Homer he occurs as the friend and adviser of **ODYSSEUS**, from which function his name now signifies one who gives useful advice.                    HOMER: *Odyssey*

## MERCURY

A late introduction to Roman mythology, much influenced by the character of the Greek god **HERMES**. He is principally the god of commerce, his name being connected with the Latin word for merchandise.

## MERLIN

Developed into one of the major characters of British myth, Merlin appears in early Celtic tales under the name of **MYRDDIN** as the figure of the mad prophet, with which became amalgamated that of the wild man, the exile from social life living in community with nature. The name was Latinized into the form Merlinus, from which its present form is derived, by Geoffrey of Monmouth, for whom he formed a spokesman for a set of prophecies concerning Britain. It was Malory who took this powerful figure and attached him to the court of King **ARTHUR**. In that setting he operates as his

predecessor the wizard **GWYDION** did, sometimes interfering by magic in the activities of the court, otherwise occasionally emerging from the background with the benefit of advice based on his wisdom and foreknowledge. Even there however Merlin appears surprisingly human, falling hopelessly in love with a nymph, Viviane, who deceitfully makes use of his infatuation to extract from him his special powers, which she then uses against him. He is thus also a tragically doomed figure, unable to forestall an end which he can nevertheless foresee.

GEOFFREY OF MONMOUTH: *History of the Kings of Britain;* MALORY: *Morte d'Arthur*

*A Romano-British carved stone relief of Mercury, the Roman god of commerce.*

### MERTSEGER

A serpent goddess in the religion of the ancient Egyptians, one of the companions of the dead. She was also regarded as a goddess of the desert, a guardian against the desert snakes. She was known as the 'Mistress of the West', the western desert being the region of the sunset and also regarded as the land of the dead. She also had a judging role, punishing wrongdoers but protecting the good. She is sometimes represented as a serpent, which occasionally has the body of a woman.

### MESHACH

Formerly called Mishael. In a Hebrew story which forms part of the traditional history preserved in the Old Testament, he was one of the three companions (see ABEDNEGO, SHADRACH) who with God's help survived the attempt to convert them to heathenism by the ordeal of the 'fiery furnace'. *Daniel*

### MESHKENT

A female Egyptian deity, a goddess specifically of childbirth, often being thought of as four separate goddesses concerned with the elements of the birth-chamber. She also took part in the funeral rituals of transition to the afterlife.

### METHUSELAH

A patriach in the descent from ADAM to NOAH, in the traditional early history of the Hebrews as conveyed by the Old Testament. He was said to have lived nine hundred and sixty-nine years. He is thus the oldest man among many of great longevity mentioned in the Bible. *Genesis*

### METIS

In the main Greek pantheon, she was the first wife of ZEUS, and the prospective mother of ATHENA, whose birth however Zeus prevented, eventually producing her from his own head. HESIOD: *Theogony*

### MHER

Or Meherr. The Armenian version of the Iranian god MITHRA, whose worship survived in Armenia as a nationalistic influence until modern times.

### MICHAEL

In Hebrew tradition, as recorded in the Old Testament, an Archangel, who is with GABRIEL one of the only two named angels in the Old Testament; as one of the chief ministers of God he has a guardian function. *Daniel*

### MICTLANTECUHTLI

God of the underworld, for the Toltec Indians of Mexico, ruler of the land of the dead. He provided QUETZALCOATL with the magic bones from which mankind was originally made.

### MIDAS

In Greek mythology, a legendary king of Phrygia. The god DIONYSUS rewarded a favour by granting him a wish. Midas then represents human greed and folly by asking that everything he touched should turn to gold, and when even his food was changed he had to beg the god to remove this favour. Later this unfortunate king chose rashly in a judgement between PAN and APOLLO, and the latter in revenge gave him ass's ears. Finding the secret to be unbearable, he told the earth of it, but a reed grew on the spot and whispers this confidence, that King Midas has ass's ears, to the wind. OVID: *Metamorphoses*

### MIMIR

In Scandinavian mythology, a wise demon, guardian of the spring of wisdom which lies in the roots of the World Tree. When ODIN begged to be allowed to drink he was obliged to leave one of his eyes as a ransom.

### MIN

An Egyptian sky-god, he was particularly connected with the thunderbolt, but also had a fertility function as a god of rain and natural growth. His festival fell at harvest time. As with many deities there is an element of absorption of the roles of other gods, HORUS, RA and AMON-RA, with whom

*Representations of the Egyptian god Min stress his role as a fertility deity. Bronze of the late New Kingdom period, 1567-1085 BC.*

*The Laud screenfold, probably painted in the 14th century, was a major ritual document for priests of the Toltec religion. A group of priests are shown surrounding one of their number dressed as Mictlantecuhtli. He is curing the sun of eclipse by sucking the darkness from it.*

he became loosely identified. As a fertility god he became associated with sexual energy, and his festival took on an indulgent character. In what appears to be a separate nature he was a god of travel, patron of both pastoral and hunting expeditions, and guarded the great caravan route through the eastern desert. His sacred animal was a bull.

### MINERVA
A Roman goddess, identified with the Greek goddess ATHENA, a goddess of wisdom, craft and trade, and later of war. Hence she was one of the leading Roman deities, and was worshipped at a central site on the Capitol. Like Athena she was portrayed in her military aspect, with helmet and armour.

### MINOS
A major figure of Greek myth, the powerful and intimidating king of Crete; he lived in the labyrinth-palace of Knossos, kept a herd of fine cattle, and evidently had an ambivalent relationship with POSEIDON, god of the sea. The latter sent a bull for Minos to sacrifice which instead he kept, and in anger the god made the king's wife PASIPHAË fall in love with the bull. The

Minotaur, half-man, half-bull, which resulted, was kept like a guilty secret in the labyrinth at Knossos designed for the purpose by Minos' craftsman DAEDALUS. Minos occurs in Greek myth as the enemy of Athens, and hence as a power outside Greece itself, exacting from the Athenians the terrible tribute which THESEUS put an end to. See also ARIADNE, PHAEDRA.

## MINOTAUR
A figure of Greek mythology. See ASTERION, MINOS.

## MIRIAM
In the Hebrew material which forms the books of the Old Testament, she occurs as the elder sister of MOSES. By implication she was responsible for watching over him when he was placed in the river, and thus for arranging that their mother became his nurse when Pharaoh's daughter adopted him. She sided with her other brother AARON in a disagreement with Moses, and although punished by God with leprosy she was forgiven by Moses and cured.

*Exodus, Numbers*

## MITHRA
An Iranian deity. Compare Hindu MITRA. His name means Contract or Covenant. An early god, at one time the supreme deity but subdued in Zoroastrian religion by the rise in importance of AHURA MAZDA. In developed form, as the Roman god MITHRAS, he took on elaborate symbolic surroundings, which however were not part of his original worship. The original Mithra, however, was never totally obscured by this separate cult nor forgotten in Zoroastrianism.

## MITHRAS
A god of both Iranian and Roman mythology. A developed form of the ancient Iranian god MITHRA, much diffused and popularized by the Roman legions, both the centre and the frontiers of the Empire being profuse with his temples, the Mithraea, in which rituals of initiation took place. These Roman Mysteries of Mithras

*Miriam, who in the Old Testament is described as the sister of Moses, plays, sings and dances with her maidens. Miniature from the Golden Haggadah, c. 1320.*

almost formed a religion in themselves, and appear to have been based on the episodes of the life of the god, who is said to have been born from a rock, ready armed and in the form of a youth. His story concerns the antagonism of and final encounter with a ferocious bull: his destiny is to slay it, by cutting its throat, an event always depicted as taking place in a cave.

## MITRA
A figure occurring in the mythology of India as a god of light, and also of close friendship, and associated with the god VARUNA. See Zoroastrian MITHRAS.

*Rig Veda*

## MNEMOSYNE
A figure of Greek myth, the name signifying 'Memory'. She was one of the wives of ZEUS and the mother of the Muses.

HESIOD: *Theogony*

## MNEVIS
An ancient Egyptian bull-god, see APIS, BUCHIS. As in other cases he was worshipped literally in the form of a special bull. The bull was a symbol of fertility, and in the case of Mnevis the bull's life was thought to repeat that of OSIRIS.

## MODRON

A figure of Celtic British myth, perhaps based on the Gaulish mother-goddess MATRONA, who gave her name to the river Marne. The name means 'great mother'. See MABON.

## MOLOCH

Or Molech. A foreign god in the tradition of the Hebrew, whose worship was associated with human sacrifice, specifically the sacrifice of children. Worshipped by the Ammonites, his cult was explicitly forbidden in the law of MOSES, but formed a part of SOLOMON's lapse into heresy.

## MOMOTARO

In Japanese stories, he was a hero born supernaturally from a peach, who quickly became a great conqueror of demons.

## MONJU-BOSATSU

A god of learning and understanding, in the mythological traditions of Japan. The title 'Bosatsu' a version of the Indian Buddhist 'Bodhisattva', the 'enlightenment-being' of Buddhism.

## MONT

Also Mentu, Month. An ancient Egyptian god originally centred on Hermonthis, near Thebes, and with mainly local connotations. Like so many other Egyptian deities he was absorbed into the orbit of the great god RA, and thus acquired solar functions. He was however individually connected with the bull sacred to him, and represented as having a bull's head. The cult has overlaps with that of BUCHIS, centred on the same town. Mont also possessed many of the attributes typical of a war-god.

## MONTEZUMA

A name adopted by the Navajo Indians of North America from Aztec sources (being that of the last emperor of Mexico, defeated by the Spanish in the sixteenth century) and used by them to stand for the founder and benefactor, but also the scourge, of the human race. After much turbulent activity he retreated from the world to live underground.

## MOOMBI

Or Mumbi. A figure in the beliefs of the Kikuyu people of Kenya in Africa. The bride of GIGUYU, and therefore an ancestral mother-figure. She bore him nine daughters, and this precedence gave rise to the system of matriliny adopted by the Kikuyu.

## MORDRED

In early forms, Medrawd, or Medraut. A figure of Celtic British tradition. In developed form he became viewed as being King ARTHUR's illegitimate son by his sister, hence also his nephew. Originally cited as an enemy who brought about his death at the battle of Camlan, Mordred is one of the earliest themes to enter the Arthurian amalgam. His story bears strong mythic elements, since it was foretold by MERLIN that he would bring about the downfall of Arthur and his knights, for which reason he was cast out to sea. Fate as usual predominated, and he was rescued and reared by a stranger. Presented by

*Images of Mithras slaying the bull have been found at many of the frontier posts of the Roman Empire. The Mithras of the Roman cults was a much developed form of the ancient Iranian god Mithra.*

151

Geoffrey of Monmouth as grasping and treacherous, he emerges in Malory as a figure of complete evil, based on bitterness and spite, in high contrast to the humanity and goodwill of the court around him.

GEOFFREY OF MONMOUTH: *History of the Kings of Britain;* MALORY: *Morte d'Arthur*

### MORGAN LE FAY
In Celtic British tradition, an enchantress, queen of the mystic land of Avalon, an afterworld where fallen heroes are healed and to which she takes King ARTHUR after his last battle. She appears in Malory's tales as Arthur's sister but as consistently wicked and conspiring. Originally the character may have been the Irish war-goddess, the MORRIGAN.      MALORY: *Morte d'Arthur*

### MORPHEUS
A Greek deity, the god of sleep and giver of dreams.

### MORRIGAN
The Morrigan, an ancient Celtic Irish battle-goddess, a weird and terrible figure who appears at or before battles and occasionally takes part by aiding or intimidating heroes, such as CUCHULAINN.

### MOSES
One of the great prophets of the Hebrews, and a major figure in their traditional early history as recorded in the Old Testament. Saviour, intermediary, and law-giver, and also ultimately doomed, he fulfils many of the essential characteristics and functions of the mythic hero. The agent of God in delivering the tribes of ISRAEL from their bondage in Egypt and further presenting them with their special relationship, the 'Covenant', with God, and its corollary, the Law. In the Judaic religion he is regarded as having written the *Torah*, the first five books of the Bible, as the scribe of God. He was the survivor of an order to kill all male children, during the period of the exile of the Israelites in Egypt, saved by being floated on the river and found by Pharaoh's daughter, thence adopted as a member of the royal palace. Later he is obliged to

spend a period in exile, where he receives instructions from God. It is there that he encounters the mystery of the burning bush, out of which the voice of God gives his name as 'I am', or 'I am that I am', which was adopted by the Hebrews in the form of the letters YHWH as the symbolic name of God (See YAHWEH). After a series of plagues has distressed the Egyptians Pharaoh is moved to allow Moses and his brother AARON to lead his people out of the country, and although he changes his mind and pursues them the intervention of God allows them to cross the Red Sea, which however immerses their pursuers. Moses communes with God and in an encounter with him on Mount Sinai he is given the basis of the sacred law in the form of ten ordinances written on tablets of stone. Supported by further verbal instruction, this body of law forms the foundation of the special relationship between God and the tribes of Israel. Moses himself, however, is not destined to reach the end of the journey, the good land which God had promised the Hebrews. As a dying man he viewed it but was laid to rest in the land of Moab.

*Exodus, Leviticus, Numbers, Deuteronomy*

### MOT
God of death in the mythology of Syria, the subject of a story in which the great god BAAL attempts to overcome him.

RIGHT: *A late bronze statue of the Egyptian god Mut, the consort of Amon-Ra.*

BELOW: *A miniature from the Rylands Haggadah, a Catalonian work of the mid-14th century, showing Moses in front of the burning bush.*

**MUDUNGKALA**

One of the institutors of the population, in the tradition of some of the aboriginal peoples of Australia. She was an old blind woman who came out of the ground, and the three babies she had with her became the first human beings.

**MUGWE**

A great religious leader in the tradition of the Meru tribe of Kenya in Africa, who played a similar role to that of **MOSES** by leading them out of a land where they were in bondage and into their present homeland, being strengthened and instructed in this purpose by God.

**MUKASA**

The great god of the people of Buganda in Africa, believed by them to be the provider also of human twins. The name applies as well to a divinity connected with seas and lakes, and to a spirit of divination, viewed as benevolent and consulted in trouble.

**MUKURU**

The first man, in the creation myth of the Herero tribe of South West Africa. See KAMAUGARUNGA.

**MULUNGU**

Or Muluku. A figure in the beliefs of the people of East Africa, also occurring in central and southern Africa. A name for god, as creator of the first man and woman. He once lived on earth among men, but when they began to displease him he left to live in heaven.

**MUNIN**

In Scandinavian mythology, the name of one of **ODIN**'s ravens. See HUGIN.

**MUPE**

The first man, in the creation myth of the Bambuti people of Central Africa. See UTI.

**MURA-MURA**

In the beliefs of Australian aborigines, they are beings with the ability to change their shape.

**MURILÉ**

According to the traditions of the Chaga of Kenya in Africa, he was a boy who made a journey to the land of the moon, where he became rich by introducing the knowledge of fire.

**MUSA**

A hunter and travelling hero, and the instructor of men in crafts and skills, in the beliefs of the Songhay people in West Africa.

**MUT**

A mother-figure in the religion of the ancient Egyptians, originally portrayed as a vulture but later as a woman with a vulture in her headdress. As a local goddess of the area of Thebes, she became associated with the god **AMON** and with him became a solar deity. At the great temple of Karnak she was worshipped as his wife, their son **KHONS** making up a trinity.

**MWAMBU**

The first man, according to the Luyia of Kenya in Africa, who along with his partner **SELA** is given the world as a home and the animals as food, with the exception of a number of taboos. They live in a tree-house for fear of monsters, possibly a reflection of early customs of the area.

**MWINAMBUZHI**

A figure of Central African mythology. See MULONGA.

**MYESYATS**

The moon, in Serbian and in other Slavonic mythologies, sometimes seen as the female consort of **DAZHBOG**, the sun, and with him the parent of the stars. In other variants, however, Myesyats is viewed as being a male deity, and in those cases the sun is sometimes seen as his female companion.

**MYRDDIN**

An early British poet said to have gone mad and run wild in the woods; he enters Celtic British myth as a prototype of **MERLIN**.

## NABU
A Mesopotamian deity, the son of Marduk, and himself a god of speech and of writing.

## NAGAS
In the mythology of India, the Nagas were serpents, particularly cobras, rulers of an underworld where they guarded great treasure.

## NAGENATZANI
In the beliefs of the North American Navajo Indians, he was the more active of two twin brothers (the other being THOBADESTCHIN) born of the divine and mysterious ESTANATLEHI after her encounter with the sun in the form of a man. They set about destroying the monstrous animals and man-eating giants which previously plagued the world, thus making it fit for mankind to inhabit. In the course of this campaign they underwent many adventures and journeys, not unlike those of the Greek heroes HERACLES and ODYSSEUS.

## NAKKI
A water spirit in the mythology of the Finns, believed to live in an underwater palace reached through bottomless lakes, and to visit the world of dry land at twilight.

## NAMBI
The first woman, in the cosmogony of the people of Buganda in Africa, the daughter of the king of heaven. She wishes to marry KINTU, the first man, but her family disapprove until he proves his ability in a series of tests.

## NAMTAR
A figure occurring in the mythology of Mesopotamia as the servant to ERESHKIGAL,

himself seen as an underworld spirit of ill-fortune. *Epic of Gilgamesh*

## NANA-BULUKU
For the people of Benin, in West Africa, the spirit of first creation, a remote female being who is not worshipped in her own right but whose act of creating the first pair of male and female twins brought about the human race. See LISA, MAWU.

## NANABUSH
The Great Hare, a figure occurring in the mythology of the Algonquin Indians of North America. He is also known as Gluskap Michaba, and by various other names. He is mainly viewed as a spirit of natural energy and enterprise, a creator and inventor, but is also occasionally portrayed as something of a buffoon. He occurs in a tale featuring a great destructive flood, from which he survives to recreate the earth.

*The bird-god Garuda of Hindu mythology is the enemy of the Nagas, the serpent rulers of the underworld. This Nepalese bronze shows the Garuda standing on a dying Naga.*

**NANNA**

The Sumerian form of the Semitic SIN, the god of the moon.

**NANNA**

A goddess of Scandinavian mythology, in which she occurs as the wife of **BALDER**. Her story tells how she died of grief when he was killed, and was cremated with him on a funeral pyre on his ship.

SNORRI STURLUSON: *Prose Edda*

**NANOOK**

Or Nanuq. In the beliefs of the Eskimo people of North America, a bear thought to have once lived on earth, and to have been chased into the sky by a remarkable pack of dogs. He is now identified, along with them, with the constellation of Pleiades.

**NARASIMHA**

In the religious system of India, an incarnation of the god **VISHNU** in which he proved his omnipresence in the world by emerging from the pillar of a doubting enemy in the form of a creature half man, half lion. The name means literally 'man-lion'. In this form he was able to kill the demon king, who had been promised that he could not be killed by god, man or animal. The demon's virtuous son worshipped Vishnu, and when the father asked if Vishnu were present in a pillar the god emerged from it as Narasimha and tore the demon to pieces.

**NARCISSUS**

In Greek mythology, a beautiful youth who failed to respond to feelings of love (see ECHO), and was caused to fall in love with his own image in a pool, eventually pining away, whereupon he became the flower of that name. OVID: *Metamorphoses*

**NAUSICAA**

In a story of Greek myth, as conveyed by Homer, she appears as a princess of the Phaeacians, encountered by **ODYSSEUS** towards the end of his journey.

HOMER: *Odyssey*

**NEBUCHADNEZZAR**

Or Nebuchadrezzar. A figure in the Hebrew material collected in the Old Testament, in which he occurs as the king of Babylon. The character is based on a historical figure of the sixth century BC. He appears in mythology as the king who captured the Hebrew prophet **DANIEL** and unsuccessfully attempted to convert him and his companions to the Babylonian religion. Daniel's resistance so impressed him that he became a convert to Judaism.

*Narasimha, the man-lion incarnation of the Hindu god Vishnu, disembowelling a demon. Stone carving of the 6th century.*

*William Blake's vision (1795) of the exiled Babylonian King Nebuchadnezzar.*

However he was punished for his former persecutions by becoming like a beast, exiled from human society and obliged to eat grass.
*Daniel*

### NEDU
Also spelt Neti. A character in Mesopotamian myth in which he is the gate-keeper of the underworld, watching over the entrance to the realm of the dead.
*Epic of Gilgamesh*

### NEFERTUM
An Egyptian god, the son of PTAH and SEKHMET, with whom he formed a trinity worshipped at Memphis.

### NEHEH
In Egyptian mythology, an alternative name for HEH.

### NEITH
Or Neit. An early Egyptian mother-goddess, she was said at different times to be the mother of various deities, but herself lay somewhat outside the standard pantheon. There are indications also that she had connections with hunting and with war, and as with so many of the minor Egyptian divinities her function and identity overlapped with others. She also took part in the rituals surrounding the transition of the souls of the dead. Her worship enjoyed a revival at her cult-centre at Sais, in the Nile Delta, at a late period. She is local to the lower Nile, and shown as wearing the crown of Lower Egypt.

### NEKHEBET
Or Nekhbet. A vulture-goddess in the religious system of the ancient Egyptians, specifically connected with Upper Egypt. She became associated with the main cults of RA and OSIRIS, and her diverse functions included fertility, motherhood, and the protection of the kingship.

### NEMTEREQUETEBA
A character in the mythology of the Indians of Colombia, one of a number of figures said by South American Indians to have come from elsewhere a long time ago spreading a doctrine of righteous living. Compare VIRACOCHA, THUNUPA.

### NEPHTHYS
In the Egyptian mythological system the daughter of NUT, wife of SET, the treacherous brother of OSIRIS, remaining loyal to the latter in the epic struggle between the two brothers. By Osiris she bore ANUBIS, who was hidden from Set and reared by ISIS, her sister. She accompanied and helped Isis in her search for the body of Osiris, and in the elaborate embalming rituals. These two sisters, in the form of kites, hover at each end of the coffin of the dead, and are often thus depicted.

### NEPTUNE
The Roman version of the god of the sea, in Greek myth POSEIDON, but a much less powerful and impressive figure than his Greek counterpart. He is viewed as an elderly man, sometimes bearded and crowned, and he bears a trident as his identifying emblem.

### NEREUS
A Greek sea-god, thought of as a person of venerable wisdom and prophecy, and the father of the sea-nymph THETIS.

**NERGAL**
In ancient Mesopotamian mythology, a god of the underworld, viewed as being responsible for the spirits of the dead, the male counterpart (sometimes said to be the husband) of ERESHKIGAL.
*Epic of Gilgamesh*

**NERTHUS**
A Scandinavian goddess, mentioned by Tacitus as having been worshipped in Denmark during Roman times.

**NESARU**
The dominant sky-dwelling spirit in the cosmogony of the Arikara tribe of North American Indians. He prepared the world for mankind, who originally lived underground, and he gave them the knowledge of growing corn.

**NESSUS**
In Greek mythology, one of the CENTAURS (mythic beings half man, half horse), whose blood was poisoned when he was shot by HERACLES with an arrow which had been dipped in the venomous blood of the Hydra. Heracles' wife later, in order to secure her husband's faithfulness, anointed a shirt with a fatal mixture of Nessus' blood and semen, which she believed to be a love-potion, and thus brought about Heracles' death.
OVID; *Metamorphoses*

**NESTOR**
In one of the episodes of Greek mythology he occurs as the wise old king of Pylos, one of the very few characters in the works of Homer presented with unqualified approval.
HOMER: *Odyssey, Iliad*

**NIBELUNG**
A figure of German myth, the king of the dwarfs, the possessors of a hoard of gold guarded for them by the dwarf ALBERICH (Scandinavian ANDVARI). The gold was eventually stolen by SIEGFRIED, in the romantic cycle of stories famously conveyed to us by Wagner's opera.

**NINDUKUGGA**
A Mesopotamian mythic character. See ENDUKUGGA.

**NINGIRSU**
In Mesopotamian mythology, an early name for NINURTA.

**NINGIZZIDA**
A figure of Mesopotamian myth. Along with TAMMUZ, he stood guarding the gate of heaven. Originally a fertility god, he later became a god of healing.
*Epic of Gilgamesh*

**NINHURSAG**
A Sumerian mother-goddess, the mother of NINURTA, and also an earth-goddess. Her

*An impression of an old Babylonian seal showing a man accompanied by a goddess standing before Nergal, the god of death. 1800-1600 BC.*

name means 'the mother'. In some variants she was regarded as the wife of ENKI.

*Epic of Gilgamesh*

### NINIGI

Grandson of the sun-goddess, AMATERASU, in the central group of deities of Japan. He acquired from her the imperial regalia of mirror, sword and jewels, which she had collected, and brought them to earth and to Japan. He married a princess called Ko-no-hana (whose name means 'Blossom Princess'), and it is from their family that the imperial family is descended.

### NINKI

A Mesopotamian figure, a form of NINHURSAG. *Epic of Gilgamesh*

*Noah, who in the Old Testament story survived the destruction of mankind in the flood, shown cutting grapes and being covered by his sons who found him drunk and naked in his tent. Miniature from the Golden Haggadah, c. 1320.*

### NINLIL

In Mesopotamian mythology she occurs as the consort of ENLIL, herself being a great goddess, worshipped together with Enlil at Nippur.

### NINSUN

A character in Mesopotamian mythology, in which she is the mother of the hero GILGAMESH, herself a goddess who was a minor deity of Uruk. She gave the hero his great wisdom and his consciousness of a super-human destiny.    *Epic of Gilgamesh*

### NINURTA

A wind god, in the mythological system of Mesopotamia, the god of the strong and fierce south wind, and hence a war-god. He is the enemy of the demon ASAG, whom he eventually destroys.

### NIOBE

In Greek myth, she is the daughter of TANTALUS and queen of Thebes. In a main episode of her story it is said that she boasted of having more children than LETO, as a result of which Leto's children APOLLO and ARTEMIS killed the sons and daughters of Niobe.

OVID: *Metamorphoses*

### NJORD

A Scandinavian god connected with the sea and with fishing, like many sea-gods said to be fabulously wealthy. Compare AEGIR. His story tells that his wife SKADI would only live in the mountains which he disliked. The arrangement by which they spend nine nights at each home fails and leaves them separated. FREYR and FREYJA are their children.    SNORRI STURLUSON: *Prose Edda*

### NKUNARE

In the beliefs of the Chaga people of East Africa, he was the elder of a pair of brothers who made an ascent of Mount Kilimanjaro and encountered a race of Little Folk, to whom he caused offence by taking them to be boys. His younger brother however befriended them and prospered.

## NOAH

A figure of Hebrew tradition as recorded in the Old Testament, he was the survivor of the destruction of mankind by flood. Compare DEUCALION, UTNAPISHTIM, MANU. He is warned of the impending deluge by God, and instructed to build a boat, the form and dimensions of which are specified in some detail. Into this he is to put representatives of all species. For six months he floats around on the waters, and in the seventh grounds on a mountain, Mount Ararat. He sends out birds from the boat, and when one fails to return he knows there is dry land. Emerging, he founded the new race of men with God's blessing, and in token of his agreement to favour them and not to destroy the world again God set a rainbow in the clouds. Noah took to agriculture and grew vines, one story telling how he became drunk and was found naked in his tent by his sons, who covered him. The named family of Noah are his three sons, SHEM, HAM, and JAPHETH, but it is mentioned that the company saved from the flood included their wives as well as his own, in all eight people. *Genesis*

## NODENS

Probably a Latinization of the Celtic name NUDD. From the evidence of a fourth-century temple excavated at Lydney in Gloucestershire he appears to have been a god of healing.

## NOKOMIS

'The Grandmother', in the mythology of the North American Algonquin Indians. She represents the earth, and is seen as a great mother figure, also being the grandmother of NANABUSH and CHIABOS.

## NUADHA

Known as 'the silver-handed' from an episode in one of his stories. In the myths of the Irish Celts he appears as a king of Ireland, and features particularly as the king of Tara at the time of the arrival of LUGH, who thereafter dominates the stories.

## NUDD

The British form of the Celtic Irish name NUADHA, he is a character who also appears in the British story-matter under the name of LLUDD.

## NUGU

In the creation story of the people of Papua in Melanesia, a being carved from wood and imbued with life by one of the gods, thus becoming a prototype of man. He annoyed his maker by attempting creations of his own and as a punishment, was condemned to hold up the world on his shoulders.

## NUGUA

Or Nu-kua, in the older variant of spelling. The creator goddess of the Chinese, being responsible for the making of the human species, which she modelled from yellow clay. The story tells how she grew tired of the slow process of individual creation and attempted mass-production by means of a rope dipped in the clay and allowed to drip. The difference between the hand-modelled and the arbitrarily produced specimens accounts for that between the rich and the poor. Although originally seen as a solitary figure, she later became viewed as sister and wife of FUXI, and like him she is sometimes shown as having the tail of a dragon. After the destruction of the order of the world brought about by the malicious monster GONG-GONG, she set about re-aligning the directions and re-establishing the difference between land and water, all of which had been disrupted.

## NUMMO

Or Nommo. A pair of characters occurring in the beliefs of the Dogon people of West Africa, in which they are the twin offspring of AMMA, and hence the prototype of mankind. Subsequently these twin spirits became diverse in the imagination of the Dogon, occurring for instance as the name of a pair of spirits present in seas and rivers, and particularly as heavenly blacksmiths, in which capacity they control the sun and form the focus of a fire-stealing

*A 'shame' peg from Mali, representing a Nummo figure, which features in the beliefs of the Dogon people of West Africa.*

myth. Blacksmiths enjoy a high status among the Dogon. The essential point about the Nummo is their twin-ness, an image of the ideal of wholeness or integration which mankind in his separateness has failed to achieve, though he still seeks it.

## NUN

For the ancient Egyptians, the abstract principle of primordial chaos, thought of as a great water, and represented in effigy as a man, or a frog or serpent based in the water. The early gods of creation were said to have emerged from Nun, in his capacity as all-embracing water. There is in his nature a curious ambiguity, since he can be seen both as a personalized and active deity and as the unformed universal medium which might again flood the ordered world and reduce it to the former chaos.

## NUT

In the cosmogony of the ancient Egyptians, the personification of the sky, one part of the primordial state of affairs, along with **GEB**, the earth. The two were the progeny of **SHU** and **TEFNUT**, and in their turn coupled to produce the Osirian family of gods: **OSIRIS**, **SET**, **ISIS** and **NEPHTHYS** (and in some versions **HORUS** as well). A peculiarity of the Egyptian calendar was that it had adjusted intercalated days, and because **RA** in jealousy forbade Nut and Geb to have children in any month of the year, their offspring were born on these days. Nut is presented as a woman with a long, arched body, stretching over Geb. She was in part a mother-goddess, and was sometimes said to be the mother of the sky-god Ra (who however in other variants was the parent of Shu and Tefnut). Like so many Egyptian deities she also had connections with the consignment of the dead, and is frequently depicted on the inner lid of sarcophagi.

## NYAMBÉ

An African Bantu name for God. See **NYAMÉ**.

## NYAMÉ

The commonest name for God among the Ashanti people of West Africa, a figure sometimes associated with the moon. He is a remote and non-humanized being, able to be everywhere at once because not localized, a background presence who operates in earthly action through the agency of a host of lesser gods, his ministers. The same figure is known to the Lunda as **NZAMBI**, and variants of the form **NYAMBÉ** occur in other Bantu groups in central and western Africa (e.g. Nzamé in the Congo area). In the area of the Zambesi a similarly-named deity is identified with the sun.

## NYIKANG

For the Shilluk people of Sudan in Africa, the ancestor figure who founded the royal dynasty, and consequently the great national hero of the Shilluk tribe.

## NYUNZA

In the story of the people of Angola in Africa he competes with Death and visits the otherworld, returning to Angola with the seeds of cultivated plants.

## NZAMBI

An African Bantu name for God. See **NYAMÉ**.

*A mummy case dating from the early 2nd century AD showing the goddess Nut who is here surrounded by signs of the Zodiac.*

## OCEANUS

In the pantheon of the ancient Greeks, the god of the great water which was thought to encompass the land, the earth-river, and hence regarded as the father of all river-gods and water divinities.

## OD

A minor character in Scandinavian myth, occurring as FREYJA's husband. He left her to travel on long journeys, causing her to weep tears of red gold.

SNORRI STURLUSON: *Prose Edda*

## ODIN

The chief of the Scandinavian gods, known in German as WODEN. He was their father-figure and ruler of their fortress Asgard, head of an aristocratic, warrior society in which he played a basically supervisory role. Also something of a magician, he was equated by the Romans with their god MERCURY, with whom he had in common such functions as that of leading the souls of the dead to their destination. In that capacity he also bears a folktale element, as the leader of the Wild Hunt, the soul-catching rampage which roars through the night sky on stormy nights, which may indicate that he was originally a wind-god. More sophisticated than his colleague THOR, Odin's characteristic is wisdom and knowledge, which he gains from his two ravens, HUGIN and MUNIN and also from having sipped the water of MIMIR's spring. His weapon too is more refined than THOR's hammer, being a miraculous spear which always finds its mark. As supervisor of the dead he holds court in his great hall Valhalla, where an endless feast awaits those who died bravely in battle. He is served there by the VALKYRIES, female war-fates who determine whose destiny it is to reach Valhalla. Odin's wife is the principal

LEFT: *In the upper part of this 11th-century funerary stone from the island of Gotland, Sweden, Odin's horse Sleipnir bears either Odin or a dead man being carried to Valhalla, where he is welcomed by a woman holding out a drinking horn. The ship in the lower panel is perhaps the ship of the dead.*

goddess of this pantheon, FRIGG, but like his counterpart in Greek myth ZEUS he is not above extramarital liaisons with mortal women. He is represented in some descriptions as being one-eyed, through the episode in which he had to give an eye in payment to Mimir for drinking at the fount of wisdom. He also gained wisdom through drinking the mead of inspiration, guarded by the giant SUTTUNG. Most striking of his characteristics is his death and rebirth, sacrificed to himself by being hung for nine days before seeing at his feet some magic runes which gave him renewed life. In northern myth the gods are mortal, and their world ends with Ragnarök, 'the gods' fatality'. Odin rode out bravely on his wonderful eight-legged horse SLEIPNIR to confront the unleashed forces of destruction, but was swallowed by the terrible jaws of the wolf FENRIR, to the end the leader of the gods and the first of them to perish in the cataclysmic ending of the old world.

SNORRI STURLUSON: *Prose Edda*

## ODUDUWA

The legendary first king of the Yoruba people of Nigeria in West Africa, who was said to have established his seat at Ife-Ife, their holy city.

## ODYSSEUS

A major figure of Greek mythology, the epitome of the wandering hero, a theme much loved by the Greeks, who perhaps found it an apt expression of the buffeted and unpredictable course of human life. Odysseus is very highly characterized by Homer, and later writers adopted the convention. He is cunning and wily, living by his wits rather than by brute force, small, compelling in argument, impressive as a person through sheer force of intellect. Clearly the gods had a soft spot for him, and his men seem to have exercised a devoted loyalty beyond normal expectation. He played a significant part in the Trojan War, and the famous voyage of return combined deeply human elements of love and longing with the triumph over the apparently impossible which is the stuff of folktale. He came home to find his wife PENELOPE remaining faithful.

HOMER: *Iliad, Odyssey*

## OEDIPUS

The protagonist of a central story of Greek myth. Since he is doomed by prophecy to kill his father LAIUS and marry his mother JOCASTA, no amount of careful evasion can save him from this outcome. The story of Oedipus is the best of many Greek stories about this type of human helplessness, and as portrayed in the myth he embodies the upright blamelessness of a rational, intelligent man. He saved Thebes from the curse of the Sphinx, and having married the queen he set about discovering the killer of the previous king, which had, by accident, been himself. See also CREON, ANTIGONE.    SOPHOCLES: *Oedipus the King*

## OENGUS

Oengus mac in Og. A god who occurs as a subsidiary figure in the Celtic Irish tales of FINN, he was conceived and born in a single day, being the son of the DAGA, the leader of the Irish gods. He gained from his father the occupancy of a supernatural dwelling now identified as the burial mound at Newgrange on the river Boyne. Portrayed as something of a trick-player in later stories, he has a story of his own, 'the dream of Oengus', in which he falls in love with a girl in a dream and after much searching finds her.

## OENOMAUS

In Greek mythology, he appears as the king of Elis in the Peloponnese, the father of the princess HIPPODAEMIA whom PELOPS married after defeating Oenomaus in a chariot race. Oenomaus had believed himself invincible, but was betrayed by Hippoddemid's treachery. He died, fulfilling the prophecy that his son-in-law would kill him.

## OGMIOS

A Celtic god of Romanized Gaul, perhaps based on the Irish figure Oghma, a great champion. Ogmios is identified by the Romans with their hero HERCULES, perhaps because he is commonly portrayed as a hero with a club. Through this connection he bears the status of a supernatural hero.

## OGUN

A god of the Yoruba people of Nigeria in West Africa. He is the spirit of iron, patron of blacksmiths and other metal-workers, and also of physical occupations such as hunting and warfare. He was at first a great hunter, who enabled other deities to come down to earth, and is therefore known as the chief of the gods.

ABOVE: *Oedipus before the Sphinx, the fearsome monster – part woman, part lion, part bird – who had devastated the land about Thebes. Vase of the 5th century* BC.

BELOW: *A Romano-British stone relief with on the left the figure of Ogmios, identified by the Romans with Hercules.*

## OHRMAZD

In the Zoroastrian religious system of Iran, he is the Pahlavi (Middle Persian) version of AHURA MAZDA, an omniscient creator god who however is not omnipotent as he has a free counterpart in the person of the evil spirit AHRIMAN (in the earlier literature ANGRA MAINYU). Ohrmazd in fact created the material world, and mankind, as a tool in his campaign to destroy Ahriman.

## OISIN

Son of FINN, a figure in Celtic Irish mythology. His stories form a nostalgic aftermath in Irish myth, in which the heroic days are almost over and the new era is approaching. Oisin is regarded by storytellers as the nearest contact the modern world has to the world of myth and magic. It is often he who is telling the story, as in the tale where he accompanies St Patrick across Ireland and recounts to him the doings of Finn and the Fiana. Appearing in Scottish lore as OSSIAN, he became a popular figure of literature in the eighteenth and nineteenth centuries.

## OJIN

A character in the mythology of Japan. See HACHIMAN.

## O-KUNI-NUSHI

Also spelt Okuni-nushi. A character of the mythology of Japan. In the most important episode of his career he eloped with the daughter of the storm god SUSANO, and after tests and adventures married her and became ruler of the province of Izumo. One story concerning him tells of his successful wooing of a princess with the assistance of a hare (or in some versions a rabbit) which he had cured of baldness. He suffered the jealous enmity of his eighty brothers, and was several times killed by them, only to be resurrected by his mother, the goddess Kami-Musubi.

## OLELBIS

The main god of the northern Wintun Indians of California, the creator of the

An impression of a cylinder seal showing the Persian King Darius (521-486 BC) and an emblem of Ahura Mazda derived from that of the Zoroastrian Ohrmazd.

world and its features, his name signifying 'the one who is above'.

## OLODUMARE

A figure of the mythology of the Yoruba people of Nigeria in West Africa. See OLORUN.

## OLOFAT

A hero of the Pacific islands of Micronesia, also in some places known as Yalafath. He is a trickster figure, who was said to have been responsible for the introduction of fire to mankind, which he achieved by obtaining it from the thunder god.

## OLOKUN

'Owner of the sea' A goddess of the Yoruba people of Nigeria in West Africa.

## OLORUN

Also known by the name OLODUMARE. For the Yoruba people of Nigeria in West Africa, the supreme being who lived in the sky at the beginning of time, ruler of the universe, transcendent and all-knowing.

## OLWEN

A Celtic British figure. See CULHWCH.

## OMOIGANE

Or Omoikane. A god of wisdom in the mythology of Japan.

*'The Three Sisters', a watercolour by the Seneca Indian Ernest Smith depicting spirits who, like Onatha, the corn spirit of the Iroquois, ensure the rebirth of crops.*

### OMPHALE

Occurring in Greek mythology as the queen of Lydia, she is said in her story to have subjected HERACLES to a period of serfdom, during which time they are sometimes said to have exchanged roles – he dressing as the queen, she as the warrior – a feature oddly in contrast to the dominant character of that hero.

### ONAN

In the Hebrew tradition preserved in the Old Testament, the son of JUDAH. ONAN declined to consummate a marriage which by tradition he was obliged to undertake with his elder brother's widow, instead letting his seed fall on the ground. He thus displeased God, who killed him.

*Genesis*

### ONATHA

The corn spirit of the Iroquois Indians of North America, by whom she is viewed as being the daughter of the earth, known as EITHINOHA. Like the Greek PERSEPHONE she was abducted by an evil spirit and confined in the underworld, but became restored to the world by the agency of the sun, a representation of the apparent death and rebirth of the corn which is a feature of several mythologies.

### ONI

Demons of Japanese Buddhism, seen as of ferocious appearance, with horns and three eyes, of various strange colours and sometimes gigantic proportions. Unlike the TENGU they have an evil disposition.

### ORANYAN

In the beliefs of the Yoruba people of Nigeria in West Africa, he was the son of ODUDUWA and second king of Ile-Ife. His staff, a tall stone column, can still be seen there.

### ORENDA

The great power present in the natural world, in the beliefs of the Iroquois Indians of North America.

### ORESTES

A Greek hero, the son of AGAMEMNON, he is burdened with the need to develop further the curse on his family (see ATREUS, THYESTES; AEGISTHUS, CLYTEMNESTRA) by avenging the murder of his father, even though this means incurring the sin of matricide. He in turn has to expiate this guilt, and he is plagued by the Furies until he stands trial by the gods.

AESCHYLUS: *The Libation Bearers, The Eumenides*; EURIPEDES: *Orestes*

## ORION

In Greek mythology, a giant and hunter, who after various vicissitudes became a companion of **ARTEMIS**, by whom he was eventually killed in error through a trick by her brother **APOLLO**, who had begun to fear that Orion would marry her.

## ORISHA-NLA

Also known as Obatala. For the Yoruba people of West Africa, the chief minister of the supreme god **OLURUN**. He was responsible for allocating wealth and poverty, and also physical defects.

## ORPHEUS

A character occurring in the mythology of the Greeks. The story tells how he sang and played the lyre so well that wild animals and even stones responded. When his beloved wife **EURIDICE** died young, Orpheus was heart-broken. He went down into the underworld to reclaim her, and by the power and charm of his music enticed **HADES** to let her go. See **EURIDICE**.

OVID: *Metamorphoses*

## ORUNMILA

A god of prophecy for the Yoruba people of Nigeria in West Africa, said to have assisted in the creation, and to speak all tongues. He lived on earth for a time for a time instructing humans, but eventually returned to heaven and left us to fend for ourselves. He is the force expressed by the **IFA** oracle. The Ifa priesthood operates its oracular functions by means of a set of poems about the doings of Orunmila's followers.

## OSHUN

The goddess of fountains, love and wealth, in the religion of the African people of Brazil, descendants of Yoruba slaves from West Africa. She is a figure not unlike the Roman **VENUS**. She is identified with the Virgin Mary in her role of Our Lady of Conception in the adaptation to Roman Catholicism known as *candomblé*. Her African Yoruba counterpart is a river goddess.

## OSIRIS

The centre of a major cult in ancient Egyptian religion, Osiris provided the prototype for the burial of the dead. Egyptians believed very literally in an afterlife, and much of their mythology deals with the prescription for attaining it. This is especially so with the myth of Osiris, who thus becomes the main exemplar in mythology of a reborn god. Murdered by his jealous brother **SET**, he was enclosed in a lead-lined chest, which Set threw into the Nile. It was washed ashore in Byblos and caught in the branches of a tamarisk sapling, which grew to enclose it, was cut down and made into a column in the local king's palace. Osiris' wife **ISIS** eventually found it, entered the palace as nurse to the royal child (compare **DEMETER**) and was allowed to take away the chest. See **ASTARTE**. She hid it from Set in the reeds of the Delta, but yet he found it and to thwart her aims cut the body into small pieces and scattered them. Isis and her sister **NEPHTHYS** painstakingly collected the pieces, reassembled them, and embalmed the body as the prototype mummy. Osiris did not return to earth, but became alive in the afterworld, the king of the dead. Like other deities connected with death he was

*A Roman mosaic from Tarsus depicting Orpheus and the animals. His power over untamed nature and his success in persuading Hades to release Euridice from the underworld made Orpheus the centre of cults that promised initiates a happy life after death.*

*A dead man presenting an offering to Osiris, the Egyptian god of vegetation, seasonal rebirth and hence god of the dead and judge of the underworld. Papyrus of the 19th Dynasty, c. 1250 BC.*

originally a corn-god (compare DEMETER), and hence a god of fertility. Son of NUT, the sky, and GEB, the earth, he was recognized by the supreme sky-god RA as his heir, and was credited with introducing to mankind not just agriculture but civilization itself. He was worshipped as part of a trinity (compare AMON, MUT and KHONS; PTAH, SEKHMET, NEFERTUM) along with his wife and sister Isis and his son HORUS. The natural phenomena both of the death and rebirth of vegetation and of the declining and returning waters of the Nile were attributed to his death and resurrection. At the same time his continuing conflict with his evil and disruptive brother Set is an emblem of the tension between the desert and the cultivated land, so crucial and so contrasting in the valleys of the Nile.

## OSLA

A Saxon leader occurring as representative of the enemy in early Celtic British tales, in which he is known as Osla Big-knife perhaps from the tradition that Saxons carried long knives. Possibly the name derives from Octha, son of HENGIST.

## OSSIAN

The Scottish form of the Celtic Irish OISIN, compare FINGAL. Popularized by the eighteenth century Scottish writer James Macpherson, the Ossianic cycle became the best known form of the originally Irish stories.

## OURANOS

An early Greek god, the alternative spelling of URANUS.

## OWEIN

The hero of a sub-Arthurian adventure in this Celtic British material closely related to a French Celtic story by Chrétien de Troyes, in which he appears as YVAIN. Owein was perhaps originally a historical character, son of King Urien of Rheged. In his story he perfectly illustrates the medieval hero, riding alone on a simple quest for adventure into the forest and wilderness and finding spiritual satisfaction through the marvels he encounters in his travels.      *Mabinogion*

## OWO

In Nigeria in West Africa, the Idoma tribe's name for God, and also for rain, indicating a close connection, perhaps even an identification, between the two. See EN-KAI, TANUKUJEN.

## OXALÁ

Or Oshala. In the African religion of Brazil still practised by the descendants of Yoruba slaves, he is a father-figure among the gods, a chief-deity and also the god of peace, identified with Christ in his aspect of Our Lord of Bonfim (Christ on the Cross). His native West African counterpart is ORISHA-NLA, the great god and creator god of the Yoruba people.

# P

### PACHACAMAC
In Peru, an ancient, pre-Inca god of a cult local to a site south of the present city of Lima, near the coast. The site grew to have much influence and prestige as a place of pilgrimage and the seat of an oracle. He was thought to have introduced mankind to skills and trades. Human sacrifice was a part of his worship, and the Incas adopted him as a son of the sun.

### PACHAMAMA
In the religion of the Incas of Peru, the sister and perhaps also the wife of PACHATATA, or INTI. She is a goddess of fertility and nature, appealed to still as a bringer of good fortune.

### PACHAYACHACHIC
'Teacher of the World', in the religious system of the Incas of Peru. The supreme creator god.

### PADMASAMBHAVA
A figure of Tibetan Buddhism, said to have been an early religious teacher who was thought to have overcome the local gods by magic. The name means 'Lotus-born', and the character derives from Indian Buddhism and probably also has a partial origin in a historical character. However Padmasambhava became very much an object of worship in his own right.

### PAH
The moon, in the beliefs of the North American Pawnee Indians. Along with SHAKURU the sun and the other celestial bodies he was placed in position by TIRAWA as part of the latter's preparation for the creation of mankind.

### PALLAS
A Greek goddess. See ATHENA.

### PAN
In Greek mythology, he was originally a local god of Arcadia, an area of the Peloponnese. Pan however became increasingly generalized as a god of nature, partly because of the accidental connection of his name with the Greek word meaning 'all'. He is depicted as being dark and hairy, often having tempered his solitude in wild places by making himself an instrument out of reeds, and his other habit of jumping out on solitary travellers in wild places gives us the word 'panic'.

*A 3rd-century AD mosaic from Paphos, Cyprus, representing the god Pan, in classical mythology a deity of fields, woods, shepherds and flocks.*

### PANDAVAS

In the mythology of India, the five children of PANDU and his wives KUNTI and MADRI, who however conceived them by worshipping various gods. On their father's death they were fostered by his half-brother DHRITARASHTRA, and the rivalry of one of the latter's own sons, DURYODHANA, with the consequent flight and exile of the Pandavas, forms part of the story of the *Mahabharata*.

### PANDORA

In Greek mythology, the first woman, viewed by the Greeks as a misfortune visited on mankind. She was sent as a punishment to EPIMETHEUS, the foolish brother of PROMETHEUS, as a counterpart to the acquisition of fire. He rashly accepted the gift, and along with her a jar she bore which, when opened, scattered among men ills such as work and disease, which they had not previously suffered.

HESIOD: *Works and Days*

### PANDU

In the mythology of India, the father of the PANDAVAS, the heroes of a part of the *Mahabharata*. See KUNTI, ARJUNA.

### PANGU

Or (in the older form of spelling) P'an-ku. A giant occurring in the myths of China, who was concerned with the creation of the world. Born from the primordial egg, and said originally to be a dwarf, he grew rapidly in the space between the earth and sky as this gap itself expanded. He thus came to be associated with the weather, his breath being wind, his voice the thunder, and the weather's changes reflecting his changes of mood. The parts of his body became the features of the world (compare Scandinavian YMIR, and Hindu PURUSHA). In some versions of the creation myth Pangu also played a part in the origins of mankind.

### PAPA

The Earth Mother, a primal being in the main creation story of the Maoris. She coupled with RANGI the sky to produce the original divinities of earth and air. When they were eventually forced apart from their loving union by the efforts of their sons, especially TANE, she took to herself the possession of their offspring when they died.

### PARAPARAWA

Early member of the Trio tribe of Indians of Brazil, credited by them with the introduction of cultivation, the knowledge of which he gained from a mystical woman. She first appeared to him in the form of a fish and taught him how to plant bananas, yams, sweet potatoes and yuca, and how to cook food.

### PARASHURAMA

'Rama with the axe'. In the mythology of India, an incarnation of the god VISHNU in which he combated the rising power of a secular caste.

### PARIS

Prince of Troy occurring in a central saga in the myths of the Greeks. Owing to a prophecy that he would bring about the downfall of his country he was committed to a shepherd to be killed, but the man instead adopted him. Growing up as a herdsman on Mount Ida, Paris was visited by the three contesting goddesses who disputed the possession of the apple thrown by ERIS, goddess of discord, inscribed 'to the fairest'. (See also PELEUS). As a bribe, HERA offered him wealth, ATHENA wisdom, but he chose APHRODITE because she offered him a bride as beautiful as she was. This turned out to be HELEN, wife of MENELAUS, and thus began the Trojan War. Paris' behaviour is conveyed as innocent but foolish; he is somewhat the plaything of the gods.

### PARJANYA

In the mythology of India, one of the twelve forms of the sun, a god of the fertilizing power of rain, viewed as a rain-cloud or a cow, to be milked for its goodness.

*Rig Veda*

RIGHT: *Pele, the fearsome goddess of volcanic force in the mythology of Hawaii.*

### PARSHU

A daughter of MANU, in the mythological story of origins of India, and therefore the wife of the first man. The name means 'Rib'; compare EVE.

### PARVATI

A figure of the mythology of India, in which she is the daughter of the Himalayas and wife of SIVA. She is portrayed as a beautiful woman and personifies the 'power' of her husband. She is also known by the name Uma, meaning light and beauty.

### PASIPHAË

In Greek mythology, the wife of MINOS, King of Crete. POSEIDON took revenge on Minos for failing to sacrifice a bull he had sent for that purpose, by making the queen fall in love with the animal. She sought the help of the court craftsman DAEDALUS, who made her a hollow cow in which she could consummate her infatuation. The liaison produced a monstrous offspring in the

OPPOSITE: *The barge board of a Maori meeting house showing the separation of Papa, the Earth Mother, and Rangi, the Sky Father.*

form of the minotaur ASTERION, a creature that was half man, half bull eventually slain by the hero THESEUS.

### PATROCLUS

A Greek hero, the friend and companion of ACHILLES at the Trojan War, in the events of which his death forms a climax of Homer's story. A model of blameless loyalty, he fell to the Trojan hero HECTOR while leading the Greek forces disguised as ACHILLES, when the latter refused to fight. The grief and anger which his death caused the Greek hero brought him back into the conflict, and hastened the end of the war.

HOMER: *Iliad*

### PAUAHTUNS

For the Maya Indians of Mexico, a quartet of gods whose function is still unknown.

### PEGASUS

In Greek mythology, the name of the winged horse tamed and ridden by BELLEROPHON. Pegasus was born of MEDUSA'S blood, when PERSEUS cut off her head. Bellerophon tamed Pegasus with a golden bridle, given to him by ATHENE, but the horse eventually threw him when he tried to reach the land of the gods.

### PELE

The volcano goddess of Hawaii, a malign force, and one of the pair of sisters who were said in one of the stories to have come to Hawaii from Tahiti.

### PELEUS

A figure of Greek myth. Chosen by ZEUS to marry the sea-nymph THETIS, of whom it was prophesied that her son would become greater than his father, Peleus fathered the ultimate hero ACHILLES. The gods of Olympus attended their wedding, and it was on this occasion that the goddess ERIS, annoyed at being excluded, rolled into the assembly the apple inscribed 'to the fairest', which set off a dispute between the three leading goddesses. See Paris.

**PELLES**

In Celtic British stories, the master of Grail Castle, possessor of the Holy Grail, a late form of the maimed king or fisher king (earlier known as BRON). His name ultimately derives from the Celtic god BELI (just as Bron's connects him with the rival god BRAN). In Malory Pelles has a daughter ELAINE who falls in love with Sir LANCELOT.

MALORY: *Morte d'Arthur*

**PELOPS**

Occurring in Greek myth as the son of TANTALUS, he came to the area of Elis to find a bride. His cult eventually became established at Olympia there, where four-yearly games were said to commemorate a chariot race in which Pelops took part on his arrival and by which he won the hand of the princess. That part of Greece is named, after him, the Peloponnese.

**PENELOPE**

A heroine of Greek myth, she is the epitome of loyalty and faith. Left behind by her husband ODYSSEUS when he went to the Trojan War, she resisted the hands of rival suitors and rejected the rumours of his death for the duration of the war and for the long period of his return voyage.

HOMER: *Odyssey*

**PERCEVAL**

A hero of Celtic myth of both France and Britain, the hero of the first major set of Grail stories (also under the Welsh name PEREDUR), and until the development of GALAHAD the archetypal Grail-seeking hero. An innocent and inexperienced youth he sets off from KING ARTHUR's court and finding himself lodged in the Castle of Wonders, he is confronted by the mysteries of the lame king, the bleeding lance and the salver which is the early form of the Grail. In later literature he retains his role as Grail seeker, but now as one among many, being developed in Malory as one of the outstanding knights of King Arthur's court.

CHRÉTIEN DE TROYES: *Contes del Graal;*
MALORY: *Morte d'Arthur*

*Persephone with her husband Hades, the Greek god of the underworld. Persephone's annual return for part of the year to her mother, Demeter, ensures the maintenance of the seasonal cycle. Attic kylix from Vulci, 430 BC.*

**PEREDUR**

The hero of a Celtic British tale of adventure, much of which has similarities with the Grail stories of Chrétien de Troyes; see PERCEVAL. Peredur however bears more of a folktale character, being the simple country-boy who reveals his naivety at the sophisticated court of KING ARTHUR, only to prove subsequently his natural superiority.

*Mabinogion*

**PERITHOUS**

In Greek myth, he occurs as the king of the Lapiths, his story recounting how his wedding was the cause of a battle between the CENTAURS and humans, when the Centaurs (invited as relatives) became drunk and abducted the bride and other women. The battle is depicted on one of the friezes of the Parthenon and of the temple of Zeus of Olympia.

**PERSEPHONE**

A goddess of Greek myth, the daughter of DEMETER by her brother ZEUS. She was abducted by her uncle HADES and carried off to his kingdom, the underworld, causing her mother to mourn inconsolably. See DEMETER.

**PERSEUS**

A figure of Greek myth, the son of DANAË by ZEUS, who visited her in the form of a shower of gold when she had been locked up by her father. He became a major Greek hero of the typical kind, one who undertakes rescues, journeys of adventure and the killing of monsters. See ANDROMEDA, MEDUSA, POLYDECTES.

**PERUN**

Or Pyerun, in Russian. The great Slavonic god of thunder and lightning, and also of war. He was for a long period the object of animal sacrifice, worshipped as a major deity up to the time of the arrival of Christianity in the tenth century, when his great silver and gold statue at Kiev was destroyed by being thrown into the Dnieper. Subsequently he became equated with St Elias or Elijah. In another aspect, as the Lithuanian god Perkuras, he is depicted as bearing an axe or a hammer, attributes of other gods of thunder and lightning (compare Scandinavian THOR and African SHANGO), and the name for the same figure in Polish, Piorun, is also the word for thunder. The name in general is connected with the Hindu Parjanya, one of the titles of the great Aryan god INDRA.

**PHAEDRA**

In Greek mythology, the daughter of King MINOS of Crete and husband of THESEUS; like her mother PASIPHAË she was, through no fault of her own, the victim of a god's revenge, when APHRODITE, jealous of Phaedra's stepson HIPPOLYTUS' devotion to ARTEMIS, caused her to fall in love with him, which tragically led to the death of both.          EURIPIDES: *Hippolytus*

**PHILEMON**

A figure in Greek mythology. See BAUCIS.

**PHOEBE**

One of the Titans, the older order of gods in the Greek mythological system, the mother of LETO and thus grandmother of APOLLO and ARTEMIS.          HESIOD: *Theogony*

**PHOEBUS**

In Greek mythology, one of the names of APOLLO.

**PHOLUS**

In Greek myth, one of the more civilized of the CENTAURS (see also CHEIRON), a gentle and kindly creature who had the ironic and fatal misfortune to drop one of HERACLES' poisoned arrows on his foot.

*The Greek hero Perseus, watched by Athena, has cut off the Gorgon's head, which he is carrying away in a bag. Water jar, c. 460 BC, found at Capua.*

**PHORCYS**
A figure occurring in Greek mythology as a sea-deity, the father of the three GORGONS (see MEDUSA).

**PILLAN**
For the Araucanian Indians of Chile, the god of thunder and the cause of earthquakes, a malignant spirit who also took possession of the souls of those killed in battle.

**PLUTO**
In Greek mythology, another name for HADES, the god of the underworld.

**POLEVIK**
In Slavonic tradition, the spirit of the fields. The name in fact comes from *pole* meaning 'field'. He was capable of mischievous activity, but could be placated and befriended if the necessary sacrifices were made.

**POLLUX**
A figure of Roman myth, see Greek POLYDEUCES. In later tradition it was said that Pollux was the immortal twin, CASTOR being the son of LEDA's mortal husband TYNDAREUS.

**POLYBUS**
In Greek myth he occurs as the king of Corinth who adopted OEDIPUS when he was discovered by one of his shepherds (exposed by his real parents to evade a fatal prophecy) – see OEDIPUS – and brought him up as his own son.

**POLYDECTES**
King of Seriphos, in the myths of the Greeks, who fell in love with DANAË, and sent her son PERSEUS to acquire the head of MEDUSA a task he was unlikely to be able to perform, as a way of preventing him from obstructing her seduction.

**POLYDEUCES**
In Greek myth, the twin to CASTOR, son of ZEUS and LEDA. He is better known in Roman myth as POLLUX.

**POLYNICES**
Together with ETEOCLES, one of the sons of OEDIPUS, in a central story of Greek myth. The two brothers were made joint kings of Thebes when their father was banished after the discovery of his crime. The brothers quarrelled over the arrangement and Polynices was exiled, attacked Thebes, and he and his brother killed each other in single combat. Their uncle CREON decreed that the bodies remain unburied. It was ANTIGONE's disobedience in an attempt to bury Polynices that led to the conflict between her and Creon.
AESCHYLUS: *Seven against Thebes;*
SOPHOCLES: *Antigone*

**POLYPHEMUS**
In Greek mythology, the name of the leader of the CYCLOPS; a dangerous man-eating giant encountered by ODYSSEUS on his voyage. Homer treats him with typical ambivalence, allowing him credit for his careful farming, mentioning that he is the son of POSEIDON. When Odysseus escapes by blinding him in his one eye he calls on his father to curse the mortal with a miserable homecoming.

**POMONA**
The Roman goddess of fruit trees.

**POSEIDON**
The Greek god of the sea, represented as a powerful and temperamental figure, like his element, much given to vengeance and displays of will. He was one of the children of CRONUS and RHEA, along with ZEUS and HADES, who divided the world between them. Although married to AMPHITRITE he showed no more respect for matrimony than his brother ZEUS, and one of his main stories concerns the courting of his sister DEMETER. Compare Roman NEPTUNE. A powerful statue thought to represent this god is now in the Greek archaeological museum in Athens.

**POSHAIYANGKYO**
In the cosmogony of the Pueblo Indians of North America, he was the first being to

emerge from the earth, and by doing so he led the way for the complex birth of the remaining creatures.

**POTIPHAR**

In the Hebrew traditional material preserved in the Old Testament, he is an officer to the king of Egypt, who bought JOSEPH when he was brought there after being betrayed and sold by his brothers, and it was in his household that Joseph rose to the position of chief steward. Potiphar's wife attempted to seduce him.

*Genesis*

**PRAJAPATI**

A creator figure, in the cosmogony of India, sharing qualities with VISHNU and BRAHMA. Prajapati emerged from the pre-existent element of water, giving rise to the structure of the day and the world. He is the master of created beings.

**PRAJAPATI**

Or Mahaprajapati (Maha means Great). In the background mythology of the Buddhist religion of India, she was the foster-mother of the Buddha, who is said to have two mothers. See MAHAMAYA.

**PRIAM**

In Greek myth, the king of Troy, father of PARIS, whose fateful abduction of HELEN of Sparta gave rise to the Trojan War. Priam comes over in Homer as a noble figure suffering many tragedies and disasters in the course of his city's eventual defeat.

HOMER: *Iliad*

**PRITHIVI**

In the mythology of India, the earth, regarded as female. Amid signs and portents she gave birth to INDRA, whom she hid in fear, recognizing that he was destined to supplant the old order. Compare RHEA, ZEUS.

**PROCRUSTES**

A figure of Greek mythology known for the image of his bed, a destructive device which he stretched or maimed his guests to fit. He lived in Attica, where this habit presented a danger to all travellers until eventually he was killed by the young hero THESEUS.

**PROMETHEUS**

A figure of Greek mythology. Although himself a minor god, Prometheus functions as the representative of mankind, subtle and cunning but ultimately powerless against the ruling gods. From the start he quarrelled with ZEUS, and the climax of his deeds was the stealing from the chief of the gods the privilege of fire, a form of original sin which the Greeks regarded as giving rise to the acquisition of the arts and sciences. For this he was punished by Zeus by having his liver permanently eaten by an eagle.

HESIOD: *Theogony*

**PROSERPINA**

The Roman version of the Greek goddess PERSEPHONE.

**PROTEUS**

A Greek sea-god, noted for his skill in prophecy and for his ability to change his form. He guarded Poseidon's herd of seals.

HOMER: *Odyssey*

**PRYDERI**

Lord of Dyfed (an early kingdom of what is now South Wales), the hero of a Celtic British tale of mystery, involving basic images such as the enchanted castle and the waste land, in which story he is abducted by means of a spell along with his mother RHIANNON.

*Mabinogion*

**PSYCHE**

A figure of Greek mythology, at the same time the personification of the human soul, and a lovely girl who caught the attention of EROS (in Roman myth CUPID).

**PTAH**

An ancient Egyptian god of the region of the lower Nile which became the location

*Ptah, a creator god of the Ancient Egyptians and the sovereign deity of Thebes. Bronze figure of the 19th Dynasty.*

of the great city of Memphis, where his spirit became represented by the bull-god APIS. He was a creator god, and a god of fertility, and in his overall function of ruler and initiator became associated with many other deities. He is represented in mummy form, his two hands only emerging, to hold the sceptre of order and stability. Together with his wife SEKHMET and son NEFERTUM, he formed a sacred trinity.

### PULEKUKWEREK

A figure in the traditions of the Yurok Indians of western North America, he is the conqueror of the elements of disorder in society, dispeller of monsters, and is much respected by the Yurok for his firm and devoted application of social rule.

### PURANDHI

In the mythology of India, a goddess of plenty and of childbirth. *Rig Veda*

### PURUSHA

A primordial man, in the cosmogony of India, a form of cosmic giant out of whom the gods created the world, and all the objects in it, by dismembering him. Compare Scandinavian YMIR. *Rig Veda*

### PUSHAN

In the mythological system of India, a deity with many functions, including those of guide to the souls of the dead, protector of roads and journeys, and involvement in the progress of the sun. *Rig Veda*

### PWYLL

In a story of Celtic British myth, the prince of Dyfed (an early kingdom in what is now South Wales), husband of RHIANNON and father of PRYDERI. Early in his story he changed places for a year with the king of the otherworld, ARAWN. His winning of Rhiannon against a rival's repeated tricks also reflects annual cycles. *Mabinogion*

### PYGMALION

In Greek mythology, the name both of the brother of DIDO and of a king of Cyprus best known for having fallen love with a statue which he had made, which by praying to APHRODITE he succeeded in bringing to life. OVID: *Metamorphoses*

*In the tragic classical story of Pyramus and Thisbe, Pyramus kills himself when he thinks mistakenly that Thisbe has been killed by a lion.*

### PYRAMUS

A figure of Greek myth, in which he occurs as a tragic lover, who with his beloved THISBE overcame parental disapproval only to think mistakenly that Thisbe had been devoured by a lion, upon which he killed himself. Thisbe, on finding his body, herself commits suicide.

OVID: *Metamorphoses*

### PYTHON

The name of the serpent-monster said in Greek mythology to have been made from mud left by the flood of DEUCALION and killed by APOLLO at Delphi.

## QAHOLOM

Father god, in the beliefs of the Maya Indians of Mexico. His name means 'the father who begat sons'. *Popol Vuh*

## QAT

One of a family of twelve brothers, he figures prominently in the stories of the New Hebrides in Melanesia. He was responsible for shaping men out of wood and for bringing them to life. One story however tells how a rival introduced the compensating factor of human mortality. Qat also brought into existence the alternation of night and day. He had connections with the sea and sea-faring, and in the end set off out to sea and disappeared. The people of the New Hebrides believed that he and his crew would come back, and when the first European explorers arrived greeted them as Qat and his company returning.

## QEBEHSEMUF

Son of HORUS. A falcon-headed god occurring in the symbolism surrounding the ritual of Egyptian burial, itself based on the story of the death of OSIRIS. Along with IMSET, HAPY and DUAMUTEF (also the sons of Horus) he was one of the gods responsible for guarding the canopic jars (in this case the jar containing the intestines of the embalmed corpse) and attending the sarcophagus as guardians of the four cardinal points, Qebehsenuf being the attendant of that of the west. These four were regarded as the sons of Horus by his wife ISIS.

## QI

In Chinese mythical history, he was the son of the early ruler YU, and his successor. Yu had (in some versions) wished his minister to succeed him, but Qi was chosen by his followers, thus instituting the principle of hereditary rule. Qi became a distinctly mythical figure in the tradition, being said to have ridden on dragons and to have visited heaven by that means. He was also said to be the discoverer of music, which he heard for the first time in heaven.

## QUETZALCOATL

The legendary founder of Tula, in the mythology of the Maya Indians of Mexico, in that capacity based on a historical figure of about 900 BC, but worshipped as part god, part ancestral hero, and identified with the god so frequently depicted on Maya monuments as a feathered serpent. Compare KUKULCAN. In his story he leaves his city of Tula and travels southeast over the mountains to the coast, to disappear from human knowledge, on a raft made of snakes, across the waters of the Gulf of Mexico. It is said that he will return to save his people. In another version of the story he is said to have burned himself to death.

*Quetzalcoatl, the powerful god and ancestor hero of old Mexico, depicted on one of the 'Santa Lucia' stones, each of which records astronomical events and the dates they took place.*

# R

## RA

Sometimes Re. As head and father-figure of the Egyptian gods, Ra absorbed many lesser deities, and his various titles reflect this. He was originally the god of the sun, local to Heliopolis, but became generalized and universalized in orthodox Egyptian religion. It was thought that he travelled the sky in the form of a disc carried in a boat, in which shape he is sometimes portrayed; more often he appears as a man with a falcon-head, surmounted by the sun-disc. At night he struggles with the serpent APEP, who tries to obstruct his course. Though varied stories of his origin are told, Ra is principally the ancestor of the gods, producing by self-fertilization the first divine couple, SHU and TEFNUT. At one time, during the golden age, he ruled as a king on earth. His most notable feature was a detachable eye, which was capable of going off on its own, and itself formed a powerful ruler – the emblem of the sun. The pharaohs wore the Eye of Ra in the ornament of the 'uraeus' cobra on their headdresses, signifying their descent from him. Ra is remarkable among gods for being thought to have grown old and weak, and his pre-eminent position was eventually occupied by HORUS.

## RACHEL

In the Hebrew tradition preserved in the Old Testament, she is the daughter of LABAN and hence niece of REBECCA and first cousin to JACOB, whose wife she became. See LEAH. Although at first barren, she was the mother of JOSEPH and BENJAMIN. *Genesis*

## RA-HARAKHTE

A composite figure of Egyptian mythology merging the gods RA and HORUS.

## RAHULA

Son of the Buddha, in the background material of the Buddhist religion of India. His birth was a necessary prelude to the Buddha's setting out on his great quest for understanding, as all Buddhas are said to have first had a son.

## RAIDEN

The god of thunder in the mythology of Japan.

## RAIKO

A figure of Japanese mythology. See YORIMITSU.

## RAMA

Also known as Ramachandra. In the mythology of India, an incarnation of the god VISHNU as a prince, the hero of the epic work the *Ramayana*. Exiled to the forest with his wife SITA and brother Lakshmana, he fought against the powers of darkness in the form of a demon king, RAVANA, who was preserved from destruction by gods and demons, but not by men. Thus the god in human form was able to defeat him. He is much aided in his campaign by the monkey-god HANUMAN, together with a monkey-army, and the final contest was attended by the host of gods. Rama then reigned as a king on earth, before returning to heaven to be reunited with his divinity. *Ramayana*

## RAMACHANDRA

A figure of the mythology of India. See RAMA.

## RAN

In Scandinavian myth she is married to AEGIR, the god of the sea. She catches seafarers in her net, and welcomes them, particularly if they come with gold.

## RANGI

Or Raki, Langi. A primal being in the mythology of the Maoris, the Sky Father who was the co-parent, along with PAPA, the earth as mother, of the first race of gods. Rangi and Papa coupled in blissful

*A seated falcon-headed figure of the Egyptian god Ra. He holds a plume and is crowned with a solar disc. 26th Dynasty.*

*The marriage procession of the Hindu god Rama, illustrated in a leaf of a 17th-century manuscript of the* Ramayana, *the epic work that gives an account of the heroic life of this incarnation of Vishnu.*

union until they were forced apart by their offspring. See TANE. Thereafter Rangi's tears of sadness at this separation fall to earth in the form of rain. In some parts of Polynesia the sky element in this story is known by the name Atea or Vatea.

### RASNU
In Pahlavi (Middle Persian) Rasn. One of the judges of the souls of the dead, in the Zoroastrian religion of Iran.

### RAT
An Egyptian goddess. In some variants of the tradition, she is the spouse of RA.

### RATA
The hero of stories told in many parts of Polynesia, in which he occurs as a forceful and spirited character whose main deed is a voyage of adventure in search of his mistreated parents.

### RATI
In the mythology of India, the wife of KAMA, and hence a goddess of love.

### RATI-MBATI-NDUA
In the mythology of Fiji, the god of the underworld and the devourer of the dead, whom he consumes with the aid of his single tooth. He has wings in place of arms, which enable him to fly.

### RATNASAMBHAVA
In Tibetan Buddhism an earlier group of three Buddhas (SAKYAMUNI, AMITABHA and AKSHOBYA) developed into a major cult of five by the addition of Ratnasamhava and AMOGHASIDDHI. The name means 'Jewel-Born'.

### RATRI
In the mythology of India, the goddess of the night, and thus giver of rest and recuperation, the sister of USHAS, the dawn.

### RAVANA
In the myths of India, a demon king, the ruler of Sri Lanka, said to have ten heads and to be indestructible. He formed the reason for the god VISHNU's incarnation as RAMA.                    *Ramayana*

*Romulus and Remus, the twin sons of Mars and founders of Rome, being suckled by a she-wolf. Relief carving, 2nd century AD.*

### REBECCA

Or Rebehkah. Wife of ISAAC, in the Hebrew traditions preserved in the Old Testament. A woman of Mesopotamia, the country of Isaac's father ABRAHAM, she was fetched from there with God's help by Abraham's servant. Although at first barren, when Isaac appealed to God she gave birth to twin sons, the rivals ESAU and JACOB.

*Genesis*

### REGIN

A figure of Scandinavian myth, in which he occurs as the son of HREIDMAR and the brother of FAFNIR who became a dragon. Together with Fafnir he killed his father for the ransom paid by ODIN for the accidental death of their other brother which included the magic but ill-omened ring. See ANDVARI, SIGURD. He helped Sigurd defeat the dragon, but was killed by him when suspected of betrayal.

SNORRI STURLUSON: *Prose Edda*

### REMUS

In Roman tradition, the twin brother of ROMULUS, who killed him in a quarrel.

### RENENET

Also Renenutet. A minor Egyptian goddess connected with nursing motherhood, sometimes depicted as a woman with a cobra's head.

### REUBEN

In the Hebrew traditional history as conveyed by the Old Testament, he was the eldest son of JACOB by his wife LEAH. He took the side of JOSEPH when his brothers planned to kill him, but was outwitted by them and Joseph was sold into captivity.

*Genesis*

### RHADAMANTYS

Also Rhadamanthys, Rhadamanthus. A figure of Greek myth, in which he is the brother of MINOS of Crete, son of ZEUS and EUROPA. He is known mainly as a legislator and judge, briefly mentioned by Homer as ruling over the Elysian fields, a form of paradise.

### RHEA

Mother and wife of the early gods of Greece. The daughter of URANUS, she married her brother CRONUS, and in order to avoid his habit of eating his children gave birth to ZEUS in secret in a cave in Crete. Worshipped in an early mother-goddess cult, she belongs to a primitive stage of myth.

### RHIANNON

One of the major figures of Celtic British myth, and probably one of the principal deities of the Celts, she is identified by her attributes and the episodes of her story with the continental horse-goddess EPONA, which is likely to be a title meaning 'the divine horse'. Rhiannon's name itself bears similar status, since it comes from the British form Rigantona, meaning 'Great Queen'. In the story Rhiannon appears first riding a horse, then gives birth to a child at the same time as a foal is born, the two being stolen together and later rediscovered together. She is rescued from the punishment for this loss (which further reinforces the connection with horses) by the man who has found the colt and child, whose name is TEYRNON, which significantly comes from the word meaning 'Great King'. These scraps of evidence clearly point to a background of some importance.

## RIND

In Scandinavian mythology, she was a princess wooed against her will by ODIN in order to fulfil a prophecy that he must father another son to take revenge for the death of BALDER. See VALI.

## ROMULUS

In Roman tradition, the legendary founder of Rome. Together with his brother REMUS he was the twin son of MARS, who lay with the Vestal, Rhea Silvia. The twins were to be drowned in the Tiber, but were cast ashore and discovered by a she-wolf, which reared them. The brothers set out later to found a city on the Tiber, but disagreed over its site and name. The disagreement became violent and Remus was killed.

## RONGO

Or Rongo-ma-tane, also known in some places as Lono. The god of peace in the Maori pantheon, one of the sons of RANGI and PAPA, the primal sky and earth, and consequently one of the family of chief gods in Maori belief. He joined with TANE and his other brothers in their plan to separate their previously coupled parents, in the great story of origins. His emblem is the sweet-potato, and he is thus the god of cultivated foods, especially root crops.

## RUDRA

A god of storms in the mythology of India, and embodiment of the ferocity and the instability of natural forces. Said to be the product of BRAHMA's anger, he was the father of the MARUTS, who are also sometimes known by his name. His nature is utterly ambivalent, since he is both the bringer of disease and danger, and also the healer and appeaser. As a god also of cattle and nature his qualities merge with those of SHIVA, and both partake of the character of an older deity, the Lord of the Beasts.

*Rig Veda*

## RUSALKI

Water nymphs, in Russian and Slavonic tradition, thought to be the form taken by drowned girls. They lived in the great rivers and took on various shapes, sometimes that of seductive beauties who lured people with their songs. In some areas they migrated seasonally from the water to the trees for the summer, and back to the rivers in the autumn.

## RUSTEM

Or Rustan. A popular figure of the poetic tradition of ancient Persia, now Iran. A son of a prince, and himself the founder of a dynasty, he appears as the heroic fighter against his country's enemies and the demonic forces of evil, his most notable exploit being the slaying of the great White Dragon or Demon. Another tale, made famous by the nineteenth-century English poet Matthew Arnold, tells of his battle with his own son Sohrab.

## RUTH

In the Hebrew material collected in the books of the Old Testament, she was a widow of Moab. Ruth accompanied her mother-in-law back to the land of Judah, where she met a wealthy man, BOAZ, who eventually married her. They were the ancestors of DAVID.

*Ruth*

## RYUJIN

In Japanese myth, a sea-god, seen as being responsible for the tides and rough waters,

# S

## SAMSON

Hero of the Hebrews (according to their traditional history as recorded in the Old Testament) during a period of their domination by the Philistines. He had superhuman strength, and caused great damage to the oppressors of his people, on one occasion using as a weapon the jawbone of an ass. He remained too powerful to be restrained until he was enticed to reveal his secret by DELILAH, a woman with whom he was in love. His supernatural strength depended on his never having his hair cut, in accordance with the practice of a cult to which he belonged, that of the Nazarites. With this information Delilah is able to betray him, with the result that God's grace leaves him and his enemies are able to imprison and blind him. God however restores his strength in the end, and he brings down the temple in which many of the Philistines are gathered to make sacrifice to their god DAGON for delivering Samson into their hands. In destroying the temple, he dies, but succeeds in killing more Philistines than throughout his whole life.          *Judges*

## SAMUEL

A prophet and leader of the Israelites at a time of war against the Philistines (as recorded in the traditional Hebrew history given in the Old Testament), he is chosen by God, with whom he communes, to be his intermediary with his people. He also wields considerable political power, and is entrusted with the choosing of the kings of Israel. See SAUL, DAVID.          *1 Samuel*

## SANJAYA

Charioteer to DHRITARASHTRA, in the mythology of India, and one of the participants in the *Bhagavad-Gita*, a work expressing the thoughts of KRISHNA.

## SAOSYANT

Or Saoshyans. In the Zoroastrian religion of Iran, the final saviour (which is the meaning of the name) who will be born of a virgin impregnated by the preserved seed of ZARATHUSHTRA while she is bathing in a lake. He will come to raise the dead to life and to preside in judgement at the final transformation of the world.

The Old Testament hero Samson, combatting a lion. Hispano-Moresque Haggadah, c. 1300.

## SARAH

Earlier Sarai. Wife of ABRAHAM, in the traditional early history of the Hebrew people as recorded in the Old Testament. By God's intervention her previous barrenness was overcome when she was ninety years old, and she gave birth to ISAAC.          *Genesis*

## SARANYU

The wife of SURYA, the sun-god, of the mythology of India, and in developed versions of her myth the mother by him of YAMA (otherwise said to be her son by VIVASVAT, another aspect of the sun-god). She is remarkable for having replaced herself, unknown to her husband, by an identical substitute.

**SARASVATI**

Also known as Vach. Goddess of speech, art and learning, in the mythology of India, a beautiful woman, worshipped by those involved in education. She is sometimes said to be the wife of VISHNU, and thought of as a temperamental goddess of whom the myths tell mostly misogynist tales.

**SARPEDON**

A figure of Greek mythology, who along with MINOS and RHADAMANTYS was one of the three sons whom EUROPA bore to ZEUS.

**SATAN**

In the Hebrew tradition recorded in the Old Testament the name occurs only three times. Although it came to denote the personification of the forces of evil in its later development, as it occurs in early texts this identification is not so clear. Satan is present among the sons of God, and therefore implicitly one of them, and he deals directly with God. His acts are challenging rather than hostile, his position being that of a tester of the righteous. The name means 'adversary'.

*Zechariah, Job*

**SATI**

In the mythology of India, the wife of SHIVA, the ideal of matrimonial loyalty. She died for his sake by setting fire to herself, and thus forms a precedent for the Hindu practice of *suttee*, or self-destruction by fire.

**SATIS**

An Egyptian fertility goddess, local to the upper Nile.

**SATURN**

A Roman god identified with the Greek CRONUS, but previously an independent Italian god, with, like many early gods of Rome, strong agricultural and rural associations. He was supposed in legend to have been a king of Rome in the golden age. In memory of this, and of his connection with the plentiful production of food and wine, his midwinter festival

*A renaissance relief statue of the ancient Roman agricultural divinity Saturn, who was honoured in mid-winter with a week-long festival that culminated with prodigious feasting. From the Tempio Malatestiano, Rimini.*

became a week-long feast, the Saturnalia, the favourite holiday of the Romans.

**SAUL**

The first king of the Israelites, according to the traditional early history of the Hebrews contained in the books of the Old Testament. Chosen by the prophet SAMUEL on the instructions of God when the people demanded a king, he led his people in campaigns against the Philistines. He several times displeased God by his failure to obey God's word, yet he remained king and contributed to Hebrew history by fostering the rise of his eventual successor DAVID, with whom however he maintained a constantly ambivalent and often strangely bitter relationship. His son JONATHAN became David's close friend and companion. A man of curiously unstable temperament, his fortunes and his merit fluctuate radically throughout his story, and he comes over on the whole as a tragic case of a man ill-fitted to the demands of his position as king of the Israelites.

*1 Samuel*

*Sedna, the fearsome goddess of the sea and the animals of the sea, was propitiated by the Eskimos in shamanic ceremonies in which masks, such as this one from south-east Alaska, were worn.*

### SAVITRI

In the mythology of India, the god of the rising and of the setting sun, known as the 'impeller' from his command of the activities of men and creatures, a benevolent deity bringing order and peace.                    *Rig Veda*

### SCYLLA

In Greek myth, the name of a monster identified with the navigational hazard of a perilous rock, negotiated by ODYSSEUS on his voyage, the counterpart to the whirlpool CHARYBDIS.

### SEBEK

A crocodile god of the ancient Egyptians, the god of lakes and rivers. In the complicated pharaonic cult system he became associated with the sun, and hence with RA and AMON. There is also a connection with the god SET, who at times took the form of a crocodile.

### SEDNA

One of the few individualized spirits believed in by the Eskimo of North America. She is visualized as an old woman who lives under the sea, a universal mother-figure who rules the lives of her progeny, the fish and aquatic animals, and hence is closely related to the well-being and even survival of the Eskimo, to whom however she often appears as hostile. Different stories are told regarding her origin, but it is agreed that she once lived on earth and was either abducted by a sea-spirit or abandoned by her parents, who grew fearful at signs of her unearthly nature.

### SEHEM

One of the gods in Egyptian belief who represented the influences necessary to bring about the creation of the world, the name in this case signifying energy.

### SEKER

An Egyptian god. Represented as a hawk, he was a god connected with the dead, one of the guardians of the otherworld.

### SEKHMET

A lion-headed goddess in the mythologyical system of the ancient Egyptians, the wife of PTAH and along with their son NEFERTUM an element in the trinity worshipped at Memphis. She is the centre of a myth describing the near-destruction of mankind, who had displeased the gods. In this she was acting in her capacity of agent of RA, her father, and along with the goddess HATHOR she was sometimes known as the Eye of Ra. The two goddesses merge at times and the chastisement of mankind is attributed to Hathor taking the form of Sekhmet. The goddess is usually shown as bearing the sun-disc on her head.

### SELA

The first woman, in the cosmogony of the people of Kenya in Africa. See MWAMBU.

### SEMELE

In Greek mythology she was a human (and therefore mortal) wife of ZEUS, and mother by him of DIONYSUS, whom Zeus snatched from her womb before birth, having struck her as lightning in response to her foolish request to see him in his true form.

### SENNACHERIB

A king of Assyria, according to the Hebrew tradition recorded in the Old Testament. He was noted for his siege of Jerusalem which was concluded by the intervention of God, whose power destroyed the bulk of Sennacherib's army. The character was based on a historical king of Assyria who rebuilt the Assyrian capital of Nineveh, fought numerous campaigns including one in Palestine, and died in 681 BC.     *2 Kings*

### SERAPHIM

In the Hebrew tradition recorded in the Old Testament, an order of angels, their function being that of attendants at the throne of God.     *Isaiah*

### SERAPIS

An Egyptian deity. Originally another name for APIS – from the amalgamation of that

god with OSIRIS – he became a state god in his own right at a late stage of Egyptian religion.

### SESHAT

Goddess of literature, in the Egyptian pantheon, said to be the sister and the wife of THOTH.

### SET

An Egyptian deity, the brother of OSIRIS and ISIS. He represented the evil force in the Egyptian pantheon, and in contrast to Osiris' association with crops and fertility symbolizes the counterpart element for the Egyptians, the aridity and sterility of the desert. His tale is one of rivalry and jealousy, and with these motives he destroyed his brother Osiris (compare ABEL, CAIN). In one developed form of the myth, he tricked him into lying in a lead-weighted chest, which he then nailed shut and threw into the Nile. See OSIRIS, ISIS. The conflict arose when their father GEB partitioned Egypt between them, which did not satisfy Set, who wanted the whole – indicating a territorial rivalry between religions. Set was an early god, and the myth suggests that his cult was once widespread but became confined by the expansion of other religions to a base in Upper Egypt. The sequel to the story shows him in conflict with HORUS, Osiris' son, competing with him for the succession. Set had a positive aspect as defender of RA against the serpent APEP.

## SHADRACH

Formerly called Hananiah. In a story included in the traditional Hebrew material of the Old Testament, one of the three companions who were subjected to the ordeal of the 'fiery furnace'. See ABEDNEGO, MESHACH. *Daniel*

## SHAI

In Egyptian belief, the personal spirit of destiny, conjoined with each individual from birth and responsible for deciding on the person's good fortune, length of life, and form of death. This force of destiny was also responsible for presenting the case for the dead person at the judgement of OSIRIS, and accompanying the soul to its final destination in another world.

## SHAKURU

The name of the sun for the Pawnee Indians of North America, to whom he was a great and powerful god. His importance is celebrated in the annual 'sun dance', a focal point of the tribal year.

## SHAKYAMUNI

A Tibetan Buddhist figure, the Buddha who came to teach the doctrine to the present world-age and to convert people to the Way, and for all Buddhists the tribal name of the historical Buddha known as 'the sage of the Shakyas'. He is worshipped as a central figure in the Tibetan Buddhist religion, and his shrine at Lhasa bears high religious status. He merges in character with various other Buddha figures, worshipped together as a group of five. See VAIROCANA, AMITABHA, AKSHOBYA, AMOGHASIDDHI, and RATNASAMBHAVA.

## SHAMASH

The Mesopotamian god of the sun, a benevolent figure of order and justice, and a great all-knowing judge, appealed to as protector of mankind. He is also the controller of oracles. *Epic of Gilgamesh*

## SHANG

Eponym of an early Chinese dynasty, one of the primal stages of the development of Chinese civilization known as the 'Three Dynasties'. He was said to have been born at the instruction of Heaven, TIAN, by the agency of a black bird. Later the name Shang was changed to Yin at the orders of the Emperor Pangeng. The dynasty lasted for 644 years, and although it has many legendary and mythic qualities archaeology has revealed it to have had a historical basis.

*Among the Indians of the American plains the 'dance of the sun', in honour of Shakuru, was the most important ceremony of the year. The rituals, as depicted in this painting by Frederic Remington, included self-mutilation by warriors in fulfilment of vows.*

## SHANG DI

In the ancient Chinese religion, he was a pre-existent and supreme sky-god, later to be known as TIAN, meaning literally 'sky', and also sometimes known simply as 'Di'. He was the supreme deity of the Shang dynasty's religious system. A remote figure, he was not approached directly, but rather through the intermediaries of the souls of ancestors.

## SHANGO

Sometimes spelt Sango. A god of storms, in the beliefs of the Yoruba people of Nigeria in West Africa, once said to have been a king of the Yorubas. Forced into exile by his tyranny, the story tells that he hanged himself and rose to the sky. He is depicted as bearing a double-bladed axe, an implement connected in this and other myths with thunder, comparable to the hammer of the Scandinavian god THOR. Shango's cult was established at Koso where the anger he expresses in the thunderstorm was placated by the ministrations of a priesthood. A modern statue of Shango stands outside the Electricity Centre of Nigeria, in Lagos.

## SHASHTI

In the mythology of India, a goddess connected with cats, the protector of children and of women in time of childbirth.

## SHELARDI

The moon-god, in the pantheon of the people of the kingdom of Urartu, a part of Armenia now in Turkey.

## SHEM

Son of NOAH, in the traditional early history of the Hebrews as recorded in the Old Testament. The 'sons of Shem' are the Semitic peoples.                    *Genesis*

## SHENNONG

Or Shen-nung, in the older spelling. In Chinese mythical history, he was one of the 'three sovereigns' who presided over the early stages of the development of Chinese

*The Hindu god Shiva is frequently represented in the form of Nataraja, the Lord of the Dance, as in this bronze statue. His dancing, which brought chaos to the universe, has been postponed until Doomsday, when it will be resumed as the dance of universal death.*

civilization. He is portrayed as having an ox's head, and was said to be the inventor of agriculture and instructor to mankind of its methods. Possibly originally a fire-god, the spirit of the brush-fire used in clearing land for cultivation, he certainly has roots deeper than those of his quasi-historical role.

## SHIVA

Or Siva. An early Hindu god, in the tradition of India second in importance only to VISHNU, typically shown in the cross-legged position associated with yoga. Along with Vishnu and BRAHMA he forms a trinity of major deities. Originally based on a Vedic storm god, known as RUDRA, he retained a fierce aspect, connections with death and battle, and with the destructive power of time. He supports the world by the power of meditation, and is the paradigm of the yoga-practising ascetic. One of his titles is *Pasupati*, Lord of the Beasts, another characteristic inherited from Rudra, who was also a god of cattle. He is shown as a man with three eyes and four arms, and his extra eye was said to have destructive power. His particular symbol is the *lingam*, a short round pillar of clearly phallic character, expressing a creative function as a fertility deity, and appropriate to his position as a rival to Brahma in supremacy among the gods. He is often worshipped in the form of the *lingam* itself.

### SHIVINI

The name of the sun-god in the mythology of the people of Urartu, a kingdom of the Armenians.

### SHOULAO

The Chinese god of longevity, a figure always portrayed as having a large bald head and a long beard, and bearing the life-symbol in the form of a peach. He decides when each person will die, having fixed the moment at the time of birth, but even so he is capable of altering this destiny if sufficiently impressed by attention or supplication.

### SHU

In the Chinese cosmogony, the southern counterpart of the northern emperor HU.

### SHU

In Egyptian mythology, the son of ATUM and brother of TEFNUT, with whom he formed a primordial pair. He was god of the air, and out of the original integration of earth and sky (represented by his children GEB and NUT) he formed the discrete elements of the world, by means of interposing himself between them.

### SHUKALLETUDA

A gardener, in a story in the mythology of ancient Mesopotamia, visited by the goddess INANNA, the Sumerian goddess of love and fertility, with whom he made love while she was asleep.

### SIA

One of the figures present on board the boat of the sun, in the religious symbolism of the ancient Egyptians. Sia is a primal force, originally among the influences active in the creation of the world, the name signifying intelligent thought. From that connection the figure also gained a moral function.

*Shoulao, the Taoist god of longevity, is characteristically depicted holding a peach, a symbol of life and sexuality. Soapstone carving of the Ching Dynasty, late 18th century.*

## SIDDHARTHA

The Buddha, the founder of the Buddhist religion of India. The son of an aristocratic family named Gautama, he is in part a historical character born in Nepal about 565 BC, also often known by the surname Gautama. He lived in idle luxury until he was twenty-nine years old, married and with a son, and on a day of destiny set out on his great quest for understanding. He left his wife, son and family, and went off alone except for his charioteer CHANDAKA. After a period of education, which did not bring him the enlightenment he sought, he practised austerity and withdrawal for a time, also without success. Eventually he settled in meditation under a Bo-Tree (or 'bodhi' tree, from the word for enlightenment). He there achieved *nirvana*, release from the material self, and fulfilled his destiny by becoming the supreme Buddha, or enlightened-one. Thereafter he spent his life in the preaching of the doctrine of Dharma, the Middle Way between materialism and asceticism which, by means of right-doing without sensory indulgence, may lead to deliverance from the suffering involved in imprisonment within the cycles of illusory material self-consciousness. He was opposed by his old rival DEVADATTA and by the tempter and evil spirit MARA. In the end he renounced earthly existence and entered the realm of pure Nirvana. Much portrayed in Indian and other Buddhist art, particularly in the form of statues, he is conventionally shown seated cross-legged in the 'lotus' position. See MAHAMAYA.

## SIDURI

In Mesopotamian mythology, the goddess who makes wine and beer for the gods. She lives beside the sea, where she is visited by GILGAMESH on his quest, and gives him instructions on how to cross the waters of death, although first trying to dissuade him from his quest. Her advice, when she gives it, is to seek URSHANABI, the ferryman, who alone can guide the hero on this most difficult voyage.

*Epic of Gilgamesh*

## SIEGFRIED

The German form of the Scandinavian hero SIGURD. He stole the NIBELUNG treasure from the dwarf ALBERICH, only to be killed in due course by an envious Dane, who pierced him between the shoulder blades, his only vulnerable spot. This version of the story (compare SIGURD) forms the first part of Wagner's great cycle of operas, based on the *Nibelungenlied*.

## SIF

THOR's wife, in the system of beliefs of pre-Christian Scandinavia. The story tells how she had wonderful golden hair which LOKI cut off as a joke, but in the face of Thor's anger he had new hair made for her by the dwarfs out of gold.

SNORRI STURLUSON: *Prose Edda*

## SIGURD

A major Scandinavian hero, known as Sigurd the Volsung, from his grandfather who gave the family its name. He is the hero of the Scandinavian version of the Ring Cycle, a less well-known but fuller

*Prince Siddharta Gautama, the founder of Buddhism, was born into a wealthy family in what is now Nepal. Episodes from his early life are frequently depicted in Buddhist art. Prince Siddharta is shown here riding to school in a chariot drawn by two rams. Schist relief carving in Romano-Buddhist style, 2nd to 4th century AD.*

story than that made famous in the German form by Wagner. The dwarfs possessed a great hoard of treasure, which included a small but magic ring. It had the property of increasing its owner's wealth, and when LOKI requisitioned the gold to pay a ransom to HREIDMAR for the death of his son, the dwarf ANDVARI attempted to keep back the ring, hoping thereby to renew his riches. Loki extorted it from him, but he sent it with a curse that it would destroy everyone who owned it. It then proved the downfall first of Hreidmar then of his son FAFNIR and finally of Sigurd himself.

SNORRI STURLUSON: *Prose Edda*

### SIGYN

Or Sigryn. LOKI's wife, in Scandinavian mythology. In spite of his consistently disruptive activities she remained loyal to him. Even in his final punishment, in which a snake drops poison onto his face, she sits until doomsday catching it in a bowl before it strikes him; only when the bowl becomes full and she has to empty it does Loki shudder in torment, which causes the earth to quake.

SNORRI STURLUSON: *Prose Edda*

### SILENUS

In the myths of Greece, the name of one of the satyrs, a debauched class of being associated with the revelries of DIONYSUS.

### SILVANUS

An early Roman deity, later a Romano-Celtic god of occupied Gaul, he was chiefly the god of the forests (the name coming from *silva*, meaning 'wood' or 'forest'). He was also the special deity of agriculture, particularly that associated with woodland clearing, and of all field boundaries. He is said to be in love with POMONA and is generally depicted as a cheerful old man with a cypress trunk and accompanied by a dog. He is often associated with PAN.

*An impression from an intaglio showing a north-British deity equated with the Roman god Silvanus, who is associated with woods, fields and flocks.*

### SIMARGL

A winged monster in Slavonic mythology, the guardian of the tree which produces all seeds of plants.

### SIMEON

In the Hebrew tradition contained in the Old Testament, one of the sons of JACOB by his wife LEAH. He remained as a hostage in Egypt when JOSEPH insisted that the brothers return with their youngest brother BENJAMIN. Along with Jacob's other sons he is regarded as the founder of one of the tribes of Israel.

*Genesis*

### SIN

The moon-god, father of SHAMASH, the sun, and the main celestial being in the mythology of ancient Mesopotamia. He was the son of ENLIL and NINLIL, and also the father of the goddess ISHTAR.

### SIRENS

A group of malign women in Greek myth who lured passing seafarers to their destruction by their beautiful songs, in which they appear to have offered their victims whatever it was that they individually wanted – in ODYSSEUS' case knowledge of all things. He outwitted them by making his seamen tie him to the mast and plug their ears, thus becoming the only man to have heard their songs and lived.

HOMER: *Odyssey*

## SISYPHUS

He occurs in Greek myth as an early king of Corinth, whose life was so wicked that he was condemned to roll the burden of a huge stone up a slope, only to find each time that just as it neared the top his strength failed and it rolled back down.

## SITA

The wife of RAMA, in the mythology of India. Like him she was an incarnation of a divinity, being really LAKSHMI, his heavenly wife in his identity of VISHNU. She was abducted by his arch-enemy RAVANA, recovered at his defeat by Rama, but for a time exiled in disgrace when suspected of infidelity. Her death led to Rama's decision to return to the gods.

*Ramayana*

## SIVA

A figure of the Hindu mythology of India, more phonetically spelt in the Sanskrit form of SHIVA.

## SKADI

See NJORD. In Scandinavian mythology she was the daughter of a giant, and after her separation from her husband is described as hunting in the mountains on skis, a northern ARTEMIS.

SNORRI STURLUSON: *Prose Edda*

## SKANDA

A figure of the myths of India. See KARTTIKEYA.

## SKRYMIR

The name taken by a giant encountered by THOR in an episode in Scandinavian mythology. In the story Thor took his glove to be a great hall and, with his two companions, spent the night in the thumb. On waking they find Skrymir asleep and Thor strikes him three mighty blows with his hammer. The giant pretends to think them, in turn, a leaf, an acorn, and the droppings of a bird. Eventually Skrymir reveals that Thor and his companions have been deluded by a spell.

SNORRI STURLUSON: *Prose Edda*

*In Scandinavian mythology Odin rode the fabulous horse Sleipnir, an eight-footed beast that travelled over water as easily as it did over land. From a mid-18th century illustrated manuscript of the* Prose Edda.

## SLEIPNIR

The name of ODIN's horse, in Scandinavian mythology, meaning literally 'slippery'. Eight-footed, it carried him over the waves of the sea as if they were dry land (compare Irish MANANNAN) and was able to bear its master to the land of the dead.

SNORRI STURLUSON: *Prose Edda*

## SOLOMON

In the traditional history of the Hebrews, as conveyed by the Old Testament, the son of DAVID and BATHSHEBA, and his successor as king of the Israelites. He completed the construction of Jerusalem begun by his father. Noted for his great wisdom and for building the Temple at Jerusalem, he nevertheless lapsed into heresy by worshipping idols, a result of his amorous affairs with foreign women. The Book of Proverbs was said to be written by him.

*1 Kings*

## SOMA

God of the drink of the same name, a feature of the mythology of India, thought of partly as the real intoxicating fluid produced from a plant, and also partly as a mystical element, a type of life force. The use of this liquor in rites and sacrifices was an ancient Aryan custom, which plays an important part in the related religion of Zoroastrianism. See HAOMA. As a god, Soma's role was similar to and related to that of INDRA, whom he sustains. Symbolically he is the sustaining, providing source of water, which fertilizes as rain, and through these connections he has associations with the regulating moon, so often seen as a source of fertility.

*Rig Veda*

## SPENTA MAINYU
One of the AMESHA SPENTAS, spiritual beings occurring in the Zoroastrian religion of Iran, in this case representing the spirit of God, a holy spirit active in the world.

## SPHINX
The Sphinx, a hybrid monster, having a woman's head on an animal's body, and in some representations wings as well, occurs in the mythology of the Greeks. It terrorized Thebes by asking all visitors a riddle, and eating those who failed to answer, until it was outwitted by OEDIPUS.

## STRIBOG
The Slavonic wind-god, Stribozh in Ukrainian, a figure of Iranian origin. The winds are thought to be his children.

## SUDDHODHANA
In the mythological background to the Buddhist religion of India, he was the father of the Buddha, a king of the Sakya clan.

## SUGRIVA
In the mythology of India, the king of the monkeys, a god and the son of SURYA. He and his monkey army assisted RAMA in his war against his enemy RAVANA.

## SUKU-NA-BIKONA
A dwarf who assisted the hero O-KUNI-NUSHI in stories of the mythology of Japan. Seen as a benevolent deity, he had knowledge of healing and of cultivation.

## SURYA
God of the sun, in the mythological system of India, a son of DYAUS, along with INDRA and AGNI, and thus one of the central group of gods, forming a trinity with his two brothers. Later he came to be attributed different parentages and characteristics. His symbol was the ancient Aryan form now known as the swastika, widely used throughout the ancient world as a sun-symbol, and hence an emblem of energy or provision.

## SUSANO
Or Susano-wo. God of storms in the mythology of Japan, he was the child of IZANAGI, and from the start formed a source of discord and destruction. He also took part in the formation of the land of Japan and its surroundings. His activities largely concern his discordant relationship with his sister AMATERASU. Originally his realm was to be the sea, but his disruptive nature earned him banishment to the underworld, and although reprieved for a

*A miniature illustrating Surya, the Hindu sun god, in a chariot drawn by a seven-headed horse. Tempera painting from Bundi, c. 1770.*

time and allowed to live in heaven, his troublesome ways led to his final expulsion to the province of Izumo, on earth. In one of his main stories he rescued a goddess from a dragon.

## SUSERI-BIME

Daughter of the great Japanese storm-god SUSANO, she fell in love with OKUNI-NUSHI and became his wife.

## SUTTUNG

A giant in Scandinavian myth who came into possession of the mead of inspiration and knowledge by taking it from the dwarfs who made it (see KVASIR) as payment for the death of his parents at their hands. He hid it inside a mountain, into which ODIN crawled in the form of a snake and drank up all the mead. Odin then became an eagle and flew back to the gods' fortress Asgard, where he spat it into the gods' crocks. As a result it is they who now control the gift of poetry.

SNORRI STURLUSON: *Prose Edda*

## SVANTOVIT

A god of the Slavonic people of the Baltic area, his main connection being with war. He was worshipped before battle, in this capacity, and attended by warriors. However he was at the same time viewed as a supreme god, and the father of the other deities. There was a great statue of him at his shrine at Arcona which was four-headed, each head facing one of the four quarters. The statue held a horn containing wine, the quantity of which was supposed to indicate the state of plenty or scarcity in the coming year.

## SVAROGU

Or Svarog. The god of the bright sky, in Slavonic mythology, and the father of the sun, from whom the great powers of sunlight and fire are derived. He is thus a father-figure among the deities, and seen as having withdrawn to allow his power to continue through his children, sun and fire. The latter was thought to have come to earth in the first place as lightning.

*A 20th-century representation by I. Bilibine of Slav warriors worshipping the four-headed figure of the powerful god of battle Svantovit.*

**TA'AROA**

In the belief of the people of Tahiti, a self-created original spirit who lived alone in a cosmic egg until he decided to bring about external creation. He did this by bringing into being first the gods and then all the plants and vegetation.

**TAIKOMOL**

A figure occurring in the creation stories of the Yuki and the Huchnon Indians of western North America. He is the constructive creator and initiator, the figure of a lone traveller who first established the land. In many related stories he is the positive half of the opposing primal pair of creators, who is occasionally hampered by his destructive or incompetent assistant. This antithetical pair occurs in many North American mythologies. Similarly in Taikomol's independent creation all did not go smoothly to begin with, and he was obliged to make several successive attempts at creating the world, which even in its finished form is sometimes subject to earthquakes. He made men out of sticks, and at first able to be resurrected after death, but when this proved unsatisfactory (owing to the smell of the decaying resurrected corpse) he was obliged to let men become mortal. He himself eventually went to heaven on a rainbow, and lives there still.

**TAJIKA-NO-MIKOTO**

A god who represents physical strength, occurring in the mythological tradition of Japan.

**TALIESIN**

One of the major characters of Celtic British myth, the son of the witch-goddess CERIDWEN. A powerful figure of wisdom, enchantment and prophecy, based on a possibly factual sixth-century poet of that name but developed in the stories as one of several wizard-figures in native British myth (compare GWYDION, MERLIN). It was Taliesin who foretold the loss of Britain to invaders ('except Wild Wales'), and who freed his patron ELFFIN by casting a spell, in the form of a riddle, over the loquacious bards of King Maelgwn, making them temporarily dumb. See CERIDWEN, GWION, ELFFIN.

**TAMETOMO**

A character of Japanese tradition, best known as being the uncle of YOSHITSUNE. However he was also a hero in his own right and known as a skilful archer.

**TAMMUZ**

A pastoral deity of ancient Mesopotamia, consort of the major goddess ISHTAR (Sumerian INANNA), and a god with general associations with fertility and growth. As the god of the dying and rejuvenating vegetation, he is mourned by Ishtar, and thus becomes the subject of lament by his worshippers. In one story she goes down to the underworld to look for him.                    *Epic of Gilgamesh*

**TANE**

Or Tane-mahuta. The most important figure in the mythology of the Maori, the leading son of RANGI and PAPA, the primeval sky and earth who mated to produce the first divine beings. Tane was the god of forests and trees and the patron of craftsmen. By his counsel the sons of Rangi and Papa set out to separate their parents, whose previous happy conjunction was oppressive to their offspring, in order to bring about the space between the sky and earth in which creatures could subsequently exist. After his brothers had variously failed in their attempts to achieve this, he himself successfully prised them apart, and set up four pillars to maintain this state. Tane later became the creator of mankind, which he achieved by modelling a woman out of red earth and mating with her to produce a daughter, whom he also made his wife. See HINE-AHUONE and HINE-TITAMA. After the feat of separating his parents Tane set the celestial bodies on his father's chest to light the world. As the god of trees he had to be propitiated when any were felled.

## TANGAROA

A chief god of Polynesia, though of lesser status among the Maori of New Zealand. He is the god of the sea, and of fish, one of the sons of RANGI and PAPA, the primeval pair of sky and earth, and so one of the family of first and most prominent gods. Along with his brother TANE he was responsible for populating the world with the beings and other effects which it now has. In New Zealand, though not the supreme deity, he was nevertheless one of the great gods, and among several credited with the responsiblity for creation. In some variants found in Tahiti he was regarded as a deified man. In much of the rest of Polynesia he was the creator god.

## TANO

A figure of the tradition of the Akan people of Ghana in Africa, the god of the river of the same name; he perpetually competes with death for the lives of ailing humans. He was the second son of God (see BIA), and is characterized as disobedient.

## TANTALUS

In Greek mythology, the father of PELOPS and of NIOBE. At one time a friend of the gods, he aroused the anger of ZEUS by presuming to test his omniscience at a banquet by serving his son Pelops as the main course. Zeus punished him for this and other crimes by condemning him to remain consumed by hunger and thirst and nearly within reach of fruit and water. His name gives us our word tantalize.

## TANUKUJEN

The name for God in the Didinga tribe of Sudan in Africa. The name has connections with the word for rain. Compare EN-KAI, OWO.

## TAUERET

An early Egyptian mother-goddess, represented as a hippopotamus, and worshipped in connection with childbirth. Like many Egyptian deities of birth and fertility she became also a goddess of rebirth, and protector of the dead. The name signifies 'the great one'. As a rebirth-deity she supervised the daily renewal of the sun, and came to have close links with RA, being sometimes said to be his daughter.

## TAWARA TODA

A hero of possibly historic origin, occurring in the traditions of Japan. In a main episode of his stories he defeated a monstrous and gigantic centipede, for which he was rewarded by the king of the dragons, whose territory it had been plaguing, by the gift of supernatural objects. Among these was a bag of rice which refilled itself endlessly, for which he is best known.

## TAWESKARE

The malicious member of a pair of creator twins, in the cosmogony of the Iroquois and Huron Indians of North America, who believed that he attempted to undo the good work of his brother Tsentsa, or ISOKEHA, and hence became responsible for the harsh and unpleasant aspects of reality. Compare NAGENATZANI, THOBADESTCHIN.

## TAWHAKI

A heroic mortal who forms the focus of a cycle of stories, told in many parts of Polynesia, in which he is regarded as a figure of exemplary ingenuity, patience, perseverence, and nobility of spirit Although said to be a chieftain and son of humans, he acquired in the tales many of the attributes of divinity. The central theme of the cycle is his rescue of his father, who had been captured by goblins.

## TAWHIRI

Or Tawhiri-matea. One of the family of chief gods in the beliefs of the Maori, who

*The Egyptian goddess Taueret, generally represented as a hippopotamus figure with hanging breasts, was a popular deity venerated in connection with childbirth.*

together with his brother **WHIRO** opposed the wiser brother **TANE** in the story of the latter's plans to divide their parents, **RANGI** and **PAPA**, the sky and the earth, to give space in which life might develop. Tawhiri is the storm god, and is portrayed as being in conflict with his more peaceful brothers. Unlike all the others he chose to remain with his father Rangi, in the sky.

### TEFNUT

In Egyptian cosmogony, the female part of the first divine couple, a goddess created by **RA** along with her consort **SHU**. She shared with other Egyptian divinities the title of Eye of Ra, and connections with his solar functions. Like **SEKHMET** she was depicted as having a lion's head surmounted by the disc of the sun.

### TEIRESIAS

A powerful figure of Greek myth, he was the blind prophet consulted by the people of Thebes in the story of **OEDIPUS**. He had been both a man and a woman and so was able to settle a dispute between **ZEUS** and **HERA** as to which sex gets more pleasure from the act of love. Women, he said, get more pleasure by far, a verdict used by the Greeks to justify the habit (common in the stories of their gods) of male infidelity.

SOPHOCLES: *Oedipus the King*

### TEISHEBA

The god of war and of thunder in the pantheon of the people of the kingdom of Urartu, a part of Armenia now in Turkey.

### TELEMACHUS

In Greek mythology, the son of **ODYSSEUS**, left behind by him when he went to the war. In this situation Telemachus is seen as being vulnerable to the loss of his inheritance if his mother **PENELOPE** married again in the absence of his father.

HOMER; *Odyssey*

### TEMAUKEL

Pre-existent and immaterial supreme deity of the Ona Indians of Tierra del Fuego, in Chile. He upholds the natural and social order and cares for the circumstances of mankind.

### TENGU

Ancient spirits occurring frequently in the Shinto stories of Japan, and still regarded there as being significant. They are visualized as winged and beaked like birds, but wearing cloaks and hats like men and using weapons, and are rural beings particularly connected with trees, being thought of as living in social groups. They are particularly viewed as tricksters, almost demons, but lacking any malicious intent.

### TEPEU

In the beliefs of the Maya Indians of Mexico, one of the two pre-existent 'forefather' gods known as the Creators and Makers, who together created all things that are. See **GUCUMATZ**. *Popol Vub*

### TERPSICHORE

The Muse of Greek mythology whose function was the inspiration of choral singing and dance. See **CALLIOPE**, **CLIO**, **ERATO**.

### TEYRON

A figure of Celtic British mythology. The name probably comes from the British form Tigernonos, meaning 'Great King'. For further details see **RHIANNON**.

*Mabinogion*

### TEZCATLIPOCA

In the beliefs of the Toltec Indians of Mexico, he was a magician, enemy of **QUETZALCOATL**, and part of the cause of that god-king's departure from Tula. He figures in Toltec imagery as a war god, and was said to have been born as a fully-formed warrior. In that capacity he was associated with the northern quarter of the compass. Adopted by the Aztecs as a variant of the sun-god, he became a figure of fear and the object of human sacrifices.

### THEMIS

A Greek goddess. Her name means 'convention' or 'law'. She was one of the early wives of ZEUS and mother of the Fates and the Seasons.                    HESIOD: *Theogony*

### THESEUS

A major figure in Greek mythology, the hero of Attica, very much the representative hero of the city-state of Athens, son of AEGEUS the king but born in his mother's town of Troezen in Argolis. He had a typically precocious career, in his youth removing various dangers in the area. He eventually released his country from the terrible tribute imposed by King MINOS of Crete, in the episode in which he killed the Minotaur. See also ASTERION, ARIADNE. Later in his reign we find him married first to the Amazon ANTIOPE, by whom he had a son HIPPOLYTUS, and then to Minos' second daughter PHAEDRA. See also LYCOMEDES.

### THESPIUS

In Greek mythology he was a king occurring in the story of HERACLES; he had fifty daughters, with all of whom the young hero slept, either on successive nights or in some versions (even more remarkably) on the same night.

### THETIS

A deity of Greek myth, a sea nymph, the mother of the hero ACHILLES. See PELEUS. With characteristic irony the story tells how Thetis, forewarned, tried to prevent Achilles going to the Trojan War, from which he did not return. It was at her wedding that the goddess of discord, ERIS, who was not invited, threw down before the assembled goddesses the golden apple inscribed 'To the fairest', the awarding of which proved to be the initial cause of the Trojan War. Ironically, it was Thetis who was the mother of Achilles, the Greek warrior and hero of that war. See PARIS.

### THISBE

A heroine of Greek mythology. See PYRAMUS. On finding her lover dead she likewise killed herself, in a tale of tragic irony prefiguring that of Romeo and Juliet.
                    OVID: *Metamorphoses*

### THJALFI

In the stories of Scandinavian mythology, he was a farmer who accompanied THOR to Utgard, the land of the giants.
                    SNORRI STURLUSON: *Prose Edda*

### THOBADESTCHIN

A figure occurring in the mythology of the Navajo Indians of North America. See NAGENATZANI. While his brother continued their campaign against destructive monsters he played a more passive role, helping his mother ESTANATLEHI and growing food. The constrasting primal twins occur in more extreme form in Iroquois and Huron myth, where they are named ISOKEHA and TAWISKARE.

### THOR

One of the foremost Scandinavian gods. Second in prominence to ODIN in the northern pantheon, Thor is remarkably highly characterized, seen as blunt, down-

*Theseus, watched by his mother, recovers his mortal father's arms from under a large rock, a deed that qualified him to set off and join his father in Athens and marked the beginning of a career of heroic accomplishments. Terra cotta relief, probably 1st century AD.*

195

RIGHT: *Thor's hammer, representing the thunderbolt and lightning and symbolic of the Scandinavian deity's strength as god of the storm. Viking period.*

*RIGHT: Thor's hammer, representing the thunderbolt and lightning and symbolic of the Scandinavian deity's strength as god of the storm. Viking period.*

BELOW: *Thoth, the Egyptian god of the moon and writing, whose responsibility it was to record the judgment at the weighing of the heart. Bronze statuette of the Ptolemaic period.*

to-earth, unsophisticated, physically mighty but intellectually a little simple. He often emerges as something of a likeable buffoon. It is no accident that his weapon was an enormous stone hammer – there is nothing very subtle about Thor. Apart from these folktale elements, however, his role is a highly significant one. He is the god of thunder. The rumbling noise is his journey across the sky in his great chariot; the flash and crash of the thunderbolt is his famous hammer thrown at an enemy in a fit of temper. Hence the people of the Roman-occupied lands of northern Europe equated Thor with JOVE, and the day of the week called after that Latin god became Thor's-day. The Romans, for their part, compared Thor's hammer with HERCULES' club, and Thor does indeed play the part also of the wandering, giant-slaying hero. In the latter capacity he is always on the move, and if he rested neither the home of the gods, Asgard, nor the human world, Midgard, would be safe from the giants. He also has a long-running battle with the World Serpent, which he twice encounters but which each time eludes him. The third time he grapples with it is on the occasion of Ragnarök, the gods' cataclysm, when he finally kills it but in the process dies himself of the serpent's terrible poison, a fittingly heroic end for the sturdiest, and most popular, of the northern gods.

SNORRI STURLUSON: *Prose Edda*

### THOTH

Or Thot. A major god of Heliopos, in the religious system of the ancient Egyptians whose symbols were the lotus flower and the ibis. He was a god of writing, and the recorder of the gods. His functions were many, including those of moon-god and magician. He officiated at the judgment of the dead, recording the verdict of the scales when the heart (i.e. the intention) of the dead person was weighed against the emblem of MAYET, the principle of justice. On one occasion Thoth recovered the Eye of RA and was rewarded by being given the rule of the night sky. His connections with the moon and with writing made him the

deity of time and of the sciences connected with numbers. He was normally depicted as a baboon, a creature which has the face of a dog.

### THRYM

In the Scandinavian tradition, the name of a giant who acquired and hid the god THOR's great hammer, and in ransom for it demanded FREYJA as his bride. Thor went instead disguised as her, and recovered his hammer.

### THUNUPA

Also known as Tonapa or Toapac. In the mythology of the Incas of Peru, a figure merging with VIRACOCHA, if not the same personage. He was said to be a miracle-working hero described as being of European appearance who once long ago travelled the tribal lands around Lake Titicaca preaching a religion which appeared to the Spanish missionaries to be Christianity.

### THYESTES

In a central saga of Greek mythology, he was the brother and rival of ATREUS, king of Mycenae. Thyestes was in love with his brother's wife and in dispute with him over the kingdom, which they ruled over alternately until ZEUS awarded it to Atreus. The latter invited his brother to a feast, supposedly in token of reconciliation but instead served the flesh of Thyestes' sons – the occasion which gave rise to the curse on the house of Atreus from which his descendants suffered. See AGAMEMNON, ORESTES. The youngest son AEGISTHUS escaped this destruction to feature in the later development of the curse.

## TIAMAT

In the traditional Mesopotamian cosmogony, the female member of the primordial pair. She embodies the element of salt water, which joined with the sweet water, APSU, to produce life.

*Epic of Creation*

## TIAN

Formerly spelt T'ien. Heaven, in the ancient Chinese beliefs; a deity pre-existing the dynastic supreme being DI, or SHANG DI. After the fall of the Shang dynasty Tian was restored as the central figure of worship.

## TIANLONG

In the cosmogony of the ancient Chinese, he is the male member of the primal pair whose coupling gave rise to mankind and to all other things. See DIYA.

## TICCI VIRACOCHA

A name for the creator god of the Incas of Peru; said to mean 'the Unknowable God', it was also the name given to the supreme deity in many parts of the Inca lands.

## TIEHOLTSODI

A water-monster occurring in the myth of the origins of the Navajo people of North America. Since the emergent human beings had stolen his children he caused a great flood, which put the people and creatures of the world in increasing danger, from which they were forced to flee. In due course and after many adventures he was placated by the return of the children.

## TIEN MU

In the mythology of the Chinese, she is the goddess of lightning, which she creates with the aid of reflecting mirrors. See also LEI KUNG.

## TINARAU

A Polynesian sea deity, controller of the fish, who is in some areas viewed as responsible for marine disasters. Stories tell of his courting and marriage to a mortal girl, and of their offspring.

## TIRAWA

Or Tirawa Atius. The supreme power in the beliefs of the Pawnee Indians of North America. They regarded him as the organizer of the world, which he first rid of giants by means of storm and flood, making it suitable to be inhabited by mankind. He also regulated the heavens, which he peopled with gods in the form of the main celestial bodies – the movement of the stars of morning, evening, north and south, being of great significance to the prairie-dwelling Indians.

## TITANS

A group of the older generation of gods of the ancient Greeks, the children of URANUS and GAEA, the main figure among them being CRONUS.

## TIW

Also known as Tiwaz. The Germanic form of the Scandinavian TYR, a war-god. This gives us the name of the day of the week, Tuesday.

*The primeval monster Tiamat and Marduk, the national god of Babylonia, who destroyed her and from her body made the universe. From a bas-relief on the walls of the palace of Assurnasirpal, king of Assyria, about 885-860 BC, discovered at Calah (Nimrud).*

*A 14th-century image of Tlaloc, the rain god of the Toltecs and Aztecs of Mexico. Found in Mixtec territory in the vicinity of Oaxaca.*

### TLALCHITONATIUH

God of the rising sun, in the mythology of the Indians of Mexico.

### TLALOC

For the Toltec and Aztec Indians of Mexico, the rain god, and therefore a deity of great importance and the object of propitiatory worship. He was also associated in more developed Aztec religion with mountains and streams, and in accordance with their custom became the object of a cult involving human sacrifice, in this case of small children.

### TLAZOLTEOTL

A goddess of love, in the traditions of the Aztec Indians; known as the 'dirt goddess', she is responsible mainly for the guilty side of amorous activity.

### TOCAPO VIRACOCHA

A figure in the mythological tradition of the Incas of Peru. See IMAYMANA VIRACOCHA.

### TOHIL

For the Maya Indians of Mexico, a major god who brought fire to the Quiche-Maya. He speaks to his adopted people, instructing them and answering their requests.                    *Popol Vuh*

### TO KABINANA

The sun, in the mythology of Papua New Guinea. The figure is also regarded as the originator of social order. In other areas he is one of a pair of brothers whose exploits include the slaying of monsters and the accidental introduction of human mortality.

### TORE

For the Bambuti tribe of Central Africa, the god who governs death.

### TONATIUH

The sun god of the Toltecs and Aztecs of ancient Mexico, whose name is a title meaning 'Royal Lord'.

### TORNARSUK

Or Torngasoak. A figure occurring in the mythology of the Eskimo of North America. He was a powerful spirit variously viewed by the Eskimo, but recognized by all to be a transcendent force.

### TRIPTOLEMUS

A figure occurring in Greek mythology as the prince of Eleusis at the time of the visit of DEMETER, who taught him the principles of agriculture.

### TRISTAN

A major Celtic British hero, Tristram in Malory. He is the tragic hero of an elopement story, arising from his position as the nephew of King MARK of Cornwall. He fell in love with the daughter of the king of Ireland, ISOUD, whom his uncle, in jealousy, decided to marry himself. Tristan is put in the familiar hero's position of having to choose between the demands of love and duty, but agrees to seek the hand of the lady for his uncle and king. On the return journey to Cornwall however the pair unwittingly drink a love potion intended to support the forthcoming marriage, and are bound in unending and invincible love. This aggravates the existing conflict of duties, and adds to it the theme of the lovers' powerlessness against the magic. Tristan is possibly based on a historical figure.     MALORY: *Morte d'Arthur*

**TSENTSA**

See IOSKEHA, another name by which he is known, and a figure occurring in the tradition of the North American Huron Indians. See also TAWESKARE, his more malevolent brother.

**TSUI 'GOAB**

A deity of the beliefs of the Hottentots of Africa, a rain god, skilled in magic, creator of the first couple. He died and was reborn like the returning rain, and was much worshipped for providing showers. This function gave him considerable status among the gods, and he is also revered as an ancestor and father figure. His great enemy is a spirit named Gaunab who is regarded as the creator of the rainbow.

**TSUKUYOMI**

Or Tsuki-Yomi. The Japanese god of the moon, himself the child of the creator god IZANAGI, being said to have been born from his right eye. Very few mythologies see the moon as male, the sun as female (see AMATERASU). Compare ANINGAN.

**TU**

Or Tu-matauenga. The Maori god of war, one of the sons of RANGI and PAPA, the primeval pair of sky and earth, and so one of the family of chief gods. In the story of the separation of their previously coupled parents, he was persuaded by the wise brother TANE to avoid violence, and joined Tane in his plan to bring about the division. Tu is the god of war throughout the whole of Polynesia, and as war-god he is seen also as the hunter of men, whom he traps, kills, and eats.

**TUAPACA**

In the religious system of the Incas of Peru, one of the names of the creator god, viewed in the area of Lake Titicaca as a white man of great height with miraculous powers who once visited the people and conferred on them great benefits and good will. In other areas the same figure is known as TICCI VIRACOCHA.

**TUDAVA**

A hero and creator-figure of the Trobriander people of Melanesia, who was thought by them to have introduced the skills of cultivation and to have set the ritual social pattern by giving totems to the first people.

**TUTUJANAWIN**

A figure of the mythology of Peru, one of the South American Indians' names for the transcendent creator god, the initiator of order and of life.

**TVASHTAR**

A character in the mythology of India. Related to INDRA, he is a craftsman and magician among the gods, the provider to Indra of the thunderbolt which was his special possession, and also of the SOMA (an intoxicating drink) which gave him his powers, and the endlessly replenished cup from which he drank it.          *Rig Veda*

**TWE**

The god of Lake Bosomtwe, in Ghana in West Africa, who was said to visit fishermen weekly.

**TYNDAREUS**

In Greek myth, he occurs as the king of Sparta and husband of LEDA, who was seduced by ZEUS in the form of a swan and bore immortal progeny as well as those by Tyndareus. See HELEN, CLYTEMNESTRA, CASTOR, POLYDEUCES.

**TYR**

In the pre-Christian Scandinavian tradition, a god known for his bravery, invoked by warriors in battle. He is one-handed, having lost his other hand in the jaws of the wolf FENRIR, where he placed it as a pledge of the gods' sincerity when they tricked the wolf into being bound.

SNORRI STURLUSON: *Prose Edda*

**TZUNUNIHA**

For the Maya Indians of Mexico, she was one of the first women, the wife of MAHUCUTAH.

# U

**UKE-MOCHI**
For the Japanese, a goddess of provision, the source of the produce of land and sea, which originally flowed from her body.

**UKKO**
The father-god of Finnish mythology, considered to be the ruler of the sky and the governor of the weather, the rain-giver. He also regulated the world and was the supreme authority over it.

**ULL**
A deity worshipped at many sites in Scandinavia, probably an early god since he does not figure prominently in later literary tradition. Said to be the stepson of THOR, son to his wife SIF, he was a fine and good-looking huntsman, travelling on skis or snowshoes like the female Scandinavian personage SKADI.

SNORRI STURLUSON: *Prose Edda*

**ULYSSES**
The Roman name of the Greek hero ODYSSEUS.

**UMA**
An alternative name for PARVATI, wife of SIVA in the Indian mythology. In this form the goddess practises the harshest asceticism in order to gain Siva's love.

**UMNGOMA**
The first man, in the cosmogony of the Vugusu people of Kenya in Africa. See MALAVA.

*The Romans knew the Greek hero Odysseus as Ulysses. This stone panel shows Ulysses resisting the luring melodies of the Siren; forewarned by Circe of the danger they presented, he had himself bound to the mast of his ship while his companions had their ears stopped with beeswax.*

*The great snake or rainbow snake occurs in aboriginal mythology all over the Australian continent. A painting on hardboard in the manner of a bark painting from Port Keats, Northern Australia.*

## UNGUD

'The Rainbow Snake', a figure in the aboriginal mythology of Australia, a species of gigantic snake thought of as living below the ground or in various forms of watercourse, and at the same time considered to be manifestations of the rainbow. Stories about them occur all over the Australian continent. The name of the great rainbow snake of the Kimberley region is **KALERU**, and that of the Western Desert, **WANAMBI**. The term Ungud is also used to refer to the Dreamtime or Dreaming, the epoch of timeless past, the equivalent of remote history in aboriginal understanding.

## UNKULUNKULU

The name of the transcendent god in the beliefs of the Zulu people of South Africa. It means the very old one, or the very great one. He is the creator and the giver of order and social structure. The same word is also used for the ancestral founder of a family, revered and worshipped by his descendants. The god himself is not worshipped, as being too remote. The name is also used by the Ndebele and other neighbour-tribes of the Zulus.

## UPUAUT

In the symbolism of ancient Egyptian religion, he is mainly depicted as the god who stands at the bow of the boat of the sun, during the dark night period when it passes under the world. He is shown as a wolf-headed man, and his appearance and function as a guide to the souls of the dead connect him with **ANUBIS**. In an earlier form, however, he was a god of war, and is sometimes portrayed as being armed.

## URANUS

In the mythological system of the ancient Greeks, the distant ancestor of the gods, identified with the night sky. He was the offspring of **GAEA** the earth, with whom he mated, but he so disliked their progeny that he kept them hidden inside her. Gaea and her son **CRONUS** plotted to overthrow him, and she gave him a sickle with which he waited until his father spread to couple with her, whereupon he castrated him. The blood which fell onto the earth gave rise to the Furies and the Giants, and the genitals themselves, falling in the sea, eventually produced the goddess of love, **APHRODITE**, from the foam that gathered around them.

HESIOD: *Theogony*

## URASHIMA

In Japanese stories, a youthful hero who unwittingly saved the life of a supernatural being in the form of a turtle, and thus came to marry the daughter of a sea-deity. Time passed at such a slow rate in his new world that when he tried to return home he found that his family had been dead for hundreds of years. He transgressed the taboo set by his wife by opening a box she had given him, and aged and died in a moment.

### URIAH

Uriah the Hittite, a figure occurring in the traditional early history of the Hebrews, as recorded in the Old Testament. He was a military leader in the service of DAVID who seduced his wife BATHSHEBA while they were visiting Jerusalem. In order to possess her as one of his wives David arranged for Uriah to be put in a vulnerable position in the battlefield, with the result that he was killed.

### URSHANABI

In Mesopotamian mythology, the ferryman of the waters of death, boatman to UTNAPISHTIM. He takes the hero GILGAMESH as a passenger, and when banished by Utnapishtim as a result, he returns with him to the mortal world.

*Epic of Gilgamesh*

### USHAS

In the mythology of India, she is the daughter of DYAUS, and herself the goddess of the dawn, seen as a young and beautiful maiden. She is regarded as the bringer of the richness of life, but as possessing also an ambivalent quality as the source of inevitable ageing.

### UTGARD-LOKI

A figure occurring in the pre-Christian mythological tradition of Scandinavia, as the king of the giants' land of Utgard, which was an otherworld visited by the god THOR on one of his numerous and characteristic adventures.

SNORRI STURLUSON: *Prose Edda*

### UTHER

Uther Pendragon, father of King ARTHUR in the stories of the Celtic British material. King of England, he fell in love with the wife of a rival leader, the duke of Tintagel, and slept with her, through MERLIN's wizardry, in the form of her husband, marrying her on the latter's death. It was in this way that Uther became the father of Arthur who succeeded him as king.

GEOFFREY OF MONMOUTH: *History of the Kings of Britain*; MALORY: *Morte d'Arthur*

*A Japanese 18th-century netsuke depicting the thunder god Raiden caught in her bath by Uzume, the goddess of laughter.*

### UTI

The first woman, in the cosmogony of the Bambuti people of Central Africa. See MUPE.

### UTNAPISHTIM

An important figure in the mythology of ancient Mesopotamia. He was the sole survivor, when the gods decided to destroy mankind by causing a great flood. His story bears a close resemblance to the Hebrew tale of NOAH, in that he was warned to build a boat, given instructions as to the dimensions, and told to stock it with the seed of all living creatures. He sailed over the waters for six days and nights, and on the seventh day the boat grounded on a mountain; like Noah he released birds, which came back, and then a raven, which found food and stayed, indicating dry land. The particular characteristic of Utnapishtim's tale is that after his adventure he was made immortal, and lived in a far-away place, to which eventually the hero GILGAMESH came in his quest for immortality. In the story he is often referred to, from his eventual destination, as 'the Faraway'.

*Epic of Gilgamesh*

### UTU

The Sumerian form of the Semitic SHAMASH, the sun-god, son of NANNA, in the mythologies of ancient Mesopotamia.

### UZUME

The Japanese goddess of laughter.

# V

## VACH
A goddess of the mythology of India. See SARASVATI, her alternative name.

## VAHAGN
The war-god of the mythology of ancient Armenia, later seen as the Armenian version of the Roman war-god MARS.

## VÄINÄMÖINEN
In Finnish mythology, he is the chief hero of a series of stories collected in a work called the *Kalevala* assembled in the nineteenth century from authentic folk material. He was the son of an air spirit, the 'Daughter of Nature', LUONNOTAR. In some tales he was said to have been responsible for creating the world – whereas in other versions this was the work of his mother. He features in a wide range of episodes of magic and adventure, and had the distinction of having visited the dark otherworld, the realm of the dead, and returned unharmed.

## VAIROCHANA
A figure in Tibetan Buddhism, and in Mahayana or northern Buddhism generally (as found, for instance, in China and Japan). He is a Buddha sometimes replacing SHAKYAMUNI in the group of five Buddhas who form the subject of a major cult. Originally a title of the sun, with the Sanskrit root meaning 'shining', he was identified in Japan with the sun-goddess AMATERASU. In Tibet he is depicted as the preaching Buddha. See also AMITABHA, AKSHOBHYA, AMOGHASIDDHI, and RATNASAMBHAVA.

## VALI
A minor figure in the mythology of Scandinavia. He was the son of ODIN by RIND, and was destined to avenge BALDER, being also one of the few gods to survive Ragnarök, the cataclysmic end of the world of the gods. See VIDAR.

SNORRI STURLUSON: *Prose Edda*

## VALKYRIES
The Valkyries were female spirits of Scandinavian myth akin to the Fates. They chose those who were to die in battle and escorted the brave to ODIN's feasting-hall Valhalla, where they act as his attendants. See BRYNHILD.

ABOVE: *A silver-gilt pendant of the Viking period believed to depict a Valkyrie.*

BELOW: *Episodes from the heroic adventures of Väinämöinen, the principal figure in the* Kalevala, *an important collection of Finnish folk stories. Painting by A. Gallén-Kallela, 1891.*

RIGHT: *Venus at her toilette. The Roman goddess of love was identified with the Greek deity Aphrodite. Roman mosaic from Tunisia, probably 4th century AD.*

## VAMANA

In the mythology of India, an incarnation of the god **VISHNU** in the form of a dwarf. This form which he took was a trick to recover territory acquired from the gods, which he did by being granted by the usurping king the ownership of land covered by three paces, whereupon he reverted to his divine nature and grew to gigantic proportions.

## VANIR

A family of gods of Scandinavian myth (compare **AESIR**), including **NJORD**, **FREYR** and **FREYJA**. They play a secondary but important role alongside the high gods of Asgard, but bear the separate function of being mainly gods of fertility.

## VARAHA

In the mythology of India, the incarnation of the god **VISHNU** as a boar.

## VARUNA

A major deity in the tradition of the Hindu religion of India. Creator god, and ruler of all things, he both initiated and continues to sustain order and life itself. He is present in all things he has made and is all-seeing. Varuna has associations with the sun, which he uses as his eye, and he is seen as dwelling in a palace in the sky. He operates through the medium of a force known as *maya*, the principle of justice and the expression of his will, and part of his function is one of judgment. In the course of the development of India's religion he joined with **MITRA** and **ARYAMAN** to form an important trinity.

*Rig Veda*

## VATA

In the mythology of India, a wind-god, the personification of the gale. See **VAYU**.

*Rig Veda*

## VAYU

God of the wind, an early god in the mythological system of India, to some extent replaced by **INDRA**, but surviving as a lesser deity of nature. He was seen as

BELOW: *A 19th-century bronze from Madras of Vamana, an incarnation of Vishnu as a dwarf.*

being of unstable temper, and in one typical story he stormily attacked a sacred mountain, Mount Meru, and eventually succeeded in blowing off its top, which fell in the sea and formed the island of Sri Lanka.

*Rig Veda*

## VELES

Or Volos. The god of cattle and of other horned animals in Slavonic mythology. Viewed as a benevolent figure, he later became equated with St Blasius (Vlas, in Slavonic), the guardian saint of cattle, and is still regarded as such in that capacity. In some aspects of his character he has become associated with **PERUN**, god of war.

## VENUS

In the native Roman pantheon originally a minor goddess of the spring. She owes her later character of goddess of love entirely to her identification with the Greek goddess **APHRODITE**.

## VESTA

An important Roman deity; as the goddess of fire, both of the hearth and of temple-rites, she bore the purity and mystery of that element, and in tradition, though much wooed, she remained a virgin. Her perpetual flame (to which the Romans attached great talismanic significance) was tended by chaste priestesses, and these

Vestal Virgins became an important part of Roman ceremonial life.

## VIDAR

In Scandinavian mythology, he is **ODIN**'s son, who appears at the catastrophe of Ragnarök as the avenger of Odin's death, killing the wolf **FENRIR** and surviving into the new era.

SNORRI STURLUSON: *Prose Edda*

*A stone image from Tiahuanaco, Bolivia, believed to represent the Inca god Viracocha.*

## VIRACOCHA

An important figure in the traditions of the Incas of Peru. In one of his aspects he was said to be an early member of the Inca people who emerged from Lake Titicaca after the great flood which the Incas believed destroyed the first people. More generally the name is that of a tall white man said to have come to the area of Lake Titicaca from the south a long time ago, to have travelled the Inca lands preaching a religion of goodwill, and to have disappeared from their country to the north. A number of similar stories are centred on this or related figures, including some in which he arouses the anger of the people and is in danger of being killed. He saves himself by exerting his supernatural power, for instance by bringing down fire onto the earth, with resulting natural features actually caused by local eruptions. It is because of these stories of a bearded white man that the conquering Spaniards were at first taken to be gods, multiple representatives of the returning Viracocha. The name is also often appended to the personal name of a god, and widely used on its own as the name of a supreme deity, said to mean 'foam of the sea' and to be derived from his departure from his earthly visit by walking out to sea. See **TICCI VIRACOCHA**, **THUNUPA**. As a supreme deity he is also a god of fertility, specifically of the providing power of rain.

## VISHAPS

In Armenian tradition, they were mythical creatures worshipped as spirits in the religion centred on the ancient kingdom of Urartu. Later they became viewed as demons and as folktale tricksters, occurring in stories in Armenian folklore.

## VISHNU

At first a minor sun-god in the background mythology of the religious systems of India, he took part in the creation of the ordered world by (according to the Vedas, the oldest Hindu scriptures) taking three steps through the cosmos which thereafter

set the form of earth, the air, and heaven. He was adopted by later Hindu mythology as one of the three main deities, along with SHIVA and BRAHMA, although he differed from the others by being thought of mainly in the form of his incarnations. See KRISHNA, RAMA. In some of his aspects of creator and supreme god he merges with Brahma, who is sometimes said to have come into existence from a lotus growing out of Vishnu's navel, as Vishnu lay asleep in his usual posture, reclining on a cosmic cobra. He is also seen as living in a paradise known as Vaikuntha, yet in his great benevolent concern for the good of the world, and in his divine role as preserver and as guide to the human soul imperilled by the work of demons, he descends at times of crisis in the form of one of his incarnations, or *avatars*. Rama is among the most popular of these and, like many of them, was a human hero long before he became an avatar of Vishnu.

*Rig Veda*

*Detail of a 17th-century miniature representing the Hindu version of the dawn of creation. Vishnu rests on the cosmic snake, Ananta.*

**VISHVARUPA**
A figure occurring in the mythology of India, in which he is the elder brother to VRITRA, and is a being seen as having three heads. Although he was a priest-figure among the gods, he favoured the evil demons, and was beheaded by INDRA.

**VIVASVAT**
The god of the rising sun, in the mythological system of India, and the father of YAMA.                    *Rig Veda*

**VOC**
Or Vac. Meaning 'Hawk'; in the tradition of the Maya Indians of Mexico he was the messenger of HURACAN, and of other gods.
*Popol Vuh*

**VODYANOI**
In Slavonic tradition, they are spirits of the waters. The name comes from *voda*, meaning 'water'. Unlike many other Slavonic spirits of nature the Vodyanoi were regarded as being hostile to men, catching and abducting unwary bathers. They were of varied but almost always monstrous appearance, and thought of as living in places such as mill pools, only appearing above water at night.

**VOHU MANAH**
A spiritual being in the Zoroastrian religion of Iran. The name is translated as 'Good Mind', and the figure is one of the AMESHA SPENTAS, and therefore partly an aspect of the deity, partly an independent intermediary with man; the beneficent and providing effects connected with this spirit gave rise to a link with cattle.

**VOLSUNG**
Grandfather of SIGURD (German SIEGFRIED), in Scandinavian mythology the leading hero of the adventure of the magic ring. (See also ANDVARI.) Sigurd takes the name by which he is often known, 'Sigurd the Volsung', from this connection. Sigi, first of the Volsung line, is also said to be the offspring of the god ODIN.
SNORRI STURLUSON: *Prose Edda*

**VORTIGERN**
A figure of Celtic British tradition. Although almost certainly a historical figure of the time of the first Saxon settlements, this early British king is transformed by Geoffrey of Monmouth into the discoverer and patron of the prophet MERLIN and the recipient of his prophecies. It was he, in this story, who suffered the treachery of HENGIST on the 'night of the long knives', when the Saxons turned on him and he was forced to flee. See also EMRYS.
GEOFFREY OF MONMOUTH: *History of the Kings of Britain*

**VRITRA**
A destructive spirit, in the mythology of India, the embodiment of the unproductive elements of nature, and the arch-enemy of the god INDRA. He is pictured as a great serpent, like the cosmic opponents of the Egyptian RA and the Scandinavian THOR.                    *Rig Veda*

**VUCUB-CAQUIX**
Literally 'Seven Macaws', a character in the tradition of the Maya Indians of Mexico, for whom he was a being who claimed affinity with the sun and boasted of a supremacy approaching divinity, but was eventually killed for his arrogance and presumption, by the folk-heroes HUNAHPU and XBALANQUE, together with his equally presumptuous sons.                    *Popol Vuh*

**VULCAN**
An important member of the pantheon of the Romans. Although identified with the Greek god HEPHAESTUS, Vulcan did not originally bear that god's specific role of smith, but rather was a general god of fire and an ancient guardian deity of the Romans.

**VYASA**
The legendary author of the *Mahabharata*, in the background mythology of the religions of India. He was said to have been a recluse who became the father of PANDU and DHRITARASHTRA.
*Mahabharata*

# W

### WAIMARIWI

The elder of two sisters, the Wawalag sisters, in a story of primal origins told by the aboriginal people of Arnhem Land, in the north of Australia, her younger sister being called BOALIRI. She had a child, and together with her sister travelled through the land naming the things which they found there. Eventually, however, all three were consumed by the giant python YULUNGGUL. The act of swallowing, being imaginatively connected with inundation by water, is seen as a representation of the coming of the monsoon season, and also has connections with initiation rites.

### WAKAHIRU-ME

Younger sister of AMATERASU, the great goddess of Japanese Shinto religion.

### WAKONDA

The name of the great spirit believed by the Dakota Indians of North America to reside in the sky, viewed by them as being dominant but insubstantial. He is seen as a mysterious presence and the giver of life.

### WANAMBI

A figure of Australian aboriginal tradition, the name of the great 'rainbow snake' of the Western Desert. Wanambi is still feared as being a powerful force.

### WANDJINA

Or Wondjina. A deity in Australian aboriginal belief, a figure connected with rain and seasonal fertility, represented in rock art in the north-west coastal area, in which the figures often appear in a horizontal position, said to be because they entered the rock shelters to die. The god is a primal figure, belonging to the period known as the Dreamtime, the timeless past of aboriginal thought.

### WARAMURUNGGUNDJI

A mother-figure, in the beliefs of the aboriginal people of northern Australia, who was thought to have come from the north-west by way of Melville Island, to reside in western Arnhem Land.

### WATAUINEIWA

Supreme god of the people of the extreme southern Andes, in Chile, prayed to as a benevolent father-figure and regarded as transcendent and responsible for natural and social order.

### WAWALAG

Or Wawalak. The joint name for a pair of sisters (WAIMARIWI and BOALIRI) occurring in a story of origins which forms part of the mythology of the aboriginal people of Arnhem Land, in the north of Australia. See WAIMARIWI.

### WELE

The name for God used by the Abaluyia people of Kenya in Africa. It bears the sense of 'he who guides'.

### WENCHANG

Or Wen Chang. The Chinese god of literature, a figure depicted as a seated man of aristocratic appearance. He is respected but remote, his place being taken in a household context by his assistant ZHONGGUEI.

### WHIRO

An underworld deity, one of the family of chief gods in the beliefs of the Maori, the son of RANGI and PAPA, the sky and the earth. He figures as an opponent of his wiser brother TANE in the story of the origin of the world, in which Tane and his brothers plan to separate their parents to give space in which beings could develop. Whiro chose to remain in the darkness within the earth, and became the god of the dead and the personification of evil.

### WISAGATCAK

Occurring in the stories of the North American Cree Indians, he is a figure

OPPOSITE: *A bark painting from north-west Australia of Wandjina, a god of rain and seasonal fertility.*

LEFT: *The Chinese god of literature, Wenchang, who was said to have had a benevolent attitude to deserving candidates in the examinations for public office that were such a feature of traditional China. Carved wooden figure, 19th century.*

209

typical of the trickster character so popular in North American folktales, but in this case of mythic importance as connected with the destruction and re-creation of the world. In the course of his attempts to catch a monstrous beaver he caused a flood which enveloped everything, from which he alone escaped on a raft onto which he took various types of animal. The raft by magic produced increasing earth which eventually covered the water. Compare Japanese GUN.

*A wooden statue of King Shamba Bolongongo of the Bushongo people of the Congo, said to be descended directly from their great ancestor figure Woto.*

### WIYOT

The creator god of the group of Indians of California known as the Juaneño, from their proximity to the mission of San Juan. Wiyot is not pre-existent, as are many creators, but is himself brought into being at the end of a succession of creations brought about by the coupling of the original brother-sister pair, the sky and the earth. He himself gave birth to a race of pre-humans, and as they increased the earth expanded southwards in front of them.

### WODEN

One of the chief gods of the Germans, also known at Wotan. Although regarded as the same personage as the Scandinvaian ODIN, he had for the Germanic peoples more an association with warfare. The name probably comes from the root 'wode' meaning 'fury' or 'frenzy', which survived in English as 'wood' meaning 'mad'. He gave his name to a day of the week, Woden's-day, our Wednesday.

### WOHPEKUMEN

In the beliefs of the Yurok Indians of the west coast of North America, he was the instigator of customs and practices, and also the provider of fish to mankind. Before he instituted the present form of human birth, women had always perished at their first childbirth. Wohpekumen had the weakness of an obsession with wooing women, which characteristic makes him something of a trickster figure.

### WOTO

An ancestor figure, founder of the Bushongo people of the Congo area of Africa, the son of their culture hero BOMAZI. The legendary king Shamba was thought to be his direct descendant. The name also occurs as the founder of the Bakubas, a related tribe to the Bushongo.

## XBALANQUE

A figure in the mythology of the Maya Indians of Mexico. See HUNAHPU.

*Popol Vuh*

## XIHE

A female personage in Chinese mythology, responsible for bathing the ten suns of heaven which the Chinese believed to have existed initially, of which she was the mother. Her role and that of the suns belong mainly to the beliefs of the Shang dynasty.

## XIUHTECUTLI

A fire god, of the mythology of Peru, with connections with the calendar and its ceremonies. The same figure occurs as the Aztec god HUEHUTCOTL.

## XI WANG MU

A figure of Chinese mythology, the 'Queen Mother of the West'. Once a year she met her counterpart DONG WANG GONG, in a meeting of opposites seen as representing the joining of contrary principles, the union of YIN and YANG. Her role appears to have included the governing of the constellations. As Xi Mu to the people of the Shang dynasty, she was a creator figure and the source of immortality, who is often shown as flying on the back of a bird. She held court on Mount Kunlun, on the summit of which she had a great city, and there she was attended by her assistants the Jade Girls and by three-legged birds. Contact was several times made between her and the legendary early emperors.

## XMUCANE

For the Maya Indians of Mexico, a grandmother figure, involved in the creation of man. She is known as 'the Grandmother of the Dawn'. The name comes from the Maya *xnuc*, 'an old woman'. See also XPIYACOC. *Popol Vuh*

## XPIYACOC

For the Maya Indians of Mexico, a grandfather figure, the consort of XMUCANE. The pair were regarded as involved in the creation of the world and of mankind. *Popol Vuh*

*Xi Wang Mu, 'Queen Mother of the West' in Chinese mythology, renewed the immortality of the Immortals by giving them magic peaches from the garden of her palace on Mount Kunlun, where they ripened once every 6000 years. Ching Dynasty soap-stone carving of the 17th century.*

# Y

## YAHWEH

Or Jahweh. A traditional vocalization of the Hebrew letters YHWH or JHWH, supposed to represent the identity of God, possibly meaning 'I am what I am' or simply 'He who is'. See MOSES. Hence the name normally given for the God of the Hebrews. Like the supreme deities in many other mythologies he is identified as the creator of all things and the upholder of order, the giver of laws and the ultimately dominant power; but unlike many of them he is not remote from his creation. Rather he is seen as constantly concerned and intervening, often through the intermediary of his chosen spokesmen, his prophets, with whom his relationship is viewed as one of close personal contact in characteristically human terms. He permits remarkable freedom of action and choice, while always able to exercise an ultimate veto. To his people, the tribes of Israel, he is also a humanly-viewed father-figure, wounded by neglect or disobedience, liable to storms of temper, pleased by small attentions, gratified by devotion, ultimately reliably forgiving. He grants favours to those he loves and exacts retribution from defaulters on his trust. In all the records of his acts and qualities he fully confirms his claim that he created man in his own image. Much of our knowledge of his nature arises from the tension and ambivalence inherent in his special relationship with the Israelites, by their own account a wilful and factious people, to whom he makes the principal and overriding demand of monotheistic fidelity, explicitly styling himself a jealous God.

## YALAFATH

A trickster figure in the mythology of some areas of the Pacific islands. See OLOFAT.

*The Hindu god Yama, in this late 19th-century painting from Kalighat shown standing, is commonly depicted as a vengeful figure come to collect the souls of the doomed.*

## YAM

Also known as Yam-Nahar. The Syrian god of the sea.

## YAMA

In the stories of origins contained in the mythology of India, the first man, along with his sister YAMI the child of VIVASVAT, the ascending sun. The pair mated, to give rise to the human race. Yama however explored the world and discovered a path to heaven, thus introducing mortality to the world and himself becoming the king of the dead. In this capacity he came to be seen as ruler of a purgatorial underworld, judge of the dead and governor of the destiny of the living. As such he comes to collect the souls of the doomed. It is in this later aspect that Yama appears in his depictions, shown as a fearsome figure with green skin. *Rig Veda*

**YAMATO TAKERU**
Hero of many Japanese stories of adventure, the son of an emperor and the upholder of order. When he died his soul took the form of a white bird.

**YAMA-UBA**
In Japanese belief, which is much concerned with natural features, the spirits of mountains, which are regarded as female.

**YAMI**
The first woman, in the cosmogony of India. See YAMA.

**YANAULUHA**
A primal priest-figure in the cosmogony of the Pueblo Indians of North America.

**YANG**
Meaning literally 'bright', the male principle, and the representative of the light and pure elements which came into existence with the emergence of matter out of chaos, in the cosmogony and religious beliefs of the Chinese. See YIN.

**YAO**
One of the legendary first 'five emperors' of Chinese mythical history; it was in his reign that the archer YI shot the suns (of which there were thought to have been ten) reducing them to the present single sun. Yao was most noted for having defeated the monster GONG-GONG. In his time moreover a great flood threatened the inhabitable world, and to combat it he sought the advice of the hero GUN.

**YARILO**
Or Erilo. Perhaps connected with the Greek name EROS, Yarilo is the Slavonic god of love in its physical form. He was also a god of agricultural fertility, imagined as a young man riding on a white horse.

**YASODHARA**
In the background tradition of the Buddhist religion of India, the wife of the Buddha, and said to have been his wife in previous existences.

**YEITSO**
A man-eating giant in the stories of the Navajo Indians of North America, by whom he was thought to have been created by the first being as a correction to the pride of the early people and finally defeated by the primal twins NAGENATZANI and THOBADESTCHIN.

**YEMANJÁ**
In the religion of the African-Brazilian descendants of West African slaves, she is the goddess of the sea, identified with the Virgin Mary under the title Our Lady of Glory in the amalgamation with Roman Catholicism known as *candomblé*; a benevolent deity worshipped by fishermen in a midsummer ceremony in which small houses and other structures decorated with flowers and shells are floated out to sea. Her native African counterpart is Yemoja, mother of all the rivers.

**YEN-LO**
In Chinese mythology, the god of death, the equivalent of the Indian Buddhist YAMA. It is his duty to collect the souls of those due to die, in accordance with the calculation of destiny made by the supreme governer of life and death, DONG-YO DA-DI.

ABOVE: *An 18th-century bronze ritual staff head in the form of a dragon, representing Yang, or the male principal, in Chinese mythology.*

BELOW: *Detail of a hanging scroll depicting the four Kings of Hell, in Chinese mythology part of the underworld bureaucracy in which Yen-Lo features as the ruler of the dead.*

## YGGR

One of the names for the great Scandinavian god ODIN.

## YI

An archer who shot the sun, in Chinese mythology, at a time when (so it was believed) all of the ten suns which populated the sky appeared at once, causing crops and vegetation to shrivel. Yi was ordered by the early emperor YAO to shoot at them, with the result that at the end only the one sun which we now have was left. He was also notable for obtaining from XI WANG MU the elixir of immortality, afterwards to be stolen from him again by his wife, HENG-O. In another story he is credited with having brought under control the winds, previously plaguing the 'Yellow Emperor', HUANG DI.

## YIMA

Or Jam. A figure in the background mythology of the Zoroastrian religion of Iran, in which he was said to have been a king in the golden age, possibly related in origin to Hindu YAMA. He forms a distant ancestor of the Iranian people, and to the prophet ZARATHUSHTRA appeared to represent the source of religious error.

## YIN

In Chinese cosmogony, this figure is the representation of the earthly elements which, being heavy, formed the earth when matter first came into existence (in contrast to the lighter elements of YANG, the sky). Although these two probably originated thus as earth and sky deities, they became deeply embedded in Chinese religious thinking as the opposing forces or principles latent in all things, Yin (literally 'dark') being the female element and also the negative force, while Yang, meaning 'bright', is the active male principle. Their coming together in harmonious combination is the desired goal of Chinese thinking. The Yin and the Yang principles are represented by the symbols of interlocking curves within a circle, in their contrasting black and white.

## YMIR

In the story of the pre-Christian tradition of Scandinavia, he was the primal giant, formed from the thawing ice of the pre-creation. He was killed by ODIN and his brothers, who constructed the world out of his body.

SNORRI STURLUSON: *Prose Edda*

## YOKUL

A figure of aboriginal belief among the people of western Arnhem Land, in the north of Australia. See DJABO.

## YORIMITSU

Also known as Raiko. In Japanese stories the heroic leader of the Minamoto clan, he was noted as a conqueror of demons, using ingenuity rather than brute force.

## YOSHI-IYE

In Japanese tradition, a hero of the Minamoto clan, a warrior and follower of the war-god HACHIMAN.

## YOSHITSUNE

Also known as Ushiwaka. A hero of Japan who avenged the defeat of his people, the Minamoto clan, having been taught military skill by demons (TENGU). He is best known for his association with the gigantic hero BENKEI, who became his servant after being defeated by him in a famous duel.

## YSBADDADEN

In a Celtic British mythic story, the name of the chief giant. See CULHWCH.

## YU

An early ruler, in Chinese mythical history, one of the emperors of the Xia dynasty. Said to have been born out of the belly of his dead father GUN, he at first took the form of a dragon. Like his father he took on the task of governing the still-threatening flood, which had been the cause of the former's death. This time he had the co-operation of HUANG DI, who was the owner of magically increasing earth, and by enormous labour and skill he set about controlling and directing the earth's waters, with the results (rivers, springs, estuaries and so on) which we now have. This undertaking gave him the status of an exemplar of dedicated labour, and he is most cited for his dedication to hard work. His son QI, who was born from a rock (his name in fact meaning 'split'), was the first emperor to rule by direct linear succession, and thus established both the system of primogeniture and also the great Xia dynasty. Yu's other achievements included the vanquishing of monsters, and in the course of his order-imposing activities he also recorded the geography of the known world in the form of metal cauldrons, the successors of which survived into modern times.

## YUDI

Formerly spelt Yuti. In Chinese mythology, the ruler of heaven, sometimes said to have created human beings by modelling them out of clay. He was a patriarchal monarch who lived in great state, exactly like an earthly emperor, surrounded by ministers whose function it was to concern themselves with the affairs of mankind. He himself protected the Emperor, who made special sacrifices to him. He has many titles, the chief one being that of 'August Personage of Jade', YU HUANG, in which capacity he is also another aspect of the sky-god, SHANG DI or TIAN. In part of China he was said to have created mankind.

## YU-HUANG

The 'August Personage of Jade', a title of the supreme god of the Chinese religious tradition; a form of the deity YUDI, SHANG DI or TIAN, the sky god. In this capacity he is seen as an institutor of order and control, the world being rightly and justly governed under his supervision. In due course he became viewed as too sublime, for direct contact, and communication with him could only be made by way of his chief minister, while lesser gods took on his various functions. See DONG-YO DA-DI.

## YUKI-ONNA

A figure occurring in the mythology of Japan, she is 'the Snow Woman', spirit of the snowstorm. She entices men by her beauty, but leads them to their death.

## YULUNGGUL

Also spelt Julungsul or Yurlunggur. A giant python occurring in a story of origins from the aboriginal people of Arnhem Land, in the north of Australia. See WAIMARIWI.

## YUQIANG

A figure in the mythology of China, he was ordered by the king of heaven to anchor the previously floating Islands of Immortality. He did so by enlisting the assistance of teams of giant tortoises, which held them still. Yuqiang himself was a hybrid creature, having the body of a bird and the face of a man. He is in origin a wind-god, thought of as living in the north.

## YVAIN

A hero of Celtic French mythology. See OWEIN, the British form of his name.

*A bark painting from north-east Arnhem Land, Australia, showing the Rainbow Snake swallowing children of one of the Wawalag Sisters. According to the myth, the sisters had camped unawares by the water-hole in which the snake Yulunggul lived. Yulunggul lulled them to sleep with song and then swallowed the sisters and children, later vomiting the children up.*

# Z

### Zaishen

Or Zai Shen, formerly spelt Tsai Shen. A Chinese god of wealth. His anniversary is much celebrated with sacrifices, and his image is distributed in the streets on New Year's Day.

### Zao-Jun

Or Tsao Chun, in the older form of transliteration. The Chinese kitchen god, a popular domestic deity whose shrine was often located above the kitchen stove. His story tells how he was once a mortal man, a mason, who killed himself over a trick played by his wife, but was made immortal by the ruling deity because of his own goodness. His role of god of the kitchen made him an intimate member of each family. As a central occupant of the house himself he knew all that went on, and he reported once a year to the supreme god on the family's behaviour.

### Zarathushtra

Less correctly spelt Zarathustra, Zoroaster in Greek. The founder of the Zoroastrian religion of Iran. He was a great religious leader and reformer, much developed as a mythic figure in the literature of the religion founded on his works. It is said that his birth was foretold from the beginning of the world, that his makeup was in preparation in the heavens, and that his mother received his elements by the agency of God's spirits, the **Amesha Spentas**. At his birth the whole world rejoiced, and at once the evil demons attempted to destroy the infant, but were prevented by **Ahura Mazda**. The child, like so many mythic heroes, showed precocious ability; as a youth he spent a period alone in meditation in the desert; he was visited there by one of the Amesha Spentas, and led into the presence of God.

This formed the prelude to his ministry. In his actual teaching he preached man's moral obligation to make the correct choice between good and evil, and by means of dedicating his life to Ahura Mazda and the way of truth. The religion based on his teaching developed into a positive and life-accepting one, in which the world is seen as all potentially good, and man as being placed there to draw out the best aspects of it. The character of the prophet is based on a historical figure now thought to have lived in North East Iran some time between 1500 and 1000 BC.

*A 19th-century gilt wood figure of the Chinese god of wealth, Zaishen.*

## ZEUS

The king of the gods, in the central mythology of the ancient Greeks. An autocratic ruler of the court on Mount Olympus, he is very much the representative of a patriarchal and dictatorial political system. The son of CRONUS and RHEA, he soon usurped his father to become himself the father-figure for both gods and men, a character indicated by his Roman name JUPITER, coming from the form Zeus-Pater, Father Zeus. Zeus was also the god of the sky and of thunder; in spite of these magnificent attributes he was seen by the Greeks as behaving with remarkably human self-indulgence and instability of temper – feasting, quarrelling and in particular philandering, a constant problem to his embittered wife HERA. Although he was regarded as having his throne on Mount Olympus, the centre of his worship was the vast temple at Olympia. See also Vedic DYAUS.

## ZHI NU

'The Weaver Maid', a figure in Chinese myth. In some stories she is the granddaughter of XI WANG MU. In an episode of her story she fell in love with a god, and consequently for a time neglected her task, which was the weaving of the patterned cloth of the heavens. As a result the god of heaven had to restrict her meetings with her lover.

## ZHONGGUEI

The god of examinations, in old Chinese beliefs. He was portrayed as being extremely ugly, but was much worshipped by those involved in learning, as it was his prerogative to choose who would do best in tests. He was also a patron of travellers, and controlled the evil demons who endanger travel.

## ZHUAN HU

Also known as Shun. In the mythical history of China he was an early emperor, one of the 'five emperors' who presided over the later formative stages of the development of Chinese civilization. It was on his succession that the separation of heaven and earth took place, their proximity previously causing confusion in the hierarchies governing gods and men. He appointed one of his governors, CHONG, to organize and administer heaven, and another minister, LI, to take care of earth.

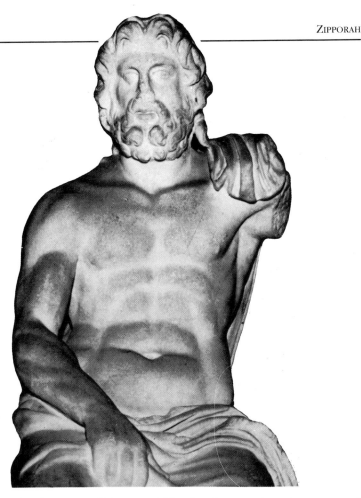

*Zeus, the supreme god of the Greeks, who ruled men and the other gods from his throne on Mount Olympus. A statue of the 4th century BC.*

## ZIN

In the beliefs of some African people of northern Nigeria and the Upper Niger, a type of water spirit, perhaps derived from the Arabic *jinn*. The sight of one of them is sometimes held to be fatal.

## ZIPPORAH

In the Hebrew tradition as preserved in the Old Testament, the wife of MOSES and daughter of JETHRO, who was a priest of Midian, the country into which Moses fled to escape Pharaoh's anger. She plays little part in his story.                   *Exodus*

## ZIUSUDRA

In the Sumerian story of the Great Flood, he is the survivor who becomes the ancestor of mankind. See Assyrian UTNAPISHTIM, and DEUCALION, NOAH.

## ZMEI GORYNICH

In Slavonic mythology, a serpent which was the assistant of BABA-YAGA, sometimes seen as being of human hybrid form. He is a danger to mankind and prone to abduct women.

## ZOA

Ancestor and tutelary spirit of the Songhay people of Upper Niger in West Africa.

## ZOROASTER

The Greek form of the name ZARATHUSHTRA, and the form which is used in accounts of the great Iranian religion based on his life and words.

## ZU

A figure of Mesopotamian myth, a god or demon seen as a great bird, apparently in conflict with the high gods, from whom he stole the tablets of fate.

## ZURVAN

'Time', a transcendent god who pre-existed creation, whose worship forms a heresy of the Zoroastrian religion of Iran. It was said that he gave birth to twins who became the principles of good and evil, OHRMAZD and AHRIMAN, and that this event took place after he had waited a thousand years. He conceived at the moment he began to doubt that he would succeed, and while Ohrmazd was the embodiment of his wisdom, Ahriman was the realization of his doubt. Through a hasty promise (that the first to come into his presence would gain the world) Ahriman possesses power over creation.

*A silver plaque of the 7th or 8th centuries BC depicting the birth of Ohrmazd and Ahriman, the opposing forces of good and evil, and, in the centre, Zurvan, a god who existed before creation and whose worship is heretical in the Zoroastrian religion of Iran.*

# INDEX OF THEMES

## Ancestor figure

ABRAHAM/Hebrew; AENEAS/Roman; AMATERASU/Japanese Shinto; ARAM/Hebrew; ATAENTSIC/North American Iroquois, Huron; BHARATA/Indian; BOLON DZECAB/ Mexican Maya; DANANN/Irish Celtic; DENG/Sudanese Dinka; DON/British Celtic; HAM/Hebrew; HAYK/ Armenian; INTI/Peruvian Inca; ISAAC/Hebrew; JACOB/ Hebrew; JAPHAPH/Hebrew; KACHINAS/North American Pueblo; KINTU/Bugandan; LEBÉ/West African Dogon; MAINA/Kenyan Luja; MANU/Indian; MASYA/Zoroastrian; MOOMBI/Kenyan Kikuyu; NYIKANG/Sudanese Shilluk; QUETZALCOATL/Mexican Maya; SHANG/Chinese; SHEM/ Hebrew; WOTO/Congolese Bushongo; ZOA/Nigerian Songhay.

## Animal form of god

AH KINCHIL/Mexican Maya; AMON/Egyptian; ANUBIS/ Egyptian; APIS/Egyptian; BAST/Egyptian; BUCHIS/ Egyptian; BUTO/Egyptian; DUAMUTEF/Egyptian; EUROPA/ Greek; GARUDA/Indian; HANUMAN/Indian; HAPY/ Egyptian; JAMBAVAN/Indian; KHNUM/Egyptian; KURMA/ Indian; MNEVIS/Egyptian; NANABUSH/North American Algonquin; NANOOK/North American Eskimo; NEKHEBET/Egyptian; PAN/Greek; PTAH/Egyptian; SEBEK/ Egyptian; SEKER/Egyptian; SUGRIVA/Indian; TAUERET/ Egyptian; VARAHA/Indian.

## Barrenness of the earth

DEMETER/Greek; ISHTAR/Mesopotamian; ISIS/Egyptian.

## Childbirth, deity of

BES/Egyptian; IX CHEL/Mexican Maya; JIZO BOSATSU/ Japanese Buddhist; JUNO/Roman; MESHKENT/Egyptian; PURANDHI/Indian; SHASHTI/Indian; TAUERET/Egyptian.

## Child prodigy

DAVID/Hebrew; GSHEN-RAB/Tibetan Bon-po; INDRA/ Indian; KRISHNA/Indian.

## Conception, supernatural

ERICHTHONIUS/Greek; EUROPA/Greek; GE-SAR/Tibetan; IHY/Egyptian; LEDA/Greek; MAHAMAYA/Indian Buddhist; MOMOTARO/Japanese; OENGUS/Irish Celtic; PERSEUS/ Greek; SARAH/Hebrew; TYNDAREUS/Greek; VÄINÄMÖINEN/ Finnish.

## Constellations

ARANRHOD/British Celtic; ARIADNE/Greek; CASSIOPEIA/ Greek; NANOOK/North American Eskimo.

## Corn deity

CERES/Roman; ONATHA/North American Iroquois.

## Crafts and skills

DAEDALUS/Greek; TVASHTRI/Indian.

## —, introduction of

MUSA/Nigerian; PACHACAMAC/Peruvian

## Creation of man

ADAM/Hebrew, DIYA/Chinese; ESTANATLEHI/North American Navajo; IOSKEHA/North American Iroquois, Huron; JUOK/Sudanese Shilluk; NUGUA/Chinese; PANGU/ Chinese; TANE/Maori; TIANLONG/Chinese; XPIYACOC/ Mexican Maya; XMUCANE/Mexican Maya; YUDI/Chinese.

## Creator god

AHURA MAZDA/Zoroastrian; AMMA/West African Dogon; AMON/Egyptian; AWONAWILONA/North American Pueblo; BRAHMA/Hindu; CHIMINIGAGUA/Colombian Indian; CON/ Peruvian Indian; DAKSHA/Hindu; DYAUS/Indian; EA/ Mesopotamian; ENLIL/Mesopotamian; GLUSKAP/North American Algonquin; GUCUMATZ/Mexican Quiche-Maya; GUDATRIGAKWITL/North American Wiyot; GUINECHEN/Chilean Araucanian; HUNAHPU/Mexican Maya; INDRA/Indian; INTI/Peruvian Inca; IOSKEHA/North American Iroquois, Huron; IZANAGI/Japanese; JUMALA/ Finnish; JUOK/Sudanese Shilluk; KWAWAR/North American Gabrielino; LEZA/Central African; MADER-ATCHA/Lapp; MARDUK/Mesopotamian; MBOMBO/Zairean Bakuba; MULUNGU/East, Central and South African; OHRMAZD/Zoroastrian; OLELBIS/North American Wintun; PACHAYACHACHIC/Peruvian Inca; PRAJAPATI/ Indian; PTAH/Egyptian; TAIKOMOL/North American Yuki, Huchnon; TANGAROA/Polynesian, Maori; TEPEU/Mexican Maya; TUAPACA/Peruvian Inca; TUTUJANAWIN/Peruvian; VARUNA/Hindu; VISHNU/Hindu; WIYOT/North American Juañeno; YAHWEH/Hebrew

## — goddess

ARURU/Babylonian; BACHUE/Colombian Indian; JUGUMISHANTA/Papua New Guinean; LUONNOTAR/Finnish; MADER-AKKA/Lapp; NANA-BULUKU/West African Benin; NUGUA/Chinese.

## Cultivation, introduction of

DEMETER/Greek; DEMOPHON/Greek; GUAN YIN/Chinese Buddhist; IMAYMANA VIRACOCHA/Peruvian Inca; NESARU/ North American Arikara; PARAPARAWA/Brazilian Trio; TRIPTOLEMUS/Greek.

## Death, god of

AH PUCH/Mexican Maya; ANUBIS/Egyptian; CUMHAU/ Mexican Maya; DIS/Roman; EMMA O/Japanese; HADES/ Greek; MICTLANTECUHTLI/Mexican Toltec; MOT/Syrian;

SEKER/Egyptian; TORE/Central African Bambuti; YAMA/Indian; YEN-LO/Chinese

## —, goddess of
HECATE/Greek; HINE-NUI-TE-PO/Maori.

## Doomed hero
ACHILLES/Greek; AGAMEMNON/Greek; BALDER/Scandinavian; CONAIRE/Irish Celtic; CUCHULAINN/Irish Celtic; GILGAMESH/Mesopotamian; HERACLES/Greek; HIPPOLYTUS/Greek; ICARUS/Greek; MERLIN/British Celtic; OEDIPUS/Greek.

## Dwarf
ALBERICH/German; ANDVARI/Scandinavian; BES/Egyptian; NIBELUNG/German; SUKU-NA-BIKO/Japanese; VAMANA/Indian.

## Early king
AHAB/Hebrew; BALAK/Hebrew; BELINUS/British Celtic; BELSHAZZAR/Hebrew; BLADUD/British Celtic; DAVID/Hebrew; ERECHTHEUS/Greek; FUXI/Chinese; GAOYAO/Chinese; GE-SAR/Tibetan; HUANG-DI/Chinese; JEHU/Hebrew; JIMMU TENNO/Japanese; LUD/British Celtic; ODUDUWA/Nigerian Yoruba; SAUL/Hebrew; SENNACHERIB/Hebrew; SHENNONG/Chinese; SOLOMON/Hebrew; VORTIGERN/British Celtic; YAO/Chinese; YIMA/Zoroastrian; YU/Chinese; ZHUAN HU/Chinese.

## Earth, god of
CHENG-HUANG/Chinese; GEB/Egyptian.

## —, goddess of
ALA/Nigerian Ibo; DIYA/Chinese; EITHINOHA/North American Iroquois; JUGUMISHANTA/Papua New Guinean; KI/Sumerian; MATI-SYRA-ZEMLYA/Russian; NINHURSAG/Sumerian; NOKOMIS/North American Algonquin; PAPA/Maori; PRITHIVI/Indian.

## —, god on
BOCHICA/Colombian Indian; IZANAGI/Japanese; KRISHNA/Indian; KUKULCAN/Mexican Maya; NANOOK/North American Eskimo; ORUNMILA/Nigerian Yoruba; QUETZALCOATL/Mexican Maya; RAMA/Indian; VAMANA/Indian; VARAHA/Indian; VIRACOCHA/Peruvian Inca

## —, goddess on
ASTARTE/Egyptian; DEMETER/Greek; ISIS/Egyptian; SEDNA/North America Eskimo; SITA/Indian.

## Earthquake
CHIBCHACUM/Colombian Indian; KWAWAR/North American Gabrielino; PILLAN/Chilean Indian; TAIKOMOL/North American Yuki, Huchnon.

## Elopement
DEIRDRE/Irish Celtic; GRAINNE/Irish Celtic; HELEN/Greek; ISOUD/British Celtic; MELWAS/British Celtic; O-KUNI-NUSHI/Japanese; PARIS/Greek.

## Evil spirit
AHRIMAN/Zoroastrian; ANCHANCHO/Peruvian Andean Indian; ANGRA MAINYU/Zoroastrian; ASAG/Mesopotamian; BEELZEBUB/Hebrew; DAEVAS/Zoroastrian; DAHAK/Zoroastrian; KALI/Indian; KUBERA/Indian; LEVIATHAN/Hebrew; LOKI/Scandinavian; MANINGA/North American Mandan; MARA/Indian Buddhist; NAMTAR/Mesopotamian; ONI/Japanese Buddhist; RAVANA/Indian; SATAN/Hebrew; VRITRA/Indian.

## Father god
ALL-FATHER/Scandinavian; ANU/Babylonian; EL/Syrian, Hebrew; MANITOU/North American Algonquin; ODIN/Scandinavian; OXALA/Afro-Brazilian; QAHOLOM/Mexican Maya; SVAROGU/Slavonic; UKKO/Finnish; ZEUS/Greek.

## Fertility deity
ALA/Nigerian Ibo; ANAHIT/Armenian; BAAL/Syrian; FREYR/Scandinavian; INDRA/Indian; KARTTIKEYA/Indian; KUNAPIPI/Australian aboriginal; MIN/Egyptian; NEKHEBET/Egyptian; NINGIZZIDA/Mesopotamian; PACHAMAMA/Peruvian Inca; PTAH/Egyptian; SATIS/Egyptian; SHIVA/Hindu; TAMMUZ/Mesopotamian; VIRACOCHA/Peruvian Inca.

## Fire, acquisition of
MURILÉ/Kenyan; PROMETHEUS/Greek; TOHIL/Mexican Maya.

## —, deity of
AGNI/Indian; ATAR/Zoroastrian; CHONGLI/Chinese; JURONG/Chinese; KAGUTSUCHI/Japanese; SVAROGU/Slavonic; VESTA/Roman; VULCAN/Roman; XIUHTECUTLI/Peruvian.

## First man
ADAM/Hebrew; APSU/Mesopotamian; ASK/Scandinavian; BALAM-ACAB/Mexican Maya; BALAM-QUITZE/Mexican Maya; BURI/Scandinavian; CAQUIXAHA/Mexican Maya; DXUI/African Bushman; EFÉ/African Pygmy; GARANG/Sudanese Dinka; GAYOMARD/Zoroastrian; GBOROGBORO/Central African Lugbara; IQUI-BALAM/Mexican Maya; KENOS/Chilean Ona; MAHUCUTAH/Mexican Maya; MUKURU/South West African Herero; MULONGA/Central African; MUPE/Central African Bambuti; MWAMBU/Kenyan; POSHAIYANGKYO/North American Pueblo; SHU/Egyptian; UMNGOMA/Kenyan Vugusu; YAMA/Indian.

## — woman
ABUK/Sudanese Dinka; ATAENTSIC/North American Iroquois, Huron; BOALIRI/North Australian aboriginal; CAHA-PALUNA/Mexican Maya; CHOMIBA/Mexican Maya; EMBLA/Scandinavian; EVE/Hebrew; HINE-AHUONE/Maori; KAMAUGARUNGA/South West African Herero; MALAVA/Kenyan Vugusu; MEME/Central African Lugbara; NAMBI/Bugandan; PANDORA/Greek; PARSHU/Indian, SELA/Kenyan; TEFNUT/Egyptian; TZUNUNIHA/Mexican Maya; UTI/Central African Bambuti.

## Flood
ATRAHASIS/Babylonian; BOCHICA/Colombian Indian; CHIA/Colombian Indian; CHIBCHACUM/Colombian Indian; DEUCALION/Greek; ETANA/Mesopotamian; GUINECHEN/Chilean Araucanian; GUN/Chinese; MANU/

Indian; NANABUSH/North American Algonquin; NOAH/Hebrew; OLOKUN/Nigerian Yoruba; TIEHOLTSODI/North American Navajo; UTNAPISHTIM/Mesopotamian; VIRACOCHA/Peruvian Inca; WISAGATCAK/North American Cree; YU/Chinese; ZIUSUDRA/Sumerian.

## Founder of the race
ADU OGINAE/West African Ashanti; AYAR CACHI/Peruvian Inca; DANAAN/Irish Celtic; GIKUYU/Kenyan; MANCO CAPAC/Peruvian Inca; ROMULUS/Roman.

## Giant
ARGUS/Greek; ATLAS/Greek; BALOR/Irish Celtic; BAUGI/Scandinavian; CALYPSO/Greek; CYCLOPS/Greek; DAGDA/Irish Celtic; GEIROD/Scandinavian; GERYON/Greek; GOG/British Celtic; GOLIATH/Hebrew; HRUNGIR/Scandinavian; HUMBABA/Mesopotamian; HYMIR/Scandinavian; MIMIR/Scandinavian; ORION/Greek; PANGU/Chinese; POLYPHEMUS/Greek; PURUSHA/Indian; SKRYMIR/Scandinavian; SUTTUNG/Scandinavian; YEITSO/North American Navajo; YMIR/Scandinavian; YSBADDADEN/British Celtic.

## Giant-killer
CORINEUS/British Celtic; CULHWCH/British Celtic; DAVID/Hebrew; LUGH/Irish Celtic; NAGENATZANI/North American Navajo.

## Good luck, bringer of
BISHAMON/Japanese Buddhist; DAIKOKU/Japanese; EBISU/Japanese; EKKEKKO/Peruvian Indian; FUKUROKUJU/Japanese; FUXING/Chinese; HOTEI/Japanese; JUROJIN/Japanese; KISHIJOTEN/Japanese; LUXING/Chinese; PACHAMAMA/Peruvian Inca.

## Hades see Otherworld-visit; Underworld

## Healing, deity of
AESCULAPIUS/Roman; ASCLEPIUS/Greek; IX CHEL/Mexican Maya; NINGIZZIDA/Mesopotamian; NODENS/British Celtic.

## Hell see Otherworld-visit; Underworld

## Hunting
ACTAEON/Greek; ADONIS/Greek; ANINGAN/North American Eskimo; APOLLO/Greek; ARTAVAZD/Armenian; ARTEMIS/Greek; ASDIWAL/North American Tsimshian; CAIPORA/Brazilian Indian; DEVANA/Slavonic; DIANA/Roman; MUSA/Nigerian; OGUN/Nigerian Yoruba; ORION/Greek; SKADI/Scandinavian.

## Intermediary
KIRANGA/East African Barundi; MOSES/Hebrew.

## Law-giver
LI/Chinese; MAYET/Egyptian; MOSES/Hebrew; NESARU/North American Arikara; PULEKUKWEREK/North American Yurok; RHADAMANTYS/Greek; TEMAUKEL/Chilean Ona; YAHWEH/Hebrew; YU-HUANG/Chinese.

## Love, god of
CUPID/Roman; EROS/Greek; KAMA/Indian; YARILO/Slavonic.

## —, goddess of
AHRODITE/Greek; ISHTAR/Mesopotamian; RATI/Indian; TLAZOLTEOTI/Peruvian Indian; VENUS/Roman.

## Matrimony
HERA/Greek; JUNO/Roman; KILYA/Peruvian Inca.

## Monster
ASTERION/Greek; BABA-YAGA/Slavonic; CENTAURS/Greek; CERBERUS/Greek; CHARYBDIS/Greek; CHIMAERA/Greek; DELGETH/North American Navajo; FAFNIR/Scandinavian; FENRIR/Scandinavian; GONG-GONG/Chinese; GORGONS/Greek; GRENDEL/Anglo-Saxon; LEVIATHAN/Hebrew; MEDUSA/Greek; SCYLLA/Greek; SIMARGL/Slavonic; SPHINX/Greek; TIEHOLTSODI/North American Navajo.

## Monster-killer
BELLEROPHON/Greek; BEOWULF/Anglo-Saxon; FINN/Irish Celtic; HERACLES/Greek; KINTARO/Japanese; KRAK/Polish; LUGULBANDA/Sumerian; MITHRAS/Iranian, Roman; NAGENATZANI/North American Navajo; PERSEUS/Greek; PULEKUKWEREK/North American Yurok; TAWARA TODA/Japanese; THESEUS/Greek.

## Moon
ANINGAN/North American Eskimo; ARTEMIS/Greek; CHIA/Colombian Indian; DIANA/Roman; HENG-O/Chinese; IRDLIRVIRISSONG/North American Eskimo; IX CH'UP/Mexican Maya; KHONS/Egyptian; KILYA/Peruvian Inca; MAWU/West African Benin, Togo; MYESYATS/Slavonic; NANNA/Sumerian; NYAMÉ/West African Ashanti; PAH/North American Pawnee; SHELARDI/Armenian Urartu; SIN/Mesopotamian; THOTH/Egyptian; TSUKUYOMI/Japanese.

## Mother goddess
ADITI/Hindu; ALA/Nigerian Ibo; ALOM/Mexican Maya; ANNAN/Irish Celtic; ARANRHOD/British Celtic; COATLICUE/Mexican Aztec; CYBELE/Greek; DANU/Hindu; DEMETER/Greek; GAEA/Greek; ISIS/Egyptian; JUGUMISHANTA/Papua New Guinean; KUNAPIPI/Australian aboriginal; MATI-SYRA-ZEMLYA/Russian; MODRON/British Celtic; MUT/Egyptian; NEITH/Egyptian; NEKHEBET/Egyptian; NINHURSAG/Sumerian; NOKOMIS/North American Algonquin; PAPA/Maori; RHEA/Greek; SEDNA/North American Eskimo; TAUERET/Egyptian; WARAMURUNGGUNDJI/Australian aboriginal.

## Mourning
DAVID/Hebrew; DEMETER/Greek; GILGAMESH/Mesopotamian; HERO/Greek; ISHTAR/Mesopotamian; ISIS/Egyptian; KITAMBA/Angolan; NANNA/Scandinavian; OD/Scandinavian; PATROCLUS/Greek; PERSEPHONE/Greek; RANGI/Maori; TAMMUZ/Mesopotamian.

## Musical instruments
APOLLO/Greek; DAVID/Hebrew; ORPHEUS/Greek; PAN/Greek.

## National hero

AENEAS/Roman; ARTHUR/British Celtic; BEOWULF/Anglo-Saxon; CUCHULAINN/Irish Celtic; FINN/Irish Celtic; NYIKANG/Sudanese Shilluk.

## Nature, deity of

HINE-RAU-WHARANGI/Maori; INARI/Japanese; ORENDA/North American Iroquois; PACHAMAMA/Peruvian Inca; PAN/Greek; SILVANUS/Roman; TAMMUZ/Mesopotamian; TANE/Maori; VAYU/Indian.

## Oracles, prophecy

APOLLO/Greek; CALCHAS/Greek; CASSANDRA/Greek; DANAË/Greek; ELIJAH/Hebrew; EMRYS/British Celtic; FA/West African Benin; IFA/Nigerian Yoruba; IPHIGENIA/Greek; JOCASTA/Greek; JONAH/Hebrew; JOSEPH/Hebrew; MERLIN/British Celtic; ORUNMILA/Nigerian Yoruba; PACHACAMAC/Peruvian; SAMUEL/Hebrew; TALIESIN/British Celtic; TEIRESIAS/Greek; ZARATHUSHTRA/Zoroastrian.

## Otherworld-visit

EFÉ/African Pygmy; ETANA/Mesopotamian; EURIDICE/Greek; GLISPA/North American Navajo; HERMOD/Scandinavian; IZANAGI/Japanese; MARWÉ/Kenyan; MURILÉ/Kenyan; NYUNZA/Angolan; ONATHA/North American Iroquois; ORPHEUS/Greek; PWYLL/British Celtic.

## Rain, god of

AO CHIN/Chinese; CHACS/Mexican Maya; CHI SONGZI/Chinese; EN-KAI/Kenyan; INDRA/Indian; LEZA/Central African; MIN/Egyptian; OWO/Nigerian Idoma; PARJANYA/Indian; TANUKUJEN/Sudanese Didinga; TLALOC/Mexican Toltec, Aztec; TSUI 'GOAB/African Hottentot; VIRACOCHA/Peruvian Inca; WANDJINA/Australian aboriginal.

## Rebirth

LEMMINKÄINEN/Finnish; ODIN/Scandinavian; ONATHA/North American Iroquois; OSIRIS/Egyptian; TAUERET/Egyptian.

## River deity

AIWEL/Sudanese Dinka; ANUKET/Egyptian; BIA/Ghanaian; BOIUNA/Brazilian Indian; BRAN/British Celtic; CHALCHIUHTLICUE/Mexican Toltec, Aztec; GANGA/Indian; HAPI/Egyptian; HENG BO/Chinese; KHOPUN/Slavonic; OCEANUS/Greek, TANO/Ghanaian.

## Sacrifice

ABEL/Hebrew; AGAMEMNON/Greek; HUITZILOPOCHTLI/Mexican Aztec; IDOMENEUS/Greek; IPHIGENIA/Greek; ISAAC/Hebrew; KIRANGA/East African Barundi; MOLOCH/Hebrew; PERUN/Slavonic; POLEVIK/Slavonic; TLALOC/Mexican Toltec, Aztec.

## Sea, god of

AEGIR/Scandinavian; AIPALOOKVIK/North American Eskimo; ALCINOUS/Greek; AO CHIN/Chinese; MANANNAN/Irish Celtic; NEPTUNE/Roman; NEREUS/Greek; NJORD/Scandinavian; OLOKUN/Nigerian Yoruba; PHORCYS/Greek; POSEIDON/Greek; PROTEUS/Greek; RYUJIN/Japanese; TANGAROA/Polynesian, Maori; YAM/Syrian.

## —, goddess of

RAN/Scandinavian; SEDNA/North American Eskimo; YEMANJÁ/Afro-Brazilian.

## Serpent

APEP/Egyptian; ARANDA/Australian aboriginal; CADMUS/Greek; GE-SAR/Tibetan; LAOCOÖN/Greek; LEVIATHAN/Hebrew; MAKA/Egyptian; MERTSEGER/Egyptian; NAGAS/Indian; PYTHON/Greek; THOR/Scandinavian; VRITRA/Indian; YULUNGGUI/Australian aboriginal; ZMEI GORYNICH/Slavonic.

## Sister-wife

IZANAGI/Japanese; IZANAMI/Japanese; LISA/West African Benin, Togo; MAMA OCLLO/Peruvian Inca; NUGUA/Chinese; SESHAT/Egyptian.

## Sky

ANU/Babylonian; ARAWOTYA/Australian Wonkamala aboriginal; ARYAMAN/Indian; BACABS/Mexican Maya; DYAUS/Indian; HATHOR/Egyptian; HORUS/Egyptian; JUPITER/Roman; MIN/Egyptian; NUT/Egyptian; RANGI/Maori; SHANG DI/Chinese; SVAROGU/Slavonic; TIAN/Chinese; URANUS/Greek; YU-HUANG/Chinese.

## Son of god

IMAYMANA VIRACOCHA/Inca; MARDUK/Mesopotamian.

## Storm god

ADAD/Babylonian; HADAD/Syrian; HUITZILOPOCHTLI/Mexican Aztec; INDRA/Indian; KIBUKA/Bugandan; RUDRA/Indian; SHANGO/Nigerian Yoruba; SHIVA/Hindu; SUSANO/Japanese Shinto.

## Sun

AH KINCHIL/Mexican Maya; AMATERASU/Japanese Shinto; ANHUR/Egyptian; ASA/Zoroastrian; ATEN/Egyptian; ATUM/Egyptian; BOCHICA/Colombian Indian; DAZHBOG/Slavonic; HELIOS/Greek; HYPERION/Greek; INTI/Peruvian Inca; KHEPRI/Egyptian; LISA/West African Benin, Togo; MITHRA/Iranian, Zoroastrian; RA/Egyptian; SAVITRI/Indian; SHAKURU/North American Pawnee; SHAMASH/Mesopotamian; SHIVINI/Armenian Urartu; SURYA/Indian; SVAROGU/Slavonic; TLALCHITONATIU/Mexican Indian; TONATIUH/Mexican Indian; TO KABINANA/Papua New Guinean; VISHNU/Indian, Hindu, VIVASVAT/Indian; YI/Chinese.

## Supreme god

AHURA MAZDA/Zoroastrian; AMON/Egyptian; BIHEKO/Ugandan Kiga; CHINGICHNICH/North American Luiseño; CON/Peruvian Indian; DI/Chinese; DXUI/African Kalahari Bushman; GUINECHEN/Chilean Araucanian; HUNAB KU/Mexican Maya; INTI/Peruvian Inca; JUMALA/Finnish; KAGGEN/African Bushman; MANITOU/North American Algonquin; NYAMÉ/West African Ashanti; PACHAYACHACHIC/Peruvian Inca; TEMAUKEL/Chilean Ona; TICCI VIRACOCHA/Inca; TIRAWA/North American Pawnee; UNKULUNKULU/South African Zulu, Ndebele; WAKONDA/North American Dakota; WATAUINEIWA/Chilean Southern Andes; YAHWEH/Hebrew.

## Taboos
ADAM/Hebrew; CONAIRE/Irish Celtic; EURIDICE/Greek; EVE/Hebrew; LOT/Hebrew; MWAMBU/Kenyan; URASHIMA/Japanese.

## Thunder and Lightning
ADAD/Babylonian; CHACS/Mexican Maya; DONGO/West African; HENG/North American Huron; HENO/North American Iroquois; ILYAPA/Peruvian Inca; LEI KUNG/Chinese; LEZA/Central African; MIN/Egyptian; PERUN/Slavonic; PILLAN/Chilean Indian; RAIDEN/Japanese; SHANGO/Nigerian Yoruba; TEISHEBA/Armenian Urartu; THOR/Scandinavian; TVASHTRI/Indian.

## Trickster
ANANSI/West African; AUTOLYCUS/Greek; BRICRIU/Irish Celtic; EA/Mesopotamian; ESHU/Nigerian Yoruba; LEGBA/West African Benin, Togo; LESHY/Slavonic; LOKI/Scandinavian; MAUI/Maori; ODYSSEUS/Greek; OLOFAT/Pacific Islands; VISHAPS/Armenian; WISAGATCAK/North American Cree; YALAFATH/Pacific Islands.

## Twins
AMPHITRYON/Greek; APOLLO/Greek; ARTEMIS/Greek; ASHVINS/Indian; CASTOR/Greek, Roman; ESAU/Hebrew; IOSKEHA/North American Iroquois, Huron; LEDA/Greek; LISA/West African Benin, Togo; MAWU/West African Benin, Togo; MUKASA/Bugandan; NAGENATZANI/North American Navajo; NUMMO/West African Dogon; POLLUX/Roman; POLYDEUCES/Greek; ROMULUS/Roman; TAWESKARE/North American Iroquois, Huron; ZURVAN/Iranian.

## Underworld
ADONIS/Greek; AH PUCH/Mexican Maya; ARAWN/British Celtic; BELIT-SHERI/Mesopotamian; CHIABOS/North American Algonquin; CIBCHACUM/Colombian Indian; DIS/Roman; ENDUKUGGA/Sumerian; HADES/Greek; HECATE/Greek; HEL/Scandinavian; MICTLANTECUHTLI/Mexican Toltec; NEDU/Mesopotamian; NERGAL/Mesopotamian; PERSEPHONE/Greek; RATI-MBATI-NDUA/Fijian; SEKER/Egyptian; WHIRO/Maori; YAMA/Indian.

## Virgin birth see Conception, supernatural

## War god
ANHUR/Egyptian; ARES/Greek; GUAN DI/Chinese; HACHIMAN/Japanese; HARMONIA/Greek; HUITZILOPOCHTLI/Mexican Aztec; KARTTIKEYA/Indian; KIBUKA/Bugandan; MARS/Roman; NINURTA/Mesopotamian; SVANTOVIT/Slavonic; TEISHEBA/Armenian Urartu; TIW/German; TU/Maori, Polynesian; TYR/Scandinavian; VAHAGU/Armenian; WODEN/German.

## —goddess
ATHENA/Greek; MINERVA/Roman; MORRIGAN/Irish Celtic.

## Wife of chief god
ATIRA/North American Pawnee; CHANDASHI/Central African; CHIA/Colombian Indian; DEVI/Hindu; FRIGG/Scandinavian; FRIJA/German; HERA/Greek; JUNO/Roman; KILYA/Peruvian Inca; METIS/Greek.

## Wild man
ENKIDU/Mesopotamian; ISHMAEL/Hebrew; MERLIN/British Celtic; MYRDDIN/British Celtic.

## Wind god
AEOLUS/Greek; AMON/Egyptian; FENG BO/Chinese; GAOH/North American Iroquois; NINURTA/Mesopotamian; ODIN/Scandinavian; STRIBOG/Slavonic; VATA/Indian; VAYU/Indian; YUQIANG/Chinese.

## Wine, god of
BACCHUS/Greek, Roman; DIONYSUS/Greek.

## Wisdom
ANAHIT/Armenian; ATHENA/Greek; BAUGI/Scandinavian; CERIDWEN/British Celtic; CHEIRON/Greek; GWION/British Celtic; KRISHNA/Indian; KVASIR/Scandinavian; MENTOR/Greek; MIMIR/Scandinavian; MINERVA/Roman; NESTOR/Greek; ODIN/Scandinavian; OMOIGANE/Japanese; SARASVATI/Indian; SUTTUNG/Scandinavian; THOTH/Egyptian.

*An ivory netsuke of a Tengu emerging from an egg. In Japanese mythology these spirits of bird-like appearance are thought of as mischievous tricksters.*

# ACKNOWLEDGMENTS

The publishers would like to thank the following for providing the illustrations on the pages listed below:

Antivarisk-Topografiska Arkivet, Stockholm: 73, 74, 196 right. 203 top

Ateneum Art Gallery, Helsinki: 137, 203 bottom

Bibliothèque Nationale, Paris: 24

Bodleian Library, Oxford: 149

Bridgeman Art Library, London: 32, 58, 109, 117 top left, 135

British Library, London: 101 (BL, Or. 2737, folio 93v), 105 (BL, Add. 27210, folio 5r), 115 bottom left (BL, Add. 27210, folio 2v), 150 (BL, Add. 27210, folio 15v), 158 (BL, Add. 27210, folio 3r), 180 (BL, Or. 2737, folio 35v)

British Museum, London: 15, 28 bottom, 35, 41, 50, 195, 213 bottom

Collection of the Rochester Museum and Science Center, Rochester, New York: 164

Corinium Museum, Cirencester: 147

Durham University Oriental Museum: 128, 186, 211, 213 top

Edinburgh University Library: 119 top left (Al-Biruni's Chronology of Ancient Nations, Or Ms. 161, folio 48v)

Mary Evans Picture Library, London: 93 right

Fitzwilliam Museum, Cambridge: 92

Werner Forman Archive, London: 36 bottom, 37, 53, 64, 85, 88, 97, 98, 102, 116 bottom, 120 bottom, 121 bottom, 122 centre right, 124 top, 126 top left, 136, 151, 154, 157, 159, 161, 163, 169, 175, 177, 185, 198, 206

Sonia Halliday Photographs, Buckinghamshire: 47, 48 top, 56, 59 bottom, 66, 69, 71, 72, 79, 93 left, 117 bottom left, 165, 167, 217

Claus & Liselotte Hansmann, Munich: 2, 12, 16, 45, 63, 65 top. 77, 81, 119 top right, 120 top left, 120 top right, 125 bottom left, 125 bottom right, 126 top right, 134, 155, 166

Robert Harding Picture Library, London: 18

Hirmer Fotoarchiv, Munich: 20 top, 27, 55, 162 top

Michael Holford, London: 1, 6, 25 bottom, 28 top, 30, 31, 34, 38 left, 48 bottom, 62, 65 bottom, 107, 114 bottom, 116 top, 118 top right, 118 bottom, 119 bottom right, 120-1 top, 122 bottom, 123 bottom, 124 bottom left, 125 top right, 127 left, 131, 148, 153, 160, 170, 182, 183 left, 193, 196 left, 202, 204 top

Horniman Museum, London: 138, 209, 216

I.G.D.A., Milan: 125 top left

Larousse, Paris: 104

Manchester Museum: 103

Mansell Collection, London: 11, 23, 29, 33, 36 top, 38 right, 40, 51, 54, 89, 90, 106, 111, 173, 174, 176, 181, 197, 200

Tony Morrison/South American Pictures, Suffolk: 96, 100, 122 top, 143, 205

Musée de l'Homme, Paris: 82

Musée Guimet, Paris: 17

Musée Romain, Avenches: 178

Museum für Völkerkunde, Vienna: 86

Museum of Fine Arts, Boston: 19 (gift of E.G. Curtis), 115 right (William Sturgis Bigelow Collection)

Museum of Antiquities of the University & Society of Antiquities of Newcastle-upon-Tyne: 162 bottom, 188

Museum of Mankind, London: 25 top, 70

National Museum of Antiquities, Scotland: 46

Peter Newark's Western Americana, Bath: 184

Newnes Books, London: 20 bottom, 61, 75 (© National Palace Museum, Taipei)

Ann & Bury Peerless, Kent: 118 top left, 123 top, 127 top right

Percival David Foundation of Chinese Art, London: 140

Photographie Giraudon, Paris: 24, 99, 117 right, 191, 218

Photoresources, Kent: 122 centre left, 124 bottom right, 127 bottom right

Axel Poignant, London: 94, 115 top left, 126 bottom, 133, 142, 145, 168, 201, 208, 215

Royal Library, Copenhagen: 39 (Ny.Kgl.Saml.1867,4°), 119 bottom left (Ny.Kgl.Saml.1867,4°), 189 (Ny.Kgl.Saml.1867,4°)

Russell-Cotes Art Gallery & Museum, Bournemouth: 112

John Rylands University Library, Manchester: 14 (RYL. HEBREW ms. 6, folio 15v), 152 (RYL. HEBREW ms. 6, folio 3v)

Scala, Florence: 59 top

Smithsonian Institution, Washington: 129

Tate Gallery, London: 76, 156

Thames & Hudson Publishers, London: 113

Victoria and Albert Museum, London: 9, 22, 42, 43, 78, 83, 84, 87, 95, 108, 132, 187, 190, 204 bottom, 212, 223

Warburg Institute, London: 60

Wheelwright Museum of the American Indian, Santa Fe: 114 top, 121 top right